Workers' Rights as
Human Rights

Workers' Rights as Human Rights

Edited by **James A. Gross**

ILR PRESS
An imprint of
Cornell University Press
Ithaca and London

First published 2003 by Cornell University Press

Printed in the United States of America

Library of Congress Cataloging-in-Publication Data
Workers' rights as human rights / edited by James A. Gross.
    p. cm.
Includes bibliographical references and index.
  ISBN 0-8014-4082-3 (cloth : alk. paper)
    1. Labor unions—Organizing—United States. 2. Labor laws and legislation—United States. 3. Employee rights—United States.
I. Gross, James A.
  HD6490.O72U69 2003
  331'.01'1—dc21   2002156374

Cornell University Press strives to use environmentally responsible suppliers and materials to the fullest extent possible in the publishing of its books. Such materials include vegetable-based, low-VOC inks and acid-free papers that are recycled, totally chlorine-free, or partly composed of nonwood fibers. For further information, visit our website at www.cornellpress.cornell.edu.

Cloth printing   10 9 8 7 6 5 4 3 2 1

To Cletus Daniel,

A true and dear friend and distinguished colleague whose commitment to economic and social justice is best reflected in his studies of farmworkers' rights.

Contents

Acknowledgment

This volume would never have been made ready for publication without the expert, untiring, patient, and good-humored efforts of my colleague, Brigid Beachler.

Workers' Rights as
Human Rights

CHAPTER 1

A Long Overdue Beginning

The Promotion and Protection of
Workers' Rights as Human Rights

James A. Gross

In 1935, the National Labor Relations Act (the Wagner Act), established the most democratic procedure in United States labor history for the participation of workers in the determination of their wages, hours, and working conditions. The Wagner Act was not neutral; the law encouraged as government policy the practice of collective bargaining and protection of workers in their exercise "of full freedom of association, self-organization, and designation of representatives of their own choosing, for the purpose of negotiating the terms and conditions of their employment and other mutual aid or protection."[1] What was then called industrial democracy was to replace employers' unilateral determination of matters affecting wages, hours, and working conditions.

The values underlying the Wagner Act, its conceptions of workers' rights, and most (but not all) of its provisions[2] are consistent with human rights values. Although not using the term *human rights*, the Wagner Act was far ahead of its time in applying human rights principles to U.S. workplaces. The act guaranteed the right to organize and bargain collectively, core social justice issues for workers.[3]

Few human rights are more important than the right of freedom of association. Senator Robert Wagner, the act's chief advocate, believed that the exercise of that right was essential for a free and democratic society in which workers were able to participate in and influence the decisions that most directly affected their lives. The Wagner Act promoted independent labor organization and collective bargaining as essential to a democratic form of government, not merely as the consequences of management mistakes. He intended the law that bears his name to be a just and democratic alternative to the tyranny of both the laissez-faire free market in which "men became the servile pawns of their masters in the factories" and an authoritarian "super government."[4] The Wagner

Act was a moral choice against servility, a relationship between owner and worker that is incompatible with human rights.

Labor never came close to achieving the system of workplace democracy envisioned by Wagner. This was due in great part to the 1947 Taft-Hartley amendments to the Wagner Act. My study of Wagner–Taft-Hartley from 1947 to 1994 in a book titled *Broken Promise*[5] shows how a policy that encouraged the replacement of workplace autocracy with a democratic system of power sharing was turned into governmental legitimization of employers' opposition to the organization of employees, collective bargaining, and workplace democracy, and governmental protection of employers' unilateral decision-making authority over many of the most important decisions affecting wages, hours, and working conditions.

Although Congress carried over into Taft-Hartley the Wagner Act statement that it was the policy of the federal government to encourage collective bargaining, it added language asserting the right to refrain from engaging in collective bargaining.[6] Critics saw this as part of a legislative design "calculated to destroy the philosophy of the Wagner Act that collective bargaining should be encouraged."[7] The concept, added to Taft-Hartley, of the federal government as a neutral guarantor of employee free choice between individual and collective bargaining, indifferent to the choice made, is clearly inconsistent with the Wagner Act concept of the federal government as a promoter of the exercise of the right of freedom of association.

Another provision of Taft-Hartley, the employer "free speech" section,[8] has been read as statutory justification for promotion of the policies of individual rather than collective bargaining and employer resistance to unionization and collective bargaining.[9] Labor policy in the early years of the Wagner Act required employer neutrality concerning the exercise of their employees' right of freedom of association. Taft-Hartley's deregulation of employer speech increased the ability of employers to use their economic power to defeat unionization efforts. Few democratic societies, other than our own, condone open opposition by employers to unionization and collective bargaining.

Near the end of 1984, as the National Labor Relations Act (NLRA) approached its fiftieth birthday, the House Committee on Education and Labor's Subcommittee on Labor-Management Relations concluded that U.S. "labor law has failed."[10] By failure, the committee meant that the Taft-Hartley Act had not achieved its purpose of encouraging collective bargaining and protecting employees from discrimination because of their union activities. In fact, the subcommittee said the act was being used "as a weapon to obstruct collective bargaining" and to create only the illusion of protecting workers against discrimination.[11] After fifty years of the Wagner and Taft-Hartley acts, workers and unions were, in the subcommittee's words, "being badly betrayed."[12]

Less than one year later, however, then secretary of labor William Brock told the Senate Committee on Labor and Human Resources that "we have greater freedom of association in this country than any country in the world."[13] Secretary Brock found it "very hard for others to criticize us when we are doing so much better than any of them."[14] Committee Chairman Orrin Hatch proclaimed the U.S. "the most liberal labor law-oriented country in the world."[15]

Chairman Hatch's committee was examining U.S. relations with the International Labour Organization (ILO). He wanted to know if the United States could ratify ILO labor conventions without having them supersede "present existing labor laws which have been delicately drawn and have a delicate balance" and which "have worked rather well in our country."[16]

Until recently, the international human rights movement and organizations, human rights scholars, and even labor organizations and advocates have given little attention to worker rights as human rights.[17] Historically, human rights organizations have concentrated on the most egregious kinds of human rights abuses such as torture, death squads, and detention without trial. This lack of attention has contributed to workers being seen as expendable in worldwide economic development and their needs and concerns not being represented at conferences on the world economy dominated by bankers, finance ministers, and multinational corporations. As one United Nations document put it, "Despite the rhetoric, violations of civil and political rights continue to be treated as though they were far more serious, and more patently intolerable, than massive and direct denials of economic, social, and cultural rights."[18]

There has been an enduring disagreement over the status, even the existence, of economic rights. The Western tradition of human rights, which focuses mainly the individual's right to freedom from being coerced by the state, is narrow and has ignored worker rights. From that perspective, the essential rights of man were "negative" in that they were to guarantee freedom from being coerced into doing things. There was and is an historically important affinity between this eighteenth-century "negative" rights theory and "free market," laissez-faire economics that has led to another historically important doctrine advocating the minimalist state. The lack of attention to so-called "positive" economic and social rights, therefore, has been caused at least in part by disagreements over the proper role of government. That is reflected in the traditional distinction maintained between civil and political rights that supposedly require nothing of the state but restraint and economic and social rights that require the state to take positive legislative, administrative, and executive action to ensure jobs, education, shelter, and health care, among other things. It follows that the state "also acts against those elements whose power and disproportionate share of national resources inhibit state action in this direction."[19]

There is no compelling reason, however, to continue this unrealistic separation of rights that distinguishes between violations caused by a tyrannical government and violations caused by tyrannical forces in an economic system. As Senator Wagner understood, it is not only the state that has the power to violate people's rights. Employers have explicit power over individuals' lives, and implicit power can be found in the supposedly free market. A human being has a right to be free from domination regardless of the source. Wagner's act was based on the understanding that servility is incompatible with human rights and democracy. Servility, or what some call powerlessness, leaves human beings dependent on the benevolence, pity, charity, or arbitrary power of others. People can be rendered powerless not only by totalitarian states but also by those minimalist states that do not outlaw or take effective steps to prevent the violation of people's rights by private nonstate actors. Modern corporations rival governments in power and directly affect their employees' lives.[20]

Yet, while assertions of individual rights and freedom are commonly made against the exercise of power by the state, rights and freedom are routinely left outside factory gates and office buildings with barely a murmur of protest. Consequently, too many workers stand before their employer not as adult persons with rights but as powerless children or servants totally dependent on the will and interests of their superiors and employers.[21]

The United Nations' Universal Declaration of Human Rights (UDHR) adopted in 1948 includes economic and social rights (Articles 22–26, for example) as well as civil and political rights.[22] The United States' position has fluctuated from the time of Franklin Roosevelt's Economic Bill of Rights to the Reagan administration's rejection of economic rights of any sort. The preamble of the International Covenant on Civil and Political Rights (ICCPR), which the United States ratified in 1992, asserts the interdependence of political and economic rights: "The ideal of free human beings enjoying civil and political freedom and freedom from fear and want can only be achieved if conditions are created whereby everyone may enjoy his civil and political rights, as well as his economic, social and cultural rights."[23] Put simply, it means that for those without bread, freedom of association, freedom of speech, and political participation are in reality meaningless as many are coerced into giving up their liberty in order to secure their subsistence.

Article 20 of the UDHR asserts the right to freedom of association, including in Article 23(4) the right to form and join trade unions.[24] The ICCPR incorporates in Article 22 the language of the Universal Declaration: "Everyone shall have the right to freedom of association with others, including the right to form and join trade unions for the protection of his interests."[25] Article 8 of the International Covenant on Economic, Social, and Cultural Rights (ICESCR), which the United States has not signed, also affirms the "right of everyone to form and join the trade union of his choice."[26] The International Labour Organization's (ILO) Convention Concerning the Application of the Principles of the Right to Organize and to Bargain Collectively (Convention 98, adopted in 1948) addresses in great part the exercise of the freedom of association rights set forth in the international covenants. (In addition, the First and Fourteenth amendments to the U.S. Constitution guarantee the right of association.) These statements of international human rights, therefore, affirm that the freedom of association is both a civil and an economic right.[27]

The United States, however, adopted the ICCPR as a non-self-executing treaty. Consequently, the provisions of the ICCPR do not become U.S. law and are not directly enforceable through a private cause of action in U.S. courts. It is uncertain, therefore, precisely what labor rights obligations the United States assumed when it ratified the ICCPR or, more specifically, whether ratification obligated the United States to bring its domestic labor laws into accord with international labor standards.

As I have written elsewhere, "It defies the reality of the last 30 years to claim that current U.S. labor law is a model of the freedom of association and it defies labor history to claim that the freedom of association has been respected even generally in this country for anything but brief periods of time."[28] The United States government, in a 1999 report to the ILO assessing its labor law in relation to ILO conventions that it had not signed, asserted that it "has an elaborate system of substantive law and procedures to assure the enforcement of that law [and] is committed to the fundamental principle of freedom of association and the effective recognition of the right to collective bargaining."[29] The United States admitted in understated language, however, "that there are aspects of this system that fail to fully protect the rights to organize and bargain collectively of all employees in all circumstances."[30] The report expressed "concern" about that and said it was "important to re-examine any system of labor laws from time to time to assure that the system continues to protect these fundamental rights."[31] An ILO Committee of Expert Advisors included this U.S. report in a group of reports it termed "striking for their open recognition of difficulties still to be overcome or situations they deemed relevant to achieving full respect in the principles and rights in the Declaration."[32]

United States labor law reform has been debated for years, but the debate has focused on specific proposals to amend or repeal certain labor and employment laws and the strategies, objectives, and relative power of those who would gain or lose as a consequence of such legislative changes. Although the basic foundation of law, whether made by legislatures, judges, or administrative agencies, is moral choice, there has been little attention given to the values and conceptions of rights and justice underlying these laws—including the fundamental human rights at stake.

The chapters in this book provide a different perspective in the assessment of U.S. labor-relations law by applying a human rights standard that is more fundamental than statutory or even constitutional standards. In part, the inspiration for this new approach came from the conviction that protestations about the perfection (or slight imperfection) of our labor law and practice and about some mythical delicate balance of employer and employee and labor organization rights in this country are false and hypocritical. It was time, therefore, to get our own house in order rather than to continue to pretend that human rights violations occur only elsewhere. In major part, however, the inspiration for this book came from a strong belief that an honest reexamination and reassessment of U.S. labor and employment law using human rights principles as standards for judgment would be a long overdue beginning toward the promotion and protection of worker rights as human rights.

In October 2000, Cornell University held a conference, Human Rights in the American Workplace: Assessing U.S. Labor Law and Policy, as an important first step in placing human rights at the center of U.S. labor policy. The authors of the chapters included in this book participated in that conference and were invited later to write chapters for this book. Their chapters, by providing human rights standards for judgment, provide new ways of understanding U.S. labor law and practice that will help redefine policy issues. They also provide innovative recommendations for what should and can be done to bring U.S. labor law in line with international human rights standards.

The unprecedented Human Rights Watch Report, *Workers' Freedom of Association in the United States Under International Human Rights Standards*,[33] adds another persuasive reason for making human rights a part of U.S. labor policy:

> An argument that international human rights and labor rights law is not relevant to U.S. labor law and practice cannot be sustained. Basic U.N., ILO, and regional human rights instruments have forged an international human rights consensus on workers' freedom of association that includes the United States. The consensus is strengthened by the accelerating international engagement of the United States at the ILO and in regional and multilateral trade fora, where it actively supports the cause of internationally recognized workers' rights. To fulfill both the obligations it has assumed and the objectives that it promotes in the international community, the United States must live up in its own labor law and practice to international labor rights norms on workers' freedom of association and rights to organize, to bargain, and to strike.[34]

Ideas of human and labor rights were debated at the Cornell conference and are discussed in this book. At the Cornell conference Barbara Shailor, director of international affairs for the AFL-CIO, asserted that the concept of "universally recognized worker rights as human rights is so powerful it has the ability to transform the global economy."[35] Earlier, however, professor James Atleson of the University of Buffalo Law School, who has a chapter in this book, asked "How do you talk to people who don't believe that labor rights are human rights? It seems instinctively right that fairness in the workplace is a human right [but] what kinds of arguments can you use with those who have a different feeling?"[36] This is a serious question that requires an adequate explanation for any theory of human rights—particularly worker rights as human rights. There is disagreement of varying degrees of intensity over the existence, source, nature, and scope of human rights and worker rights.

The idea of human rights, however, has endured over the years in one form or another. In this country, for example, whether understood as having divine, moral, or legal roots, human rights influenced the abolition of slavery, factory legislation, universal public schooling, trade unionism, the universal suffrage movement, and other reform movements. But there was no widespread domestic and international acceptance of the concept of human rights until after the rise and fall of Nazi Germany and World War II. Possibly because it was unquestioned that the Holocaust was a crime against humanity, the existence of human rights was commonly considered self-evident. The United Nations' UDHR, ICCPR, and ICESCR, for example, are long on lists of human rights, but short on the foundations of those rights in moral and political thought.

Edward Potter in his chapter, "A Pragmatic Assessment from the Employers' Perspective," points out that the Third Restatement of the Foreign Relations Law of the United States defines human rights as referring to "freedom, immunities, and benefits which, according to widely accepted contemporary values, every human being should enjoy in the society in which he or she lives." Potter maintains that regardless of country, culture, or heritage, certain rights can constitute human rights by international agreement or by custom if that right is "stated generally," "addresses a serious infringement of the human condition," or "seriously offends common values." According to Potter, an international consensus on whether something is a human right breaks down, however, if that right is not viewed as being basic or widely considered serious, or if it is defined in too detailed a manner.

Beyond a core of accepted basic rights, Potter says what constitutes a human right "is in the eye of the beholder." He maintains that there is no consensus, even among Americans with a common heritage, about what constitutes workplace human rights once we move away from general principles.

In his chapter, "Closing the Gap between International Law and U.S. Labor Law," Lee Swepston of the International Labour Organization refers to the ILO's Declaration on Fundamental Principles and Rights at Work as an innovative new approach, which the U.S. government and employers supported enthusiastically. In that declaration, all members of the ILO pledged to respect, promote, and realize in good faith principles and rights concerning:

1. freedom of association and the effective recognition of the right to collective bargaining;
2. the elimination of all forms of forced or compulsory labor;
3. the effective elimination of child labor; and
4. the elimination of discrimination in respect of employment and occupation.

AFL-CIO general counsel John Hiatt anticipates that "the main achievement of the declaration could be to end the debate over whether those core universal labor rights are applicable to every worker in every country."[37] In his chapter, Potter cautiously agrees that although it might take years to occur, U.S. courts might eventually view the declaration as an articulation of principles common to the world's major legal systems. Potter cautioned, however that the declaration committed all ILO member nations to good faith efforts to achieve the document's goals and objectives but not the detailed legal requirements of the ILO conventions.

Swepston, by contrast, emphasizes in his chapter that international labor law is a part of international human-rights law, which, in turn, is based on ILO standards that have been adopted over the years. At the same time, he points out that international labor law is not much known in the United States and sees the chapters in this book as a step in diminishing the gap between international labor law and U.S. labor law.

As Swepston's chapter illustrates, moreover, it is not only ignorance of international labor law that has created a gap between the rest of the world's understanding of international labor rights and our own but also deliberate U.S. policy. Swepston points out, for example, that most countries in the world—except for the United States and China—have ratified most of the ILO's basic human rights standards, including those the ILO always considered fundamental for all workers. Included among the basic ILO conventions not ratified by the United States are Convention 87 (Freedom of Association and Protection of the Right to Organize)[38] and Convention 98 (Right to Organize and Bargain Collectively),[39] which, taken together, constitute the essential elements for the creation, administration, and functioning of employers' and workers' organizations.

Swepston also notes that ILO standards cover many subjects other than fundamental rights, including occupational safety and health. Emily Spieler objects to the exclusion of health and safety from the ILO's four basic or core worker rights and their relegation to a second tier of rights. In her chapter, "Risks and Rights: The Case for Occupational Safety and Health as a Core Worker Right," she contends that these core rights do not assert a right to a minimum level of protection at the workplace. Spieler is especially critical of what she terms the "drive for consensus" that leads to a least-common-denominator standard where only the most serious abuses of the four core rights are recognized as human rights violations. Yet, as she notes, consensus in the tripartite ILO discussions required the agreement of developed and undeveloped states, as well as business and trade unions. These negotiations occurred in a context in which poorer countries saw the assertion of working condition rights as potentially damaging to their fledgling economies and large employers and multinational corporations lobbied for weak enforcement of minimum work standards in developing countries. Many parties to the negotiation embraced the underlying critical assumption that safe and healthful working conditions would follow automatically from economic growth.

Spieler maintains that human rights derive from a moral and political commitment to principles of justice. She acknowledges variations in the level of economic and cultural development among nations but contends that human rights are universal, inviolable, nonwaivable, and rooted in a recognition of fundamental human decency. Her starting premise, therefore, is that labor rights should be seen as human rights. Consequently, she rejects the argument of neoclassical economists that the unregulated market resolves workplace issues efficiently and that the bargain between workers and employers is consensual and fair. For her, human life is "incommensurable" and "the right to life is deeply imbedded in every human rights declaration." The issue in health and safety, Spieler writes, is to protect individuals' lives from those who wield unequal power.

Spieler's conception of human rights is in the tradition which holds that human rights are a species of moral rights which all persons have equally simply because they are human *not* because these rights are earned or acquired by special enactments or contractual agreements. In that human rights tradition, rights and moral obligation are correlative, in other words, "certain things ought not to be done to any human being and certain other things ought to be done for every human being."[40] In that context, Spieler writes that to say health and safety is a right is to say workers have a right to have access to information concerning hazards, to be free from retaliation for raising safety concerns or for refusing to perform work that poses imminent danger, and to work in an environment that "is free of predictable, preventable, and serious hazards."

Spieler recognizes that there is a spectrum of health and safety risks ranging from those that are the result of the current state of technology to those that are the result of an employer's "bad acts." Along that spectrum, she maintains "that *human rights* violations occur when employers' deliberate and intentional actions expose workers to preventable, predictable, and serious hazards." Spieler asserts that there is a fundamental right to be free from those hazards and that right should be guaranteed.

Spieler's chapter is a model for systematically considering worker rights as human rights. She begins by ascertaining the nature of the existing situation with respect to worker health and safety in this country and elsewhere; she identifies the issues and problems that need to be addressed; and she provides a basis for principled policy-making. In regard to policy-making, for example, Spieler discusses the gap between the safety and health words of the U.S. legal regime and workplace realities. She concludes that there is a strong connection between improving occupational health and enforcing other fundamental labor rights such as "rights against discrimination for minorities and immigrants; rights to free speech at work; to association, to engage in concerted activity, and to organize trade unions; and any evolving rights to job security and social benefits." She makes it clear that she does not consider the right to safety and health contingent on these other rights but contends that "as the legal and social norms at work change to allow for expanded demands of workers, there is no question that working conditions will also improve."

Other chapters in this book point to the gap between the ideals of statutory language and labor practices in the United States. They emphasize, for example, that human rights principles raise serious challenges to the National Labor Relations Act—not only to its interpretation by the National Labor Relations Board (NLRB) and the courts but also to some of its provisions.

Lance Compa in his chapter, "Workers' Freedom of Association in the United States: The Gap between Ideals and Practice," makes the point that freedom of association for workers has long been universally acknowledged as a fundamental right. The Human Rights Watch report called the freedom of association "the bedrock workers' right under international law on which all other labor rights rest." He recites a body of international norms that have established standards for workers' freedom of association covering the right to bargain collectively and the right to strike. He also asserts that the United States has committed itself, through international agreement, to enforce U.S. laws protecting workers' rights to organize, bargain collectively, and strike.

Prominent among these international human rights instruments are the Universal Declaration of Human Rights ("Everyone has the right to form and to join trade unions for the protection of his interests"), the International Covenant on Civil and Political Rights ("Everyone shall have the right to freedom of association with others, including the right to form and join trade unions for the protection of his interests"), and the International Covenant on Economic, Social, and Cultural Rights (which obliges governments to "ensure the right of everyone to form trade unions and join the trade union of his choice"). He also cites in particular ILO Convention 87 ("Workers and employers . . . shall have the right to establish and . . . join organizations of their own choosing") and ILO Convention 98 ("Workers shall enjoy adequate protection against acts of anti-discrimination in respect of their employment.") In addition, Compa emphasizes that the United States championed adoption of the ILO's Declaration on Fundamental Principles and Rights at

Work that set forth freedom of association as the first principle and right.

The United States has not ratified conventions 87 and 98 but, as Compa explains, the ILO has determined that member countries such as the United States are bound to respect a certain number of general rules that have been established for the common good. Among these principles, freedom of association has become a customary rule above the conventions. Compa also points out that "over decades of painstaking treatment of allegations of violations of workers' rights," the ILO's Committee on Freedom of Association has elaborated authoritative guidelines for implementation of the right to organize, the right to bargain collectively, and the right to strike. This committee, in considering alleged violations of the freedom of association, does not distinguish between charges leveled against governments and those leveled against persons but seeks in both cases to determine if a government has ensured within its territory the free exercise of trade union rights.

There have been several charges brought against the U.S. government alleging the inadequacy of U.S. labor legislation in safeguarding the principles of freedom of association, including many of the specific issues and practices discussed in Compa's chapter.[41] The U.S. government in all the cases reported by the Committee on Freedom of Association has denied all charges, claiming that there is no evidence to support any contention that its labor laws "are inadequate to safeguard the principles of freedom of association."[42] Despite these denials, the committee in many cases "noted with concern" and "drew the attention of the U.S. government" to problems the committee perceived, and in some cases, the committee recommended changes in U.S. labor policy and practice.

Compa concludes that workers' freedom of association "is under sustained attack in the United States and the government is failing its responsibility under international human rights standards to deter such attacks and protect workers' rights." In support of that conclusion, Compa cites the exclusion of farm, household domestic workers, and other workers from the law's protection in the face of international standards affirming the right of *every person* to form and join unions and to bargain collectively; the legality of the permanent replacement of economic strikers that nullifies the right to strike; and the harassment, suspension, firing, or deportation of workers who try to form unions in reprisal for their exercise of the right to freedom of association. Other tactics used to intimidate workers include legal or bureaucratic remedies so weak that they constitute an incentive to violate the law; forced attendance at captive-audience speeches on work time; refined methods of legally "predicting"—as distinct from unlawfully threatening—workplace closures, firings, wage and benefit cuts, and other dire consequences if workers form and join a trade union. Finally Compa also mentions delays in NLRB and court procedures that hold up elections, frustrate the commencement of bargaining, and require years to resolve issues in the courts; weak remedies for surface bargaining (going through the motions of bargaining without any intention of reaching an agreement); the use of subcontracting arrangements and temporary workers to avoid the freedom of association; and the special vulnerability of immigrant workers when employers during NLRB election campaigns threaten to call the Immigration and Naturalization service to have workers deported.

Thomas Moorhead in his chapter, "U.S. Labor Law Serves Us Well," disagrees sharply with Compa and maintains that our law serves us better than any of the "so-called" international norms in the world. He commends our labor law that allows individual employees to make up their own minds while guaranteeing free speech, union rights, and secret ballots. He distinguishes U.S. labor law based on the principle of individual employee rights from ILO Conventions focused on institutional rights and privileges for organizations, such as Convention 87, in which he says the rights of the organization not the individual are paramount.

Moorhead grants that some employer hostility exists but dismisses the claim that such hostility is the main factor in explaining low union membership. He says he is bemused by the "naiveté" of the Human Rights Watch report when it cites a study reporting that a majority of managers would oppose unionization in their workplace and that it would detrimentally affect their advancement if their workers organized. It is going to hurt their advancement, Moorhead argues, because in his thirty years of dealing with unions he is convinced that bad management, not unions, organize a workplace.

Moorhead lists some of the human rights U.S. workers enjoy: the right to exclusive representation once a union is certified; the right to have an individual grievance processed to arbitration; and the right to object if dues assessments are used for anything other than proper union business. He agrees that there are generally accepted international labor standards that can be compatible with U.S. labor law and cites the ILO Declaration on Fundamental Principles and Rights at Work as a source of such rights. He emphasizes that U.S. employers "were in the forefront of those advocating [the Declaration's] adoption."

Moorhead urges caution, however, in identifying what are assumed to be generally accepted international standards as evidenced by the relatively few ratifications of ILO conventions. Potter, while acknowledging general agreement that these conventions are fundamental, emphasizes that as a consequence of the low rate of ratifications "about half of the world's workers are not covered by these conventions." The adoption of the Declaration of Principles, Potter says, was the result of an effort to address that gap. Potter acknowledges that the United States had not ratified any major human rights treaty before 1988 and has not gone far in integrating human rights law into domestic law. He also confirms that U.S. courts have been "quite reluctant" to incorporate customary international law into U.S. law.

Potter also explains that unqualified ratifications by the United States of treaties such as UN and ILO conventions would not only create international obligations, but would also require the incorporation of those conventions into domestic law, superseding inconsistent federal and state statutes. He makes it clear that regardless of who has been in the White House or which party controlled the Senate, the ratification process in this country has been geared to ensure that a treaty will not directly affect federal or state law, or interfere with U.S. prerogatives in any way. The United States ratified the International Covenant on Civil and Political Rights in 1992, for example, with non–self-executing declarations, that is, the treaty would create no new domestic rights and no new domestic legislation was contemplated. Potter emphasizes that the administration and the Senate went out of their way to make it clear that ratification of this covenant did not infer specific protections of the trade union rights found in the UN Covenant on Economic, Social and Cultural Rights and ILO Convention 87 concerning freedom of association and the right to organize.

In the conclusion of his chapter, Potter refers to the book he wrote in 1984 on the implications for U.S. law and practice of ratifying ILO conventions 87 and 98—implications which he contends are still valid. In that book Potter stated that whether or not these ILO conventions were declared self-executing, it would "afford no assurance that the United States would be found by the ILO to be in compliance with its international obligation."[43] He warned that ratification of ILO Convention 87, for example, would (among other things): "broaden the classes of employees entitled to NLRA-type protections"; "repeal the employer free speech provision under Section 8(c) of the NLRA and prohibit all acts of employer and union interference in organizing"; and "limit restrictions on the right to strike, including secondary boycotts, in both the public and private sectors."[44]

In his book, Potter also admitted that the differences between U.S. labor law and ILO conventions 87 and 98 were not merely technical but involved "substantial, substantive differences." Potter acknowledged it was very likely that the ILO's Committee of Experts would conclude "that U.S. law and practice does not conform with the conventions' requirements on some if not all [these] substantive differences."[45] Potter and Compa address the same differences from very different viewpoints.

As one writer put it, "the idea of human rights should intimidate governments or it is worth nothing. If the idea of human rights reassures governments, it is worse than nothing."[46] Kenneth Roth, executive director of Human Rights Watch, maintains that the key current question is not creating new rights but enforcing existing rights.[47] Neither the ILO nor any other international body has enforcement powers such as those possessed by a national legal system. In great part, fears of inroads on national sovereignty block the creation and implementation of effective international enforcement measures.

The ILO, for example, monitors the application of its conventions but must rely on the voluntary acceptance and publication of its findings to promote and protect human rights. Lee Swepston describes the implementation of international labor standards in his chapter and concludes that the ILO "has been seriously remiss in not paying sufficient attention to analyzing how well this system works." He also concludes that no international organization is likely to adopt a sanctions-based approach to a violation of labor standards, unless in exceptionally severe cases.

In that context, several of the chapters in this book discuss alternative ways of promoting and protecting the human rights of workers, particularly in this country. Roy Adams argues in his chapter "Voice for All:

Why the Right to Refrain from Collective Bargaining Is No Right at All," that proposals for tinkering with the Wagner Act model such as those put forth by the Dunlop Commission in 1994 and Human Rights Watch in 2000 are not the solution. He maintains that to deliver on its promises to honor international human rights standards, the U.S. needs to make fundamental changes in its labor policy.

Adams contends that the core principle of employee choice set forth in section 7 of the NLRA is an improper standard for compliance with international obligations because it compels employees to choose between collective bargaining or no representation. He refers to it as the "illegitimate 'right' of employees to defer to arbitrary authority." He points out that U.S. employers "have seized on the need for workers to choose to adopt methods designed to deny employees a voice at work." In reference to the four core human rights set forth in the Declaration on Fundamental Principles and Rights at Work, Adams writes:

> We do not . . . permit people to sell themselves into slavery. We do not allow states to choose apartheid, and we do not allow children to choose to prostitute themselves or enter into other forms of exploitative labor arrangements. From a human rights perspective the alternative to voice for employees—deferral to authority unaccountable to the governed—is as obnoxious as any of these possibilities and its continued existence is shameful.

Adams argues that the option to choose workplace autocracy should not be available, but as with slavery, child labor, and discrimination arbitrary authority in industry should be eliminated. Among other things, Adams advocates legislation requiring the establishment of employee representation councils that would have responsibility for codetermining a range of issues set forth in the law. He realizes that proposals such as this are considered impractical but reminds us that in the past halfcentury the civil rights, women's rights, and gay rights movements have demonstrated that social values and behavior can be changed.

Lance Compa, on the other hand, recommends major but more traditional legislative change, including stronger remedies for discriminating against workers for engaging in union activities and engaging in surface bargaining and antiunion speech; equal access to workplaces for nonemployee union organizers, equal time for unions in captive-audience situations, faster representation elections and card-check certifications; protections for the rights and interests of contingent workers, contract workers, and others; NLRA coverage for agricultural workers, domestic workers, and low-level supervisors; prohibition of the permanent replacement of economic strikers; and greater protections for immigrant workers.

It has been argued, however, that only the people whose rights are at stake can force a government or a private enterprise to respect human rights.[48] In his chapter, "'An Injury to One . . .' Transnational Labor Solidarity and the Role of Domestic Law," James Atleson emphasizes the efforts of workers themselves as key to the advancement of workers' rights. He argues that the increasingly global nature of work makes it essential that worker solidarity exist across national boundaries.

Barbara Shailor has pointed out that while corporations have discovered how to reorganize themselves globally, unions have not. The AFL-CIO is now talking about global organizing campaigns and ways to empower working people across the globe.[49] Atleson agrees that unions in the United States have not emphasized international labor rights. He is persuaded that legal change in the United States is not going to occur through the benevolence of the state, which, historically, has never been benevolent to labor. He characterizes trade agreements and ILO standards as "thin reeds" for the advancement of labor. He agrees with the other authors that most American labor lawyers have not read, or perhaps even heard of, the ILO's standards or even the relevant U.N. documents. Consequently, he maintains that labor may have to rely on self-help, directed internationally. Atleson makes the important point that despite attempts to set international standards for labor and employment, legal regimes are local in character. He explains, for example, how our own labor law system with its prohibitions of sympathy strikes and secondary boycotts designed to protect "neutral" employers creates serious problems for unions that try to forge international labor solidarity or to take action across national borders. Yet, Atleson finds, transnational activity is clearly occurring, despite the difficulties and complexities that he discusses.

Atleson describes and analyzes several recent transnational solidarity actions: the U.S. Teamsters Union strike against UPS in 1997; Belgian, French, and other European unions' coordinated action against the Renault automobile company in 1997; the Paper, Allied-Industrial,

Chemical, and Energy Workers International Union's global campaign against the Paris-based Imerys involving the Georgia Marble plant in Alabama; and the international boycotts of the Neptune Jade, a Singapore-owned Orient Lines freighter—what Atleson calls "a stimulating example of transnational labor solidarity."

Atleson finds it ironic that the pressures inducing the creation of multinational firms also provide openings for international labor solidarity. He believes globalization may create a more international worker, more aware of common interests with workers in other countries. He also concludes that unions may challenge existing statutory and judicial prohibitions by maintaining that the current policy choice of protecting alleged neutral companies violates a valuable human right, the right to withhold one's labor in aid of others.

The labor movement must be more than just another self-interest group protecting its own members regardless of the cost to others.[50] As Lance Compa put it, "Unions cannot make progress on social issues, on social justice for workers, on workers' rights, simply under their own motive power."[51] The culture of union organizing must change, particularly by developing alliances with other social movements such as civil rights groups, the women's rights movements, environmental groups, immigrant worker support organizations, and religious organizations. While unions need the support of these groups, however, it has to be a reciprocal relationship in which unions are ready and willing to assist other groups in their struggles.[52]

Two chapters in this book deal with alliances between labor and religious organizations at the grassroots level on the West Coast and in the Delmarva Peninsula of Delaware, Maryland, and Virginia. Linda Lotz in her chapter, "All Religions Believe in Justice," provides a most informative history of faith-labor relations in the United States and the changes that have occurred recently in that relationship, case histories of labor-religion alliances at workplaces in Los Angeles, a "tool box" of activities that have been used to support union organizing, and some thoughts about challenges facing the faith community in its relations with labor. Lotz describes the tactics used by Clergy and Laity United for Economic Justice (CLUE) in helping Local 11 of the Hotel Employees and Restaurant Workers obtain a new contract at five prominent hotels in Beverly Hills; assisting the Service Employees International Union's Local 399 in ongoing efforts to organize the Catholic Healthcare West hospitals; supporting janitors, cafeteria, and dormitory workers' in their efforts to resist the subcontracting out of their jobs and to obtain a new contract; and advocating for workers, particularly Latinos, working for the Los Angeles garment industry.

Her tool box includes the use of prayer which many workers said "gave them more inner strength and courage to take action or to speak the truth about their work situations and their needs"; strategic planning in the early stages of an organizing campaign or contract negotiations which also gave clergy and laity opportunities to learn what it means to live in low-wage poverty and to develop personal relationships with workers; "speaking truth to power" in which employers are held accountable in their own congregations or communities; the engagement of elected officials who understand the inherent power of the clergy to mobilize public opinion in their districts; the establishment of models for employers (for example, many day care centers, schools, nursing homes, and hospitals contacted CLUE to determine if their wages and benefits matched the Living Wage ordinance CLUE had supported); public education campaigns including worker presentations to congregations, clergy sermons, special ceremonies, study groups, and visits to union meetings; and investigation of working conditions through worker hearing boards and research projects or commissions. Lotz concludes by discussing the challenges to this work.

Reverend Jim Lewis explains the title of his chapter, "Grasshopper Power," in terms of the "small creature that, in large numbers, brought to Pharaoh one of the many plagues sent by God as a warning to let people held in slave labor go free." He maintains that all piety must finally come to rest on earth. His piece of earth is the Delmarva Peninsula where he chairs the Delmarva Poultry Justice Association (DPJA), which labors on behalf of the predominantly African Americans, Mexicans, and Central Americans who work for what he calls "Big Chicken," mainly Perdue and Tyson.

Most people do not know where the food they eat comes from and have no idea under what conditions the food on their plate is grown and harvested or how much pain and injustice is associated with their meal. He quotes author Wendell Berry, who asks why thank God for food "that has come at unbearable expense to the world and other people?" Berry contends that "every eater has a responsibility to find out where food comes from and what its real costs are, and then to do something to reduce the costs."

Lewis describes the dangerous and unhealthful working conditions in this industry and relates the personal stories of several workers because he feels strongly that there is a human face to this human rights struggle and that human face must never be allowed to get lost in conceptualizing about human rights. He explains that the poultry industry is notorious for threatening and firing workers who try to organize. Workers are expendable and those who are injured are disposed of and replaced by other workers made up largely of immigrants.

Lewis explains that the Episcopal church put him to work on the Delmarva Peninsula because "there are deep moral issues at stake around the chicken we bless and eat." He perceptively defines the sharp distinction between the charity role of religion and its role in challenging an unjust system:

> What the poultry industry is comfortable with is the religious community being available to do the personal and charitable tasks so long associated with the church and religious work. What that means is that companies are not troubled by clergy and churches calling on the injured and sick, assisting the unemployed with meals and canned goods, and burying members of the community. What they object to is seeing clergy and churches move from a charitable and traditionally pastoral role to a more activist role of addressing the justice issues involved with the injured, unemployed and deceased. When a local preacher or congregation start asking questions and directing attention to what causes people to be injured in the workplace, what economic forces have caused people to be unemployed, and what the workplace situation was that caused a person to die, that's when the preacher, according to company standards, has gone to meddling.

Lewis maintains that it is the mission of religion to address fundamental justice issues at the workplace even though doing so means living with the fear of losing a contract, or a job, or the poultry plants that threaten to pack up and move jobs to a more "friendly" community if people raise their voices in protest at how wrong things are. The DPJA that he chairs seeks to get growers, workers, religious communities, environmentalists, consumers, animal rights advocates, and others around the same table to address underlying economic justice issues—groups that cut across race, class, cultural, and language differences and denominational affiliations—because the poultry companies thrive off dividing the community. Lewis says that without a contract union workers are unable to stand up to the injustices they experience daily while working in the hatcheries, catching chickens, or laboring on the line in a processing plant. He warns that unions cannot assume that they are in touch with this work force until contracts are in Spanish and leadership in local unions has a Latino face. He calls for unity across all parts of a community, across all divisions, to bring about real structural change.

The chapters in this book constitute more than differences of opinion among advocates for particular values. The basic foundation of law is moral choice and the moral choices made in our labor laws concern fundamental human rights: the right of workers to associate and participate in workplace decisions that affect their lives and livelihoods, their right to physical security and safe and healthful working conditions, and the right not to be discriminated against, in other words, not to be treated as less than fully human. The moral choices we make, particularly when they involve human rights, determine what kind of society we want to have and what kind of people we want to be. The chapters in this book use a human rights standard to judge our own labor law and policy choices. Together they constitute a long overdue beginning in this country toward the promotion and protection of worker rights as human rights.

CHAPTER 2

Workers' Freedom of Association in the United States

The Gap between Ideals and Practice

Lance Compa

Workers' Freedom of Association under International Human Rights Law

The International Background

International human rights analysts and advocates have been slow coming to grips with issues of workers' rights. Attention has focused on pressing problems of arbitrary detention and torture, massacres of indigenous peoples and ethnic minorities, atrocities of war and civil war, and other gross human rights violations, not on workers' rights to form and join trade unions and bargain collectively. For their part, worker representatives have been slow to see human rights aspects in their work. The day-to-day challenge of organizing and bargaining in complex frameworks of national labor laws leaves little time to learn from international human rights discourse. In the United States and in many other countries, union and management officials and attorneys, as well as administrators and judges, seldom turn to international law to inform their work.

All that is changing under the pressures of a globalizing economy and new sensitivity to the human rights implications of workers' rights advocacy. For example, employers' organizations, trade unions, and governments joined together at the International Labour Organization (ILO) in 1998 to issue a landmark Declaration on Fundamental Principles and Rights at Work. Their common declaration set out freedom of association and the right to organize and bargain collectively as the first such principles.

At the same time, the 1998 action at the ILO was not a complete novelty. Freedom of association for workers has long been universally acknowledged as a fundamental right. A widely accepted body of international norms has established standards for workers' freedom of association covering the right to organize, the right to bargain collectively, and the right to strike.[1]

Sources of international labor law on workers' freedom of association include human rights instruments developed by the United Nations and by regional human rights bodies, principles elaborated through worker, employer, and government representatives at the ILO, and labor rights clauses in international trade agreements. The United States has acknowledged its international responsibility to honor workers' freedom of association by ratifying human rights instruments, in particular the International Covenant on Civil and Political Rights. It has also accepted obligations under ILO conventions on freedom of association and under the 1998 declaration.

The United States has committed itself, through international agreement, to effectively enforce U.S. laws protecting workers' rights to organize, bargain collectively, and strike. It has affirmed obligations to honor workers' freedom of association in its own trade laws and in laws governing U.S. involvement in the World Bank, the International Monetary Fund, and other multilateral bodies. In all these laws, freedom of association is held out as the foremost internationally recognized workers' right.

International Human Rights Instruments

• The Universal Declaration of Human Rights (1948) states that "everyone has the right to freedom of peaceful assembly and association," and "everyone has the right to form and to join trade unions for the protection of his interests."[2]
• The International Covenant on Civil and Political Rights (ICCPR, 1966) declares: "Everyone shall have the right to freedom of association with others, including the right to form and join trade unions for the protection of his interests."[3]
• The International Covenant on Economic, Social, and Cultural Rights (ICESCR, 1966) obliges governments to "ensure the right of everyone to form trade unions and join the trade union of his choice . . . the right of trade unions to function freely . . . the right to strike."[4]

The United States ratified the International Covenant on Civil and Political Rights in 1992. The ICCPR requires ratifying states "to respect and to ensure to all individuals within its territory and subject to its jurisdiction the rights recognized in the present Covenant" and "to adopt such legislative or other measures as may be necessary to give effect to the rights recognized in the present Covenant." The ICCPR also constrains ratifying states "to ensure that any person whose rights or freedoms as herein recognized are violated shall have an effective remedy."[5]

When the U.S. Senate ratified the International Covenant on Civil and Political Rights in 1992, it took several reservations, understandings, and declarations sidestepping certain obligations in the covenant, perhaps most notably reserving the right to impose capital punishment on minors.[6] But it took no reservations, understandings, or declarations with respect to Article 22 on the right to form and join trade unions, or to Article 2 requiring an "effective remedy" for rights violations.[7]

Acknowledging the obligation, the U.S. State Department's first report on compliance with the ICCPR stated that "provisions of the First, Fifth and Fourteenth Amendments guarantee freedom of assembly in all contexts, including the right of workers to establish and join organizations of their own choosing. . . . The rights of association and organization are supplemented by legislation."[8] Distressingly, however, the United States devalued the importance of protecting the right to freedom of association by claiming that the widespread exclusion of workers from coverage under U.S. labor laws—primarily agricultural workers, domestic workers, and supervisory employees—"means only that they do not have access to the specific provisions of the NLRA . . . for enforcing their rights to organize and bargain collectively."[9] "Only" lacking access to enforcement mechanisms means these workers' rights can be violated with impunity. There is no labor board or other authority to remedy violations.

Regional Instruments

Regional human rights instruments reaffirm the consensus on workers' freedom of association as a basic right:

- The American Declaration of the Rights and Duties of Man
(1948) states: "Every person has the right to assemble peaceably with others in a formal public meeting or an informal gathering, in connection with matters of common interest of any nature. Every

person has the right to associate with others to promote, exercise and protect his legitimate interests of a political, economic, religious, social, cultural, professional, labor union or other nature."[10]

• The later American Convention on Human Rights (1969) declares: "Everyone has the right to associate freely for ideological, religious, political, economic, labor, social, cultural, sports, or other purposes."[11]

• Reflecting the international consensus on workers' freedom of association, though it does not involve the United States, the European Convention for the Protection of Human Rights and Fundamental Freedoms (1950) says: "Everyone has the right to freedom of peaceful assembly and to freedom of association with others, including the right to form and to join trade unions for the protection of his interests."[12]

• The European Union's Community Charter of Fundamental Social Rights of Workers (1989) holds: "Employers and workers of the European Community shall have the right of association in order to constitute professional organisations or trade unions of their choice for the defence of their economic and social interests . . . the right to negotiate and conclude collective agreements under the conditions laid down by national legislation and practice . . . the right to strike, subject to the obligations arising under national regulations and collective agreements.[13]

ILO Conventions and OECD Guidelines

Building on this international consensus, the ILO, a UN-related body with nearly universal membership and tripartite representation by governments, workers, and employers, recognizes freedom of association and protection of the right to organize as core workers' rights. Over decades of painstaking treatment of allegations of violations of workers' rights, the ILO's Committee on Freedom of Association has elaborated authoritative guidelines for implementation of the right to organize, the right to bargain collectively, and the right to strike.

• ILO Convention 87 on freedom of association and protection of the right to organize says that "workers and employers, without distinction whatsoever, shall have the right to establish and, subject only to the rules of the organization concerned, to join organizations of their own choosing without previous authorization."[14]

• ILO Convention 98 declares that "workers shall enjoy adequate protection against acts of anti-union discrimination in respect of their employment. . . . Such protection shall apply more particularly in respect of acts calculated to—a) make the employment of a worker subject to the condition that he shall not join a union or shall relinquish union membership; b) cause the dismissal of or otherwise prejudice a worker by reason of union membership or because of participation in union activities."

In greater detail, Convention 98 goes on to say:

"Workers' and employers' organizations shall enjoy adequate protection against any acts of interference by each other. . . . Machinery appropriate to national conditions shall be established, where necessary, for the purpose of ensuring respect for the right to organize . . . . Measures appropriate to national conditions shall be taken, where necessary, to encourage and promote the full development and utilization of machinery for voluntary negotiation between employers' and workers' organizations, with a view to the regulation of terms and conditions of employment by means of collective agreements."[15]

• The ILO's Declaration of Fundamental Principles and Rights at Work says expressly: "All members, even if they have not ratified the Conventions in question, have an obligation arising from the very fact of membership in the Organization, to respect, to promote, and to realize, in good faith and in accordance with the [ILO] Constitution, the principles concerning the fundamental rights which are the subject of those Conventions, namely: (a) freedom of association and the effective recognition of the right to collective bargaining."

ILO core conventions were officially recognized at the 1995 World Social Summit conference in Copenhagen. In addition to those covering freedom of association and the right to organize and bargain collectively, ILO norms on forced labor, child labor, and employment discrimination were defined as essential to ensuring human rights in the workplace. Signed by the United States, the Copenhagen summit's final declaration called on governments to ratify these ILO conventions, to respect them even if they have not ratified them, and to use international labor standards as a benchmark for their national legislation.[16] The U.N. High Commissioner for Human Rights includes these ILO conventions in an authoritative list of "international human rights instruments."[17]

At the Organization for Economic Cooperation and Development (OECD), the United States subscribes to a statement that "enterprises should, within the framework of law, regulations and prevailing labor relations and employment practices, in each of the countries in which they operate: respect the right of their employees to be represented by trade unions . . . and engage in constructive negotiations . . . with such employee organizations with a view to reaching agreements on employment conditions."[18] The OECD has characterized freedom of association and the right to organize and bargain collectively as labor standards that "reflect basic human rights which should be observed in all countries, independently of their levels of economic development and sociocultural traditions."[19]

U.S. Commitments in the Multilateral Setting

The United States championed the 1998 adoption of the ILO's Declaration on Fundamental Principles and Rights at Work that set out freedom of association as the first such principle and right. On adoption, U.S. labor secretary Alexis Herman declared, "The ILO has underlined and clarified the importance of the fundamental rights of workers in an era of economic globalization . . . ILO members have accepted the need to be accountable, and with this action there will now be a process within the ILO to demonstrate that accountability."[20]

Whether or not a country has ratified conventions 87 and 98, the ILO has determined that ILO member countries are "bound to respect a certain number of general rules which have been established for the common good . . . among these principles, freedom of association has become a customary rule above the Conventions."[21] Though it has so far not ratified conventions 87 and 98, the United States has accepted jurisdiction and review by the ILO Committee on Freedom of Association (CFA) of complaints filed against it under these conventions.

Several ILO cases involving the United States in the past fifteen years have challenged its compliance with international labor standards. The United States has defended itself in these cases by describing its elaborate system of labor laws and procedures and asserting that the system generally conforms to ILO standards.[22] In many cases, the CFA "noted with concern" and "drew the attention of the U.S. government" to problems the committee perceived. In some cases, the committee recommended changes in policy and practice. However, the ILO has no enforcement powers, and the United States took no action to implement the recommendations.

Reporting on compliance and defending against complaints, the United States likewise has taken the position that its labor law and practice are generally in conformance with the conventions but that some elements of U.S. federal and state labor laws conflicted with the conventions' detailed requirements. Ratification of ILO conventions would amount to "back door" amendments to U.S. labor laws without following the normal legislative process because the ratification of an international treaty would supersede preexisting domestic law under the United States' constitutional system.[23] The leading U.S. employer representative to the ILO cautioned against making U.S. law subject to ILO supervision because "this machinery is not in our control" and the United States could be embarrassed by holding "our domestic laws and practices up to greater international scrutiny and criticism than is presently the case."[24]

Before 1999, U.S. reports to the ILO on compliance with freedom of association standards offered boilerplate descriptions of American labor law and asserted that U.S. law and practice "appears to be in general conformance" with conventions 87 and 98.[25] Significantly, however, the United States in a 1999 report acknowledged for the first time that "there are aspects of this [U.S. labor law] system that fail to fully protect the rights to organize and bargain collectively of all employees in all circumstances."

The 1999 U.S. report stated that "the United States is concerned about these limitations and acknowledges that to ensure respect, promotion and realization of the right to organize and bargain collectively, it is important to reexamine any system of labor laws from time to time to assure that the system continues to protect these fundamental rights."[26] An ILO Committee of Expert-Advisors that reviewed country reports called the U.S. statements "striking for their open recognition of difficulties still to be overcome or situations they deemed relevant to achieving full respect for the principles and rights in the Declaration."[27]

U.S. Trade Laws

The United States has also affirmed the importance of international norms and obligations regarding workers' freedom of association in its own trade statutes. Although these laws create obligations for trading partners, they underscore the U.S. commitment to freedom of association under international standards. In these statutes governing trade relationships with other countries, Congress defined freedom of association and the right to organize and bargain collectively as "internationally recognized workers' rights."[28]

Labor rights amendments have been added to statutes governing the Generalized System of Preferences (GSP) in 1984,[29] the Overseas Private Investment Corporation in 1985,[30] the Caribbean Basin Initiative in 1986,[31] section 301 of the Trade Act of 1988,[32] Agency for International Development (AID) funding for economic development grants overseas,[33] and U.S. participation in the World Bank, International Monetary Fund, and other international lending agencies.[34] All these measures hold out the possibility of economic sanctions against trading partners that violate workers' rights. In every case, freedom of association and the right to organize and bargain collectively are the first rights listed.

In formulating the labor rights clauses in U.S. trade laws, Congress has relied on ILO guidance. In its report on legislation governing U.S. participation in international financial institutions, Congress pointed to "the relevant conventions of the International Labour Organization, which have set forth, among other things, the rights of association [and] the right to organize and bargain collectively."[35] Analyzing the application of workers' rights provisions in U.S. trade laws, the General Accounting Office underscored the fact that "the international standards have been set by the International Labour Organization, which is part of the U.N. structure."[36]

Since passage of the 1984 GSP labor rights amendment, the U.S. State Department's annual *Country Reports on Human Rights Practices* refer to ILO Convention 87 as the basis of U.S. policy on workers' freedom of association. The reports say that "the 'right of association' has been defined by the International Labour Organization to include the right of workers to establish and to join organizations of their own choosing," and "the right to organize and bargain collectively includes the right of workers to be represented in negotiating the prevention and settlement of disputes with employers; the right to protection against interference; and the right to protection against acts of antiunion discrimination."[37]

Regarding strikes, the State Department's human rights policy is that "the right of association includes the right of workers to strike. While strikes may be restricted in essential services (i.e., those services the interruption of which would endanger the life, personal safety or health of a significant portion of the population) and in the public sector, these restrictions must be offset by adequate guarantees to safeguard the interests of the workers concerned."[38] The State Department's formulation of the right to strike reflects the determination by the ILO that the right to strike is an essential element of the right to freedom of association.

The North American Free Trade Agreement

The North American Free Trade Agreement (NAFTA) among the United States, Canada, and Mexico brought with it a labor side agreement, the North American Agreement on Labor Cooperation (NAALC). Freedom of association and protection of the right to organize, the right to bargain collectively, and the right to strike are the first three "labor principles" of the NAALC. This international agreement was negotiated at the insistence of the United States government following a commitment made during President Clinton's 1992 electoral campaign.[39]

The NAALC characterizes the first labor principle as "the right of workers exercised freely and without impediment to establish and join organizations of their own choosing to further and defend their interests." The agreement formulates the right to bargain collectively as "the protection of the right of organized workers to freely engage in collective bargaining on matters concerning the terms and conditions of employment." It describes the right to strike as "the protection of the right of workers to strike in order to defend their collective interests."[40] With its North American trading partners, the United States committed itself to promote the NAALC labor principles and to "effectively enforce its labor law" to achieve their realization.[41]

U.S. Labor Law and International Norms— Violations and Case Studies

American workers secured the right to organize, to bargain collectively, and to strike with passage of the National Labor Relations Act (NLRA) of 1935. The NLRA declares a national policy of "full freedom of association" and protects workers' "right to self-organization, to form, join, or assist labor organizations, to bargain collectively through representatives of their own choosing, and to engage in other concerted activities for the purpose of collective bargaining or other mutual aid or protection."[42]

The NLRA makes it unlawful for employers to "interfere with, restrain, or coerce" workers in the exercise of these rights. It creates the National Labor Relations Board (NLRB) to enforce the law by investigating and remedying violations. All these measures comport with international human rights norms regarding workers' freedom of association.

However, some provisions of U.S. law openly conflict with international standards on freedom of association. Millions of workers, including farm workers, household domestic workers, and low-level supervisors are expressly barred from the law's protection of the right to organize. United States law allows employers to permanently replace workers who exercise the right to strike, effectively nullifying the right. New forms of employment relationships have created millions of part-time, temporary, subcontracted, and otherwise "atypical" or "contingent" workers whose freedom of association is frustrated by the law's failure to adapt to changes in the economy.

The reality of U.S. labor law enforcement falls far short of its goals. Many workers who try to form trade unions are spied on, harassed, pressured, threatened, suspended, fired, deported, or otherwise victimized in reprisal for their exercise of the right to freedom of association.

A culture of near-impunity has taken shape in much of U.S. labor law and practice. Any employer intent on resisting workers' self-organization can drag out legal proceedings for years, fearing little more than an order to post a written notice in the workplace promising not to repeat unlawful conduct. Many employers have come to view remedies like back pay for workers fired because of union activity as a routine cost of doing business, well worth it to get rid of organizing leaders and derail workers' organizing efforts.

Private employers are the main agents of abuse. But international human rights law makes governments responsible for protecting vulnerable persons and groups from patterns of abuse by private actors. The United States is failing to meet this responsibility. As noted above, many groups of workers are unprotected by the law. And even when the law is applied for workers who come under its coverage, enervating delays and weak remedies invite continued violations.

Patterns of violations exemplified in the case studies that follow are not exceptional and the accelerating pace of violations is not a new phenomenon. Congressional hearings in the 1970s and 1980s revealed extensive employer violations and ineffective enforcement of laws supposed to protect workers' rights. Other government studies and reports from independent commissions in the 1980s and 1990s reached similar conclusions.[43] But those research efforts did not analyze violations in light of international human rights standards, which is the goal of this study.

Discrimination against Union Supporters

Firing or otherwise discriminating against a worker for trying to form a union is illegal but commonplace in the United States. In the 1950s, workers who suffered reprisals for exercising the right to freedom of association numbered in the hundreds each year. In the 1960s, the number climbed into the thousands, reaching slightly more than 6,000 in 1969. By the 1990s more than 20,000 workers each year were victims of discrimination for union activity—23,580 in 1998, the most recent year for which figures are available.[44]

An employer determined to get rid of a union activist knows that all that awaits, after years of litigation if the employer persists in appeals, is a reinstatement order the worker is likely to decline and a modest back-pay award. For many employers, it is a small price to pay to destroy a workers' organizing effort by firing its leaders.

Case Study: A Nursing Home in Southern Florida

Workers at the King David Center in West Palm Beach voted 48–29 in favor of union representation in an NLRB election in August 1994. "I had a determination to get respect," said Jean Aliza, the first of several workers fired for organizing activity at King David. "I am a citizen, and I deserve respect."[45]

According to the administrative law judge's decision in the case, King David management proceeded systematically to fire the most active union supporters.[46] Jean Aliza, Lude Duval, Marie Larose, Marie Pierre Louis, Michelle Williams, Carline Dorisca, and Ernest Duval were all fired on fabricated charges. They were ordered reinstated by the administrative law judge who heard testimony and reviewed documents, and the NLRB upheld the judge's order. In 1999 the workers were still not reinstated because of appeals to the courts. No collective agreement has been reached.

Jean Aliza was "set up" by managers and fired early in the organizing effort, after a yearlong "satisfactory" record suddenly became "unsatisfactory" based on warning notices he never saw.[47] King David "was determined to rid itself of the most vocal union supporter from the beginning," said the administrative law judge's ruling, referring to Ernest Duval.[48]

Ernest Duval was still vocal about his union support when he spoke in July 1999, but he was also frustrated. "I see the government protecting management," he said. "It's been four or five years now, and I've got bills to pay. Management has the time to do whatever they want."[49]

Forced Attendance at Captive-Audience Meetings

Almost without limits, employers can force workers to attend captive-audience meetings on work time. Most often, these meetings include exhortations by top managers that are carefully scripted to fall within the wide latitude afforded employers under U.S. law—allowing "predictions" but not "threats" of workplace closings, for example—to deter workers from choosing union representation. Employers can fire workers for not attending the meetings. They can impose a "no questions or comments" rule at a captive-audience meeting and discipline any worker who speaks up.

Case Study: Food Processing Workers in Wilson, North Carolina

Smithfield Foods is the world's largest hog processing company. A Smithfield Foods plant in Wilson, North Carolina, employs some three hundred workers who produce bacon, sausages, hot dogs, and other retail pork items. Workers here tried to form a union in early and mid-1999, but they lost an NLRB election. Several workers detailed threats by Smithfield managers in captive-audience meetings to close the plant if workers voted in favor of collective bargaining.[50]

Recounting management's captive-audience meetings with workers, shipping department employee Robert Atkinson said, "I saw about seven different videos on how the union just takes your dues, goes on strike, gets into fights and stuff. It really hurt us that the people only heard one side. It would be a lot fairer if the union could come in and talk to us. The company has a big advantage, making people come to meetings and showing videos. A lot of people don't come to union meetings. They're scared the company will know."[51]

"Predicting" Reprisals

Under U.S. law, employers and antiunion consultants they routinely hire to oppose workers' organizing have refined methods of legally "predicting"—as distinct from unlawfully threatening—workplace closures, firings, wage and benefit cuts, and other dire consequences if workers form and join a trade union. A "prediction" that the workplace will be closed if employees vote for union representation is legal if the prediction is carefully phrased and based on objective facts rather than on the employer's subjective bias.

This fine distinction in the law is not always apparent to workers or, indeed, to anyone seeking common-sense guidance on what is allowed or prohibited. Unfortunately for workers' rights, federal courts have tended to give wide leeway to employers to "predict" awful things if workers vote for a union.

One prediction a court found to be "carefully phrased" was made by the owner of an Illinois restaurant where workers sought to form a union and bargain collectively. In a tape-recorded speech in a captive-audience meeting the owner stated, "If the union exists at [the company], [the company] will fail. The cancer will eat us up and we will fall by the way-side . . . I am not making a threat. I am stating a fact. . . . I only know from my mind, from my pocketbook, how I stand on this." The NLRB found this statement unlawful. A federal appeals court reversed the board, finding the employer's statement a lawful prediction that did not interfere with, restrain, or coerce employees in the exercise of the right to freedom of association.[52]

Case Study: Manufacturing Plant in Maryland

In the mid-1990s, a new company called Precision Thermoforming and Packaging, Inc. (PTP), employed more than five hundred workers in a Baltimore, Maryland, factory. The workers packaged and shipped flashlights, batteries, and computer diskettes. PTP's wages were five dollars to seven dollars per hour. Health insurance cost employees thirty-six dollars per week from their paychecks—a benefit most of them declined, since they made only $200–$280 per week. There was no pension plan.

In mid-1995, a group of PTP workers began an effort to form and join a union. PTP management fired eight workers active in the union organizing effort. In addition to the firings, PTP managers and supervisors:

- threatened to close the plant if a majority of workers voted in favor of the union;
- threatened to move work to Mexico;
- threatened to fire workers who attended union meetings;
- threatened to fire anyone who joined the union;
- threatened to transfer workers to dirtier, lower-paying jobs if they supported the union;
- told workers to report to management on the activities of union supporters;

• stationed managers and security guards with walkie-talkies to spy on union handbilling and report on workers who accepted flyers;
• denied wage increases and promotions to workers who supported the union.

"I'd say I was the one who got the union going," said Gilbert Gardner, who began working at PTP in April 1993. "Then they fired me the day after I went to a hearing at the NLRB to set up the election," he told interviewers.[53] Union supporters lost the NLRB election by a vote of 226–168. Before the vote, 60 percent of the workers signed cards authorizing the union to represent them in collective bargaining. Management admitted committing the acts noted in the NLRB complaint and settled NLRB charges, but then declared bankruptcy and closed operations. Victimized workers were still waiting for back pay payments five years later.

Delays in NLRB and Court Procedures

Delays in the U.S. labor law system arise first in the election procedure. NLRB elections take place at least several weeks after workers file a petition seeking an election. In many cases, employers can hold up the election for months by challenging the composition of the "appropriate bargaining unit."

An employer can also file objections to an election after it takes place, arguing that the union used unfair tactics. It takes several months to resolve these objections. But even when the NLRB rules in workers' favor and orders the company to bargain with the union, the company can ignore the board's order. This forces workers and the NLRB to launch a new case on the refusal to bargain, often requiring years more to resolve in the courts. In many of the cases studied for this report, workers voted in favor of union representation years ago, but they are still waiting for bargaining to begin while employers' appeals are tied up in court.

Long delays also occur in unfair labor practice cases. Most cases involve alleged discrimination against union supporters or refusals to bargain in good faith. Several months pass before an administrative law judge hears the cases. Then several more months go by while the judge ponders a decision. The judge's decision can then be appealed to the

NLRB, where often two or three years go by before a decision is issued. The NLRB's decision can then be appealed to the federal courts, where again up to three years pass before a final decision is rendered. Many of the workers in cases studied here were fired many years earlier and have won reinstatement orders from administrative judges and the NLRB, but they still wait for clogged courts to rule on employers' appeals.

Case Study: Shipyard in New Orleans, Louisiana

With more than six thousand workers, Avondale Industries is Louisiana's largest private-sector employer. The U.S. Navy is Avondale's biggest single customer, accounting for more than three-quarters of its business—$3 billion in Navy contract awards in the past decade.

In 1993 Avondale workers launched an effort to form a union. Avondale management unleashed a massive campaign against the workers' organizing effort. "They told us they'd shut the door if the union came in, that we'd lose Navy contracts," said sheet-metal worker Bruce Lightall, who has worked at the plant since 1979.[54] The company also fired twenty-eight union activists.

In a speech to assembled Avondale workers at a captive-audience meeting before the 1993 election, company president Albert L. Bossier, Jr., said, "If you really want to destroy Avondale, vote for the damn union. Those of you who don't want to destroy Avondale, you better make sure these whiners, malcontents, and slackers don't even come close to winning this election . . . Secure your future by rejecting this union and its bosses."[55]

Despite management's threats and firings, the union won the election by a vote of 1,950–1,632. Avondale management refused to accept the results and began a series of appeals to the NLRB. In April 1997—nearly four years after the election—the NLRB certified the results and ordered Avondale to bargain with the union. The company still refused, appealing the board's order to the federal courts. In 1999 a federal appeals court overturned the election results because voter lists contained workers' first initials rather than their first names. No NLRB election had ever been overturned on such grounds before.[56]

In a 1998 decision, a judge characterized Avondale's behavior as "egregious misconduct, demonstrating a general disregard for employees' fundamental rights." The judge ordered Avondale to reinstate fired workers and to pledge not to repeat the unlawful conduct.[57] Avondale did not comply with this order, and the case remained on appeal.

Frank Johnson, an Avondale machinist with twenty-five years in the yard, said in 1999, "After the election I thought we'd sit down after a week or so and start bargaining. Now it's six years later, and we're still waiting."[58] Echoing Johnson, Bruce Lightall said, "I thought we'd sit down after the election and negotiate a contract like reasonable people, to get some justice, respect, dignity. In time I found out how the law doesn't work for workers. It just helps the companies. They can appeal forever."[59]

Surface Bargaining, Weak Remedies

Even after workers form a union and bargaining begins, employers can continue to thwart workers' choice by bargaining in bad faith—going through the motions of meeting with the workers and making proposals and counterproposals without any intention of reaching an agreement. This tactic is called "surface bargaining." The problem is especially acute in newly organized workplaces where the employer has fiercely resisted workers' self-organization and resents their success.

Case Study: Telecommunications Castings in Northbrook, Illinois

Acme Die Casting, a division of Lovejoy Industries, makes a variety of small aluminum and zinc castings, mainly for the telecommunications industry. In October 1987, Acme employees voted 69–39 in favor of union representation. Jorge "Nico" Valenzuela became the head of the organizing committee and then the president of the shop union in 1987. "When we won the election we thought, 'Finally we can start making things better.' We elected a negotiating committee and asked management to start bargaining," Valenzuela said.[60] He and the other Acme workers did not know that years would go by before any bargaining would begin and that, when it did, bargaining would be futile.

After the election, the company filed objections to the election so unfounded that the NLRB dismissed them without a hearing. But Acme refused to accept the decision, forcing the union to file refusal-to-bargain charges and a new round of labor board and court proceedings.

In an April 1993 decision, a judge ordered Acme to "cease and desist" from refusing to bargain and to return to the table and bargain in good faith. The judge ruled that the company's violations "are repeated and pervasive and evidence on its part an attitude of total disregard for its statutory obligations."[61]

Acme management shifted to a strategy of appearing to bargain by making proposals and counterproposals to the workers on minor subjects. However, the company "made demands they knew would be suicidal for the union" in other areas, said union representative Terry Davis. The company proposed tiny wage increases and demanded enormous hikes in employee payments for health insurance that would far exceed any pay increase.[62] A carefully coached employer can nearly always frame such demands as "hard bargaining," which is legal, as long as it makes proposals and counterproposals in other areas.

Bargaining went nowhere for six years. In March 1999, the union sent a letter to Acme and to the NLRB disclaiming representation rights. "At this rate," said union negotiator Davis, "the company would still have deal-killers on the table twenty-five years from now."[63]

A top Acme official conceded, "We worked long and hard for years to convince our employees that they're better off with us than with a union. The union did nothing but lie about us. People now believe they're better off with us than with a union."[64]

These were years when, under the law, the company was supposed to be bargaining in good faith with the workers with a sincere desire to reach an agreement. The manager's statement shows how far from sincere the company's bargaining was. Yet in the end, its methods prevailed against workers' right to bargain collectively, and the legal structure supposed to protect workers' rights proved no impediment to these tactics.

Exclusion of Millions of Workers from Protection of Organizing and Bargaining Rights

International norms refer to the right of "every person" to form and join trade unions and to bargain collectively. Several of the cases examined for this report involved workers excluded from coverage by the NLRA, such as agricultural workers, domestic employees, and "independent" contractors who actually work in a dependent relationship with a single employer for years. Low-level supervisors and managers are also excluded from legal protection.

In all, millions of workers in the United States are excluded from coverage of laws that are supposed to protect the right to organize and bargain collectively. Workers who fall under these exclusions can be summarily fired with impunity for seeking to form and join a union. Even where the employer does not fire them, workers' requests to bargain collectively can be ignored.

Case Study: Household Domestic Workers

More than 800,000 officially reported "private household workers" held jobs as domestic employees in 1998. Nearly 30 percent were foreign migrant workers, and the vast majority were women.[65] Officials of multinational corporations, international organizations, and other elites residing in the United States have brought thousands of domestic workers into the United States.

An employer from Hilda Dos Santos's native Brazil held her as a "live-in slave" for nearly twenty years in a suburb of Washington, D.C. She was never paid a salary, was physically assaulted, and was denied medical care for a stomach tumor the size of a soccer ball. Her plight only came to light when neighbors acted at the sight of her tumor and resulting publicity led to a successful prosecution.[66] Dos Santos's case illustrates the difficulty of uncovering such abuses. After twenty years of servitude, she was granted temporary legal status to testify against her employer but was then subject to deportation. An unknown number of similar victims remain silent because exposure would mean deportation for them, too.

Whether or not they are enforced, minimum wage laws, overtime laws, and child labor laws apply to most domestic workers in the United States. But if they attempt to form and join a union, or exercise any freedom of association even without the intent of forming a union, they can be threatened, intimidated, or fired by their employer because of their exclusion from coverage by the NLRA. The same abuses affect agricultural workers, low-level supervisors, and so-called independent contractors who are really dependent on a single employer for their livelihoods.

Subcontracted and Temporary Workers Are Denied Freedom of Association and Effective Remedies

Many employers can use subcontracting arrangements and temporary employment agencies to avoid any obligation to recognize workers' rights of organization and collective bargaining. This problem afflicts workers in the apparel manufacturing industry, in janitorial services, in high-technology computer services, and other sectors characterized by layers of subcontracting arrangements. Prime contractors often simply cancel the contracts of subcontractors whose employees form and join unions. The result is widespread denial of workers' freedom of association.

Case Study: High-Tech Computer Programmers in Seattle, Washington

The dilemma regarding freedom of association is stark for workers at temporary employment agencies, even at the high end of the economic ladder. A recent example of temporary agency workers' dilemma is found at the cutting edge of the new economy. More than twenty thousand workers are employed at Microsoft's Redmond, Washington, campus and other facilities in the Seattle area. But six thousand of them are not employed by Microsoft. Instead, they are employed by many temporary agencies supplying high-tech workers to Microsoft and other area companies. Many have worked for several years at Microsoft. They have come to be known as "perma-temps." Often they work side-by-side in teams with regular, full-time employees.

Some Microsoft perma-temps formed the Washington Alliance of Technology Workers (WashTech) in early 1998. But WashTech has a Catch-22–type problem. By defining perma-temps as contractors employed by various temporary agencies, Microsoft avoids being their employer for purposes of the NLRA's protection of the right to organize. Meanwhile, the agencies tell temps that in order to form a union that agency management will deal with, they have to organize other employees of the agency, not just those working at Microsoft.

"First we asked our Microsoft managers to bargain with us," said perma-temp Barbara Judd, describing an effort by her and a group of co-workers to be recognized by Microsoft.[67] Management refused. Responding to press inquiries, a spokesman for Microsoft said, "bargaining units are a matter between employers and employees and Microsoft is not the employer of the workers."[68]

Attempts to be recognized by the temp agencies were equally unavailing. " 'We don't have to talk to you, and we won't' is what they told us," said Judd. "They told us we had to get all the temps that worked at other companies besides Microsoft. We had no way to know who they were or how to reach them. Besides, they had nothing to do with our problems at Microsoft."[69]

Barbara Judd's perma-temp post at Microsoft ended in March 2000 when the company announced it was abandoning the tax preparation software project that she and her co-workers developed.[70] "We received two days notice" of being laid off, Judd said. Some workers moved to another tax preparation software company, but Judd decided to look for full-time employment. "I don't want to be a part of that system," she said. "Workers who take temp jobs do not realize there is a larger impact than just the absence of benefits. You essentially lose the ability to organize . . . the legal system is just not set up to deal with these long-term temp issues."[71]

Case Study: Sweatshop in New York City

Under current U.S. labor law, retailers and manufacturers who profit from sweatshops' race to the bottom on labor standards are not held responsible for labor law violations committed by contractors or subcontractors, including violations of workers' organizing rights. United States Labor Department studies in 1997 and 1998 indicated that nearly two-thirds of garment industry shops in New York violated minimum wage and overtime laws.[72] A comprehensive study of the Los Angeles garment industry concluded in 1999 that "this important industry is plagued by substandard working conditions. . . . There is widespread non-compliance with labor, health, and safety laws."[73]

In 1997, a group of workers at a midtown Manhattan sewing shop called MK Collections formed a union. Mario Ramírez said that workers took action because they had not been paid for two months and "because the owners screamed at people."[74] Eduardo Rodríguez, who like Ramírez came to New York from Puebla, Mexico, was another union adherent. "We would talk outside before work and at lunchtime, but never in big groups," he explained. Rodríguez estimated union support at about forty workers, a majority of the sixty-five to seventy people working at MK Collections.

In January 1997, MK workers brought their organizing effort to a head with a work stoppage demanding back pay for work performed. At first, their movement bore fruit. Seven members of the organizing group signed a handwritten agreement with the owner recognizing the workers' union, setting a just cause standard for disciplinary action, promising to maintain clean bathrooms, and—besides paying wages on time—to pay an additional fifty per week until full back pay was reached for each worker.

The agreement held up for only four months. The employer fired two committee members who did not want to protest because of immigration fears. In early May 1997, the company closed, claiming that a manufacturer had canceled a production contract. According to Ramírez and Rodríguez, the owner reopened at a new location and hired a new work force just a few days later.

Their experience left a mark on Ramírez and Rodríguez. "I've thought about organizing in my new job," said Ramírez, who found other work in the garment industry. "But I need to be guaranteed that I won't be fired." Rodríguez, who took a new job in a restaurant, said, "As long as there is no law to protect us better, I don't think it is likely that I will organize again."

Nullification of the Right to Strike by the Permanent-Replacement Doctrine

Under U.S. labor law, employers can hire new employees to permanently replace workers who exercise the right to strike. This doctrine runs counter to international standards recognizing the right to strike as an essential element of freedom of association. Considering the U.S. striker replacement rule, the ILO's Committee on Freedom of Association determined that the right to strike "is not really guaranteed when a worker who exercises it legally runs the risk of seeing his or her job taken up permanently by another worker, just as legally" and that permanent replacement "entails a risk of derogation from the right to strike which may affect the free exercise of trade union rights."[75]

Case Study: Steelworkers in Pueblo, Colorado

Oregon Steel Company permanently replaced more than a thousand workers who exercised the right to strike at its Pueblo, Colorado, steel mill in October 1997. Many of the replacements came from outside the Pueblo area, drawn by the company's newspaper advertisements throughout Colorado and neighboring states offering wages of thirteen dollars to nineteen dollars per hour for permanent replacements. A company notice declared, "It is the intent of the Company for every replacement worker hired to mean one less job for the strikers at the conclusion of the strike."[76]

On December 30, 1997, three months after it began, Oregon Steel workers ended their strike and offered unconditionally to return to work. The company refused to take them back except when vacancies occur after a replacement worker leaves. Some workers returned under this legal requirement, but most of the Oregon Steel workers were still out of work in 2000 because the company permanently replaced them with new hires.

According to a judge who held an eight-month-long hearing on the case, the company was guilty of interference, coercion, discrimination, and bad-faith bargaining.[77] Oregon Steel management's unfair labor practices before the strike began included:

- spying on a union meeting where bargaining strategies were discussed;
- threatening to close the plant and "reopen non-union in thirty days" if workers struck;
- assigning undesirable, dirty jobs cleaning arc furnaces and cooling towers to union supporters because of their support for the union;
- threatening to "bust" the union if workers struck (as one witness testified, a supervisor said, "within 15 minutes they would have two bus loads of people in the mill to do our jobs and the union would no longer exist");
- promising promotions to workers if they would cross the picket lines and return to work during a strike.

In all, said the judge, Oregon Steel's unfair labor practices "were substantial and antithetical to good faith bargaining." Under this ruling, workers are entitled to reinstatement because a company that violates the law loses the right to permanently replace strikers. However, the company appealed the decision and vowed to keep appealing for years before a final decision is obtained in the case. In the meantime, the workers remain replaced and without their means of livelihood for themselves and their families.

Special Vulnerability of Immigrant Workers

International human rights principles apply to all persons regardless of immigration and citizenship status. In the United States, workers' rights violations with particular characteristics affect immigrant workers in nearly every economic sector and geographic area examined in this report. For many, the vulnerability of their undocumented status and related fear of deportation are the most powerful forces inhibiting their exercise of the right to organize and bargain collectively.

During NLRB election campaigns, employers commonly threaten to call the Immigration and Naturalization Service (INS) to have workers deported. Immigrant workers are often afraid to come forward to file unfair labor practice charges or to appear as witnesses in unfair labor practice proceedings because they fear their immigration status will be challenged.

Case Study: Warehouse Workers in the Washington Apple Industry

Thousands of workers are employed in the warehouse sector of the Washington apple industry. Like apple pickers, many seasonal workers in the warehouses are migrants from Mexico.

Apple warehouse workers are not defined as agricultural workers. They are covered by the NLRA, which makes it an unfair labor practice to threaten, coerce, or discriminate against workers for union organizing activity. But when workers at one of the largest apple processing companies sought to form and join a union in 1997 and 1998, management responded with dismissals of key union leaders and threats that the INS would deport workers if they formed a union.[78] Here is how one worker described the company's tactics:

> At the meetings they talked the most about the INS. . . . [T]he company keeps talking about INS because they know a lot of workers on the night shift are undocumented—I would guess at least half. . . . It is only now that we have started organizing that they have started looking

for problems with people's papers. And it is only now that they have started threatening us with INS raids. . . . They know that we are afraid to even talk about this because we don't want to risk ourselves or anyone else losing their jobs or being deported, so it is a very powerful threat.[79]

The union lost the NLRB election even though a majority of workers had signed cards to join the union and authorize the union to bargain on their behalf.

Even Legal Immigrants Unprotected

About thirty thousand temporary agricultural workers enter the United States each year under a special program called H-2A giving them legal authorization to work in areas where employers claim a shortage of domestic workers. H-2A workers have a special status among migrant farm workers. They come to the United States openly and legally. They are covered by wage laws, workers' compensation, and other standards.

But valid papers are no guarantee of protection for H-2A workers' freedom of association. As agricultural workers, they are not covered by the NLRA's antidiscrimination provision meant to protect the right to organize.

H-2A workers are tied to the growers who contract for their labor. They have no opportunity to organize for improved conditions and no opportunity to change employers to obtain better conditions. If they try to form and join a union, the grower for whom they work can cancel their work contract and have them deported.

Case Study: H-2A Workers in North Carolina

More than ten thousand migrant workers with H-2A visas went to North Carolina in 1999, making growers there the leading employers of H-2A workers in the United States.[80] North Carolina's H-2A workers are mostly Mexican, single young men, who harvest tobacco, sweet potatoes, cucumbers, bell peppers, apples, peaches, melons, and various other seasonal crops from April until November.[81]

At home "there's no work," which workers described as their main reason for emigrating.[82] Many of the workers come from rural villages in Mexico. Some spoke Spanish with difficulty, as in their village at home people mainly speak Misteco, a local Indian language. In most cases earnings in U.S. dollars from their H-2A employment are the only source of income for their families and for their communities.

There is evidence of a campaign of intimidation from the time H-2A workers first enter the United States to discourage any exercise of freedom of association. Legal Services attorneys and union organizers are "the enemy," they are told by growers' officials. Most pointedly, officials lead workers through a ritual akin to book-burning by making them collectively trash "Know Your Rights" manuals from Legal Services attorneys and take instead employee handbooks issued by growers.[83]

On paper, H-2A workers can seek help from Legal Services and file legal claims for violations of H-2A program requirements (but not for violation of the right to form and join trade unions, since they are excluded from NLRA protection). However, in this atmosphere of grower hostility to Legal Services, farm workers are reluctant to pursue legal claims that they may have against growers. "They don't let us talk to Legal Services or the union," one worker said. "They would fire us if we called them or talked to them."[84]

In December 1997, the U.S. General Accounting Office (GAO) reported that "H-2A workers . . . are unlikely to complain about worker protection violations fearing they will lose their jobs or will not be hired in the future."[85] The fear of blacklisting is well founded, according to a 1999 Carnegie Endowment study, which based its findings on interviews conducted in Mexico with current Mexican H-2A workers. The Carnegie study found that "blacklisting of H-2A workers appears to be widespread, is highly organized, and occurs at all stages of the recruitment and employment process. Workers report that the period of blacklisting now lasts three years, up from one year earlier in the decade."[86]

Recommendations

Here is a summary of recommended changes in U.S. labor law to address the problems cited above:

Interim Reinstatement and Tougher Remedies

A worker who is fired for union activity should be reinstated immediately while the case continues to be litigated. Only such an interim reinstatement remedy can overcome the devastating impact on individual workers who are dismissed and on the workers' overall organizing effort.

Remedies and sanctions should have a deterrent effect. Workers should receive full back pay regardless of interim earnings. They should receive punitive damages in cases of willful violations. In addition to paying workers victimized by violations, employers who repeatedly engage in discrimination against union supporters should pay substantial fines to the NLRB.

Equal Access to the Workplace, Faster Elections, "Card-Check" Certification

A principle of equal access should apply where employers force workers into captive audience meetings at the workplace. Workers should have access to information from union representatives in the workplace about their right to form and join trade unions and to bargain collectively. The NLRB should conduct an election as quickly as possible after the filing of a petition, normally within a matter of days. Experience demonstrates that where workers and employers can agree to use card checks—neutral verification that workers freely signed cards authorizing representation and collective bargaining—they can combine the benefits of freedom of choice and a mutually respectful relationship that carries over into collective bargaining. Public policy should encourage the use of voluntary card-check agreements as an alternative means of establishing workers' majority sentiment and collective bargaining rights.

Tighter Scrutiny and Tougher Remedies

The NLRB should more closely scrutinize employers' antiunion statements for potentially coercive effect, removing the artificial distinction between "predictions" and "threats." Where it finds violations, the board should apply strong, swift remedies like additional union access to the workplace or bargaining orders where employers' conduct makes fair elections impossible.

Legal Responsibility of the Dominant Economic Force

Labor law must change to encompass the rights and interests of contingent workers, contract workers, and others involved in new occupations and industries. Congress should enact legislation cutting through the fiction of subcontracted employment relationships that are structured to avoid responsibility for recognizing workers' rights.

Fixing responsibility should be based on a test of effective economic power to set workers' terms and conditions of employment, not on the formality of an employment relationship. The dominant economic entity in the employment relationship holding real power over workers' terms and conditions of employment should have legal responsibility to bargain with workers when a majority choose representation.

Stronger Remedies for Surface Bargaining

Stronger remedies should be fashioned for willful refusal to bargain in good faith. For example, where workers have formed and joined a new union in a previously unorganized workplace and the employer is found to bargain in bad faith, workers should have recourse to first-contract arbitration as a remedy, where an independent arbitrator sets contract terms.

Arbitration for a first contract gives workers an opportunity to establish a bargaining relationship that would most likely have taken shape had the employer bargained in good faith. It also provides a chance to demonstrate to the employer that both parties can act responsibly under a collective agreement, making good-faith negotiations more probable in subsequent bargaining.

Eliminate Statutory Exclusions, Protect All Workers' Organizing Rights

Congress should bring agricultural workers, domestic workers, and low-level supervisors under NLRA coverage with the same rights and protections as all other covered workers. Legal reform should also subject employers' claims of workers' "independent contractor" status to strict scrutiny under standards that make the workers' real-life dependence on employers—not how employers classify them—the test for NLRA coverage.

In general, workers who *want* to organize and bargain collectively should have the *right* to organize and bargain collectively, except where there are manifestly no employers to bargain with or where the essence of such workers' jobs is so truly managerial or supervisory that they effectively would be bargaining with themselves.

Reverse the Permanent-Replacement Doctrine

Congress should enact legislation prohibiting the permanent replacement of workers who exercise the right to strike. The balance should be restored to a genuine equilibrium in which temporary replacements give way to employee strikers when the strike ends. In effect, prohibiting permanent striker replacements effectuates a "balance of pain" in a strike that promotes more rapid resolution of a dispute while respecting both workers' right to strike and management's continued operations.

More Protection for Immigrant Workers, Stronger Remedies

Congress should establish a new visa category for undocumented workers who suffer violations of their right to organize and bargain collectively, and the INS should exercise discretionary authority to allow them to remain in the United States. Workers who obtain a reinstatement order because their right to freedom of association was violated should be immediately reinstated and granted a work authorization card for sufficient time to allow them to seek renewed, extended, or permanent authorization under discretionary authority in such cases.

Mobility and Organizing Rights for H-2A Workers

The H-2A program should allow workers to seek work with a different employer if their employer violates their rights. Where workers are dismissed or discriminated against for exercising rights of association, a strengthened regime is needed to ensure swift reinstatement or placement with another employer who will respect their rights.

Labor Department regulations governing the H-2A program should halt H-2A recruiters' characterizations of unions and legal services as "enemies" of H-2A workers. The H-2A program should instead require that workers be fully informed of their rights to organize and bargain collectively and have access to legal services and to the justice system, as they desire.

Conclusion

Both historical experience and a review of current conditions around the world indicate that strong, independent, democratic trade unions are vital for societies where human rights are respected. Human rights cannot flourish where workers' rights are not enforced. This is as true for the United States as for any other country.

Labor rights violations in the United States are especially troubling when the U.S. administration is pressing other countries to ensure respect for internationally recognized workers' rights as part of the global trade and investment system—at the World Trade Organization, for example, or in the new Free Trade Agreement of the Americas. United States insistence on a rights-based linkage to trade is undercut when core labor rights are systematically violated in the United States.

Without diminishing the seriousness of workers' rights violations in the United States, a balanced perspective must be maintained. United States workers generally do not confront gross human rights violations where death squads assassinate trade union organizers or collective bargaining and strikes are outlawed. But the absence of systematic government repression does not mean that workers in the United States have effective exercise of the right to freedom of association. On the contrary, workers' freedom of association is under sustained attack in the United States, and the government is failing its responsibility under international human rights standards to deter such attacks and protect workers' rights.

So long as worker organizing, collective bargaining, and the right to strike are seen only as economic disputes involving the exercise of power in pursuit of higher wages for employees or higher profits for employers, change in U.S. labor law and practice is unlikely. Reformulating these activities as human rights that must be respected under international law can begin a process of change.

What is most needed is a new spirit of commitment by the labor law community and the government to give effect to both international human rights norms and the still-vital affirmation in the United States' own basic labor law of full freedom of association for workers. A way to begin fostering such a change of spirit is for the United States to ratify ILO conventions 87 and 98. This will send a strong signal to workers, employers, labor law authorities, and to the international community that the United States is serious about holding itself to international human rights and labor rights standards as it presses for the inclusion of such standards in new global and regional trade arrangements.

CHAPTER 3

Closing the Gap between International Law and U.S. Labor Law

Lee Swepston

ILO Standards and General Human Rights

International labor law is very much a part of international human rights law. It is dealt with principally but not exclusively by the International Labour Organization (ILO). It is also dealt with under broader international human rights law, which is in turn based on the ILO standards that have been adopted over the years.

Almost all the relevant United Nations human rights standards were adopted after the ILO conventions on the four basic human rights subjects of concern to the ILO. The two principal ILO conventions on freedom of association are the Freedom of Association and Protection of the Right to Organize Convention, 1948 (Convention 87) and the Right to Organize and Collective Bargaining Convention, 1949 (Convention 98).

Freedom from forced labor is the second of the major human rights concerns of the ILO and also concerns both general human rights and the more specific labor rights. It is embodied in the Forced Labor Convention, 1930 (Convention 29) and the Abolition of Forced Labor Convention, 1957 (Convention 105).

The theme of equality has been the subject of a number of international human rights instruments. The ILO's principal conventions on it are the Equal Remuneration Convention (Convention 100), and the Discrimination (Employment and Occupation) Convention (Convention 111).

Finally, the basic standards include the theme of child labor, covered principally in the Minimum Age Convention, 1973 (Convention 138), and the Worst Forms of Child Labor Convention, 1999 (Convention 182). But these four categories are only the fundamental human rights conventions of the ILO, forming part of a much larger body of law.

What Does International Labor Law Cover?

International labor law is a wide and interesting field, which until lately has usually been ignored by writers on international law generally and on human rights particularly. It was in fact the first international law and human rights subject, with the campaign in the 1830s to eliminate slavery, and it is one of the fundamental subjects of international law.

These days the ILO is calling the basic content of international labor law "decent work." This is, of course, a new expression for the ILO's traditional rallying cry of social justice,[1] with some new elements. Coined by ILO director-general Juan Somavia in his first (1999) report after being elected to lead the ILO, it is meant to address the changing environment for labor in the broader framework of globalization and the basic rules that should govern working life.

Why do we need a new way of looking at the requirements of international labor law? Even though globalization has resulted in some real gains in the world's economies, it has also left behind very many of the world's working people, including the small employers and entrepreneurs whose success is essential for economic development around the world. Unemployment has risen and conditions of work have worsened especially in areas not directly caught up in export industries. So one of the ILO's goals in its legal and promotional work is to ensure that no one is left behind—or at least to reduce the negative impact of globalization on vulnerable workers.

The international legal context in which we are operating is that the labor law of most of the world is based on ILO standards. The standards were often incorporated directly into the labor legislation of newly independent countries that wanted to separate themselves from their colonial masters in the period beginning in the 1960s. As these countries became more sophisticated, they again turned to the ILO for help in reforming and updating their standards, and now at any one time the ILO is usually working with forty or fifty countries on their labor legislation. Needless to say, the ILO's advice on labor legislation is either based directly on its standards, or at least ensures that its advice is consistent with those standards.

In some cases the influence may be the other way around. When the ILO adopts new standards, its basis is the best national standards worldwide, and it tries not to establish international standards that are too high for developing countries to ratify. Thus the international standards are based on the best practice and most recent trends in its member states.

International labor law is not much known in the United States, as the U.S. system works very much in its own context. The fact that the U.S. system is different from the rest of the world has led to the decision of the U.S. government not to ratify most of the ILO's basic human rights standards, though the ILO and the U.S. government have been working on some of them. Among them, the Discrimination (Employment and Occupation) Convention, 1958 (Convention 111) has been before the Senate for advice and approval for ratification for some time now, and it will be interesting to see whether the Bush administration will renew the proposal to ratify it.

Scholars of the ILO will go back further, but we can begin to discuss the content of international labor law with the ILO constitution adopted in 1919. It was updated in the 1944 Declaration of Philadelphia—a fundamental source of international human rights that was incorporated into the constitution in 1946.

The constitution includes the basic expressions of human rights—though the term was not in use then—which includes equal pay for work of equal value; freedom from discrimination on the basis of race, creed, and sex; and of course freedom of association.

Beyond the constitution, the ILO's traditional method of addressing social problems is through international labor standards, or conventions and recommendations adopted by the International Labor Conference. This body of standards is sometimes characterized as the International Labor Code, though the ILO's standard-setting is in fact much richer than any one country's labor code. These international instruments do, of course, lay down requirements of international law that are similar to the content of national labor codes—hours of work, minimum wages, social security systems, safety and health, and the like. But they also contain guidance for larger questions of social policy that do not normally appear in national labor law. These include such matters as dedicating governments to the concept of full, productive, and freely chosen employment,[2] the needs that should be met by statistical systems,[3] the virtues of good labor administration,[4] the requirements for labor inspectorates,[5] and many other questions.

Given below is a sketch of the basic contents of ILO standards, forming international labor law.

Basic Rights

The ILO has always seen several categories of rights as fundamental for all workers. This has been progressively formalized over the last few years. There are the four categories of rights mentioned above, all based on concepts to be found in the ILO constitution. There are two conventions considered as fundamental for each of the basic rights.

FORCED LABOR

The basic ILO documents about forced labor are the Forced Labor Convention, 1930 (Convention 29), and the Abolition of Forced Labor Convention, 1958 (Convention 105). The Forced Labor Convention, adopted shortly after the League of Nations adopted the Slavery Convention of 1926, laid down the labor concerns necessary for protection against this most basic of human rights problems.[6] This convention prohibits all forced or compulsory labor, with a few common-sense exceptions (compulsory military service, prison labor in most situations, emergencies, etc.). After World War II, and in the face of the horror of the concentration camps and the mass forced labor programs of the Communist states, the ILO adopted the Abolition of Forced Labor Convention (Convention 105)[7] in 1957, supplementing the basic protection laid down in Convention 29. Convention 105 prohibits forced labor for political or development purposes, as a punishment for expressing political opinions or participating in strikes, and in other related circumstances.

FREEDOM OF ASSOCIATION AND COLLECTIVE BARGAINING

The basic ILO covenants covering these issues are the Freedom of Association and Protection of the Right to Organize Convention, 1948 (Convention 87), and the Right to Organize and Collective Bargaining Convention, 1949 (Convention 98). Convention 87 establishes principles and guarantees concerning the right to organize vis-à-vis the state, and Convention 98 protects workers and their organizations especially from employers. Convention 98 also promotes voluntary collective bargaining to determine conditions of employment. The two instruments taken together contain the essential elements for the creation, administration, and functioning of employers' and workers' organizations. These two conventions were adopted just before and after the adoption of the Universal Declaration of Human Rights in December 1948 and well before the United Nations had begun to adopt conventions. Indeed, in addition to taking up the theme of freedom of association and the right to organize in terms compatible with ILO standards, there is an explicit reference to Convention 87 in both 1966 international human rights covenants (article 23[2] of the Civil and Political Rights Covenant and article 8[3] of the Economic, Social and Cultural Rights Covenant):

> 3. Nothing in this article shall authorize the States Parties to the International Labour Organization Convention of 1948 concerning Freedom of Association and Protection of the Right to Organize to take legislative measures which would prejudice, or apply the law in such a manner as to prejudice the guarantees provided for in that Convention.

DISCRIMINATION

The issue of discrimination is covered by the Equal Remuneration Convention, 1951 (Convention 100), and the Discrimination (Employment and Occupation) Convention, 1958 (Convention 111). In 1951 the International Labor Conference adopted the Equal Remuneration Convention (Convention 100) to protect the right of women and men to equal remuneration for work of equal value, going beyond the principle of equal pay for equal work laid down in 1948 in the Universal Declaration of Human Rights. It went on in 1958 to adopt the Discrimination (Employment and Occupation) Convention (Convention 111),[8] which laid down the right to protection against discrimination in the world of work, on the basis of a wide range of grounds. These standards were then supplemented by the United Nations conventions that addressed the theme of equality in the broader context, including labor: the International Convention on the Elimination of all Forms of Racial Discrimination (1965); the International Covenant on Economic, Social, and Cultural Rights (1966); the International Convention on the Suppression and Punishment of the Crime of Apartheid (1973); and the Convention on the Elimination of All Forms of Discrimination against Women, adopted in 1979.

CHILD LABOR

The ILO has addressed child labor with its Minimum Age Convention, 1973 (Convention 138), and Worst Forms of Child Labor Convention,

1999 (Convention 182). The international community, including the ILO, was slower to adopt human rights standards concerning child labor, the fourth of the ILO's principal human rights concerns. The ILO had traditionally treated child labor as a technical subject, and as of its first conference in 1919 adopted a long series of instruments regulating the age of entry into employment and work of young people in various economic sectors. This way of dealing with the subject culminated in 1973 with Convention 138. The adoption of the UN Convention on the Right of the Child in 1989 was crucial in giving expression in a convention to the notion that the rights of children, including the right to protection against economic exploitation, fell properly into the human rights sphere. The ILO filled the gap in its own human rights standards on child labor by adopting the Worst Forms of Child Labor Convention (Convention 182) in 1999, and this has followed the lead of the Convention on the Rights of the Child in gathering ratifications faster than any other in ILO history.

This set of rights was endorsed as fundamental by the World Summit on Social Development in Copenhagen in 1995, which stated that all states should ratify these standards and apply them if they could not yet ratify them. The ILO then launched a ratification campaign for them, and nearly 400 ratifications of these eight conventions have been registered since then, with many more in the pipeline. More than 139 countries have ratified the conventions on freedom of association, forced labor, and discrimination, with Convention 29 having received the most at 160,[9] meaning that they are approaching virtually universal ratification fairly rapidly. This also puts them among the most ratified international human rights standards. By now, sixty-nine countries have ratified all eight, and forty-five have ratified seven of eight.

On child labor, the ILO had not earlier promoted Convention 138 aggressively, as there was a feeling among the constituents that its technical nature made it difficult to ratify, but since 1995 it has gone from under 40 to 116 with assiduous promotional work by the ILO and a real effort by the member states. In 1999, the ILO completed its human rights panoply with the adoption of Convention 182, which has already received 117 ratifications, the fastest ratification pace of any convention the ILO has ever adopted.

Beginning in 1994, its seventy-fifth year, the ILO began reflecting on updating and revitalizing a standards system that had grown heavy.

The Governing Body and the conference discussed a possible "social clause,"[10] as well as the possibility of strengthening the supervisory system to allow complaints against countries that had not ratified conventions,[11] but neither of these proposals gathered sufficient support. But the ILO did come up with an innovative new approach, which the U.S. government and employers especially supported enthusiastically. This became the Declaration on Fundamental Principles and Rights at Work.

The declaration is a pledge by all members to "respect, promote and realize in good faith" the principles and rights relating to:

1. freedom of association and the effective recognition of the right to collective bargaining;
2. the elimination of all forms of forced or compulsory labor;
3. the effective abolition of child labor; and
4. the elimination of discrimination in respect of employment and occupation.

Under the declaration's follow-up mechanism, governments that have not ratified all the ILO's fundamental conventions on each of these subjects must provide annual reports indicating how they are implementing the principles involved. An annual *Global Report* on one of these four principles is to be prepared by the director-general to examine how it is being implemented and to analyze ILO assistance. The result is to be an action plan adopted at each November session of the ILO Governing Body, to serve as the basis for targeted ILO assistance to correct the problems encountered.

The innovation is that the declaration is a purely promotional and not a supervisory instrument. Reports under it are not a new form of complaints mechanism, but a basis for finding out what is happening in the world in these four areas and for carrying out another new feature of the declaration: an obligation for the ILO to assist its members in reaching these goals.

The ILO has now had three complete rounds of reporting and discussion. Countries that had not ratified some of the conventions reported, and those reports have been published and examined by a new group of independent experts in January-February of each year since 2000.[12] The Governing Body discusses this compilation in its March session each year, and makes comments on it. The first *Global Report*, on freedom of association and collective bargaining, was published in the spring of 2000, and was discussed in the conference in June 2000, and the last part of the first cycle took place with the discussion of the action plan on freedom of association in the Governing Body in November 2000. The second report, which dealt with forced labor, was discussed by the conference in June 2001 and an action plan adopted in November of that year, to be followed by reports in successive years on child labor (2002) and discrimination (2003), before starting the cycle again.

Other Standards

The standards adopted by the ILO, and by others, cover a great number of subjects other than fundamental rights. The ILO has over time adopted 184 conventions and 192 recommendations, on all the matters that would be covered by a national labor code, and beyond. A brief reference to most of these subjects follows.

The ILO has regularly undertaken thorough reviews of its standards, the only international organization to do so. The latest such review, completed in 2002, has identified seventy-one conventions as thoroughly up to date and worth promoting, though many others remain the highest standards that developing countries have yet been able to ratify. The ILO has also recently adopted a constitutional amendment that will allow it to abrogate out-of-date conventions that should be removed from the books and is awaiting sufficient ratifications for it to enter into force, but in the meantime has "withdrawn" several older conventions that never received sufficient ratifications to enter into force.

EMPLOYMENT

Many conventions have been adopted in the field of employment. The most important is the Employment Policy Convention, 1964 (Convention 122), under which ratifying states (ninety-two up to now) have to declare and pursue, as a major goal, an active policy designed to promote full, productive, and freely chosen employment. Other ILO instruments deal with the maintenance of employment services (Convention 88 of 1948), the abolition of fee-charging employment agencies (Convention 96 of 1949) and private employment agencies (Convention 181 of 1997), vocational guidance and training (Convention 142 of 1975) and vocational rehabilitation and employment of the disabled (Convention 159 of 1983). Standards relating to termination of employment by employers, originally dealt with in a recommendation (Recommendation 119) of 1963, are now laid down in a convention (Convention 158) and a recommendation (Recommendation 166) of 1982.

WAGES

While the level of wages cannot be regulated internationally, conventions and recommendations concerning minimum wage fixing machinery were adopted in 1928 and 1951. The most recent instruments on this question—Convention 131 and Recommendation 135 of 1970—provide for a system of minimum wages to cover all groups of wage earners whose terms of employment are such that coverage would be appropriate. Instruments adopted in 1949 covered the payment of wages (Convention 95) and the question of labor clauses in public contracts (Convention 94).

GENERAL CONDITIONS OF WORK

The first convention adopted by the ILO, in 1919, was the Hours of Work (Industry) Convention (Convention 1), which provided that, subject to exceptions, working hours should not exceed eight in the day and 48 in the week. It was followed by a number of other standards on related subjects over the years. A convention (Convention 171) and a recommendation (Recommendation 178) of 1990 lay down conditions to be observed in regard to night work, including limitation of duration of such work and rest periods. They replace a number of earlier conventions that prohibited night work for women, now an outmoded concept (see below).

OCCUPATIONAL SAFETY AND HEALTH

Many of the instruments deal with safety and health at work. Some concern the general framework for policy, legislation, and implementation of measures designed to secure occupational safety and health (Convention 155 and Recommendation 164 of 1981), the establishment of occupational health services (Convention 161 and Recommendation 171 of 1985), and prevention of major industrial accidents (Convention 174 and Recommendation 181 of 1993). Others deal with protection against risks or processes, such as carcinogenic agents or substances, noncarcinogenic chemicals that endanger health, dangerous machinery, air pollution, noise and vibration. Another group of agreements establish health and safety standards for particular branches of activity, such as commerce and offices, the construction industry, dock work, and work at sea. The Safety and Health in Mines Convention (Convention 176)[13] was adopted in 1995, and a new convention (Convention 184) and recommendation (Recommendation 192) on safety and health in agriculture were adopted in 2001.

Standards have also been established to provide compensation for injury due to occupational accidents and diseases. The most recent texts on this question are Convention 121 and Recommendation 121 of 1964 (with an expanded list of occupational diseases adopted in 1980).

Under a new "integrated approach," the totality of ILO action on occupational safety and health will be discussed in the International Labor Conference in 2003 and will include an overall review of standards on the subject and how they relate to operational activities of the ILO.

SOCIAL SECURITY

Between 1919 and 1936, a series of instruments based on the concept of social insurance was adopted to protect given categories of workers against particular contingencies. Since 1944, the wider concept of social security has been adopted, aimed at providing a basic income to all in need of such protection, as well as comprehensive medical care. Comprehensive standards based on that approach were laid down in the Social Security (Minimum Standards) Convention, 1952 (Convention 102). It deals with nine branches of social security: medical care, sickness benefit, unemployment benefit, old-age, invalidity and survivors' benefits, employment injury benefit, family benefit, and maternity benefit. Since then, further instruments establishing more advanced standards have been adopted in respect of all these branches except family benefit (conventions 121, 128, 130, and 168 of 1952, 1964, 1967, and 1988). The Maternity Protection Convention, 2000 (Convention 183), is the most recent of these instruments.

Standards have also been adopted with a view to ensuring equality of treatment of nationals and nonnationals in social security (Convention 118 of 1962 in respect of workmen's compensation for industrial accidents) and the maintenance of acquired rights and rights in course of acquisition in the nine branches of social security covered by Convention 102 (Convention 157 of 1982 and Recommendation 167 of 1983).

SOCIAL POLICY

Several instruments relating to social policy as a whole were adopted (in particular the Social Policy [Basic Aims and Standards] Convention 117 of 1962) to encourage governments to pursue systematic action in this field.

INDUSTRIAL RELATIONS

In addition to the adoption of the conventions on freedom of association, described above, the ILO has dealt—mainly in recommendations—with various aspects of industrial relations, such as voluntary conciliation and arbitration, cooperation at the level of the undertaking, consultation at the industrial and national levels, and communications and examination of grievances in the undertaking.

EMPLOYMENT OF WOMEN

International action in this regard has been guided by two main considerations. Originally, the desire to protect women against excessively arduous conditions of work was the ruling factor. Subsequently, this was supplemented and partly replaced by the concern to ensure equality of rights and of treatment between women and men. The basic ILO approach now is that women should be provided special protection only in so far as conditions of work place them specifically at risk with relation to reproduction.

One form of prohibition over the years has concerned night work for women.[14] In addition to a 1906 convention adopted before the ILO was established, three ILO conventions dealt with the subject (1919, 1934, and 1948), successive revisions rendering the standards more flexible. Nevertheless, most countries now consider these standards to be inconsistent with the principle of equality, and they have been widely denounced. A protocol to the 1948 convention, adopted in 1990, permits more extensive derogations from the prohibition of night work by women. At the same time, the conference adopted standards to regulate the conditions of night work for workers generally. Protective standards for women are also contained in the conventions on maternity protection (Convention 3 of 1919, Convention 103 of 1952, and Convention 183 of 2000) and on underground work in mines (Convention 45 of 1935—another convention now considered as out of date by many countries), as well as in certain conventions dealing with occupational safety and health (e.g., lead poisoning, benzene, maximum weight for the manual transport of loads).

MIGRANT WORKERS

The principal instruments are the Migration for Employment Convention (Revised), 1949 (Convention 97), and the Migrant Workers (Supplementary Provisions) Convention, 1975 (Convention 143). The former provides for assistance and information to migrants for employment, for regulation of recruitment, and for granting to lawful immigrants treatment not less favorable than that applied to nationals in respect of labor matters and social security. The latter provides for the suppression of trafficking in migrant workers and of illegal employment of such workers, and for measures to promote equality of opportunity and treatment of migrant workers lawfully within the national territory. Both conventions are supplemented by recommendations. Instruments relating to the protection of the rights of foreign workers in the field of social security have been referred to earlier in this chapter. In a general survey of 1998, the Committee of Experts found that these instruments had such a great level of detail that many states could not ratify them, and those that had could not apply all their provisions. The ILO experts found that many of the same concerns applied to the United Nations convention on the same subject, which has not yet received sufficient ratifications to enter into force.[15] The experts proposed that consideration be given to revising them in the fairly near future. In a decision taken at its March 2002 session, the ILO Governing Body decided to include this subject on the conference agenda for detailed discussion in 2004.

OTHER SPECIAL CATEGORIES OF WORKERS

In general, ILO conventions apply to all workers falling within their scope, irrespective of nationality, and a number expressly state this. In other cases, however, conventions or recommendations have been adopted to deal with particular problems arising in various areas.

More than fifty conventions and recommendations deal with various aspects of employment and social security of seafarers. They are adopted through a special procedure aimed at ensuring participation of the representatives of seafarers and ship owners (as workers and employers in this sector are known in the ILO), and there are special conditions for their entry into force. One convention adopted in 1976 (Convention 147)[16] deals with the general question of minimum labor standards for merchant ships. Special standards have also been adopted in respect of fishermen and dockworkers.

A number of instruments deal with workers in agriculture and extend to these workers the rules applying to industry, for instance, as regards rights of association and workmen's compensation (conventions 11 and 12 of 1921). Others take into account the special features of work in agriculture. Special standards have been adopted for plantation workers (Convention 110 and Recommendation 110 of 1958 and a 1982 protocol to the convention), and for tenants and sharecroppers (Recommendation 132 of 1968). As indicated above, a new convention and recommendation on safety and health in agriculture were adopted by the 2001 session of the conference.

Indigenous and tribal peoples are protected under the Indigenous and Tribal Peoples Convention, 1989 (Convention 169), which replaced Convention 107 of 1957 on the same subject. These standards were adopted in collaboration with the UN and other interested specialized agencies and deal comprehensively with the situation of these peoples. The earlier standards had an integrationist approach, which was eliminated when the convention was revised. Convention 169 provides for action to protect the rights of these peoples and to guarantee respect for their integrity, based on the principles of consultation and participation. A series of earlier conventions, which sought to protect indigenous workers primarily in dependent territories in regard to recruiting, long-term contracts, and penal sanctions for breaches of employment contracts and to lay down special standards for workers in nonmetropolitan territories with respect to social policy, rights of association, and labor inspection have now lost their pertinence and are proposed for abrogation.[17]

Reference may also be made to Convention 149 and Recommendation 157 of 1977 relating to nursing personnel, to Convention 151 and Recommendation 159 of 1978 on labor relations in the public service, to Convention 175 and Recommendation 182 of 1994 concerning part-time workers, and to series of other instruments on particular categories of workers.

LABOR ADMINISTRATION

General provisions on the organization and functions of labor administration are laid down in the Labor Administration Convention (Convention 150) and Recommendation (Recommendation 158) of 1978. Standards relating to labor inspection are contained in Convention 81 of 1947 (for industry and commerce, with a protocol of 1995 to permit extension to the noncommercial services sector) and Convention 129 of 1969 (for agriculture) and their supplementary recommendations. Labor statistics are dealt with in instruments of 1985 (Convention 160 and Recommendation 170), which revised earlier conventions on the same subject.

Arrangements for tripartite consultations at the national level with respect to ILO standards, and regarding ILO activities more generally, are provided for in Convention 144 and Recommendation 152 of 1976.

The Implementation of International Labor Standards

All these standards are, of course, of limited use if there is no way of supervising their implementation. The ILO has an extensive scheme for doing this.

Obligations in Respect of Standards

The ILO constitution requires member states to submit all ILO conventions and recommendations to their competent authorities (normally the legislature) within a year to eighteen months of adoption, for consideration of implementing action and, in the case of conventions, of ratification. This obligation—unique to the ILO—means that there is an opportunity for new ILO standards to be taken into account by national legislatures even if they are not in a position to ratify a convention.

Under article 22 of the constitution, all states must submit reports on the conventions they have ratified, and also must send copies of those reports to the national employers' and workers' organizations. This is a very important provision, as it gives these other ILO constituents the possibility of supplementing or contradicting the governments' reports and gives the ILO other sources of information it is allowed to take officially into account.

Governments must also supply reports not only on conventions they have ratified but also, when requested by the Governing Body, on unratified conventions and on recommendations, to indicate the position of their law and practice, the difficulties encountered, and future prospects. The latter reports yield a "general survey" by the Committee of Experts.[18]

Supervisory System for Ratified Conventions

Since its founding, the ILO has had a system for supervising the manner in which governments apply the conventions they have ratified. The principal bodies are the Committee of Experts on the Application of Conventions and Recommendations, and the Conference Committee on the Application of Standards. There are also various complaint mechanisms, as well as a special system for examining freedom of association even when the countries concerned have not ratified the conventions.

Regular Supervision

The Committee of Experts carries out the first part of the regular supervisory procedure. Originally, this was done directly by the conference, but with the increasing complexity of the task the conference adopted a resolution in 1926 under which the Governing Body established the committee in time for it to begin its work in 1927.

The committee has twenty members, from all parts of the world, to allow the committee to apply the experience of different political, economic, and social systems. The members are jurists and are appointed by the Governing Body on the proposal of the director-general, with regard being given to their expertise in the relevant fields. They are appointed for three-year terms, subject to renewal.

In accordance with the 1926 resolution, the committee was created for the purpose of "making the best and fullest use" of the reports submitted on ratified conventions and for "securing such additional data as may be provided for in the forms approved by the Governing Body and found desirable to supplement that already available."

When the constitution was amended in 1946 to add new reporting obligations, the Governing Body at its 103rd session (1947) expanded the committee's terms of reference. Since then, the committee covers the examination of reports on ratified conventions (art. 22 of the constitution); reports on unratified conventions and on recommendations (art. 19); information on submission of instruments to the competent national authorities (art. 19); and reports and information on the application of conventions in nonmetropolitan territories (arts. 22 and 35).

The committee is required to examine, with complete impartiality and objectivity, whether states comply with their obligations under the constitution on standards-related matters, and in particular to examine the degree to which the legal and factual situation complies with the terms of ratified conventions. The committee has stated that in evaluating the application of conventions:

> its function is to determine whether the requirements of a given Convention are being met, whatever the economic and social conditions existing in a given country. Subject only to any derogations which are expressly permitted by the Convention itself, these requirements remain constant and uniform for all countries. In carrying out this work the Committee is guided by the standards laid down in the Convention alone, mindful, however, of the fact that the modes of their implementation may be different in different countries. These are international standards, and the manner in which their implementation is evaluated must be uniform and must not be affected by concepts derived from any particular social or economic system.[19]

The Committee of Experts examines some two thousand government reports each year. It makes comments on these reports in two forms. Observations are used for the most serious or persistent cases of noncompliance and are published in the committee's report. The committee may add a footnote inviting the government to "supply full particulars to the Conference" at its next session, or to send a detailed report before it would otherwise be due, or both. Direct requests are used to request information, clarify questions, or deal with technical points or questions of minor importance. They are not published,[20] but are sent directly to governments. They are, however, available on request.

The committee's report, containing the observations and general comments, is submitted to each session of the International Labor Conference.[21]

The conference creates each year a Committee on the Application of Standards. Like most ILO bodies, it is tripartite. It examines the report of the Committee of Experts and selects about thirty cases each year in which it requests the government concerned to appear before it and discuss the situation. The dialogue is reproduced, in slightly condensed form, in the report of the conference committee. In 1957, the committee decided that in some cases the discrepancies noted were so fundamental or had been discussed for so long a time, it should call the attention of the conference to them. Since then the committee has pointed out in its report the cases it considers most important, or other special cases of noncompliance.

The report is submitted to the conference for adoption. Important cases of noncompliance are pointed out in the general part of the report, according to various criteria. One category of these findings covers failure to comply with formal obligations, concerning, for instance, reporting or submission of conventions and recommendations to the competent national authorities. The report also deals with cases of failure to apply ratified conventions. Some special cases, which are considered by the committee to be sufficiently serious for it to express special concern, are summarized in "special paragraphs," along with a conclusion or recommendation by the committee. Other cases may be mentioned under the severest criterion of "continued failure to apply," when serious deficiencies have been encountered in the application of a convention for a given country. Cases are mentioned under this criterion only on rare occasions.

Special Procedures on Freedom of Association

In 1947, as the result of initiatives taken by the Economic and Social Council of the United Nations and on the basis of discussions concerning the principles leading to the adoption of the basic conventions on freedom of association (conventions 87 and 98), the conference adopted a resolution by which it invited the Governing Body to examine the possibility of creating a special body for the protection of trade union rights. This was based on the fact that, on the one hand, the procedures contemplated in the ILO constitution were only applicable for ratified conventions, and on the other, that the question of freedom of association was so important and often so specific (since the problems that arose were often more of fact than of law), that it was necessary to create a special procedure that could be applied independently of the ratification of the conventions on the subject.

The Governing Body decided in January 1950 to create the Fact-Finding and Conciliation Commission on Freedom of Association, and adopted its terms of reference, the basis for its procedures, and the criteria for its composition. The commission's mandate was to examine complaints submitted to the ILO Governing Body, whenever it considered an inquiry justified and the government concerned had consented (if it had not ratified the conventions on freedom of association). The latter requirement prevented the commission from functioning for many years. The Governing Body therefore decided in November 1951 to create a special committee from among its own members to carry out prior examinations of the cases submitted.

The Committee on Freedom of Association was originally conceived as a "filtering body" for the Fact-Finding and Conciliation Commission, but in practice it shortly began to recommend to the Governing Body that it bring to the attention of governments the anomalies that it had noted. In fact, in turned into a specialized body that regularly examines complaints, without the consent of the government concerned being required. It has developed its procedures over the years, with the approval of the Governing Body. Up to the end of 2001 the committee had examined well over two thousand cases, and it has developed a "jurisprudence" that clarifies and develops the principles and standards of the freedom of association conventions.

The committee is composed of nine titular and nine substitute members, and meets three times each year in Geneva. For several years, it has had an independent chairman designated by the Governing Body. Complaints may be presented only by governments or by employers' and workers' organizations. These organizations may be international organizations that have consultative status with the ILO (International Confederation of Free Trade Unions, World Confederation of Labor, World Confederation of Trade Unions, and International Organization of Employers), or other international organizations when the questions concerned directly affect national organizations affiliated to them.

The committee examines cases related to trade union legislation, collective bargaining, and strikes, but the most frequent questions concern practical measures that affect trade unions and, in particular, trade unionists. Apart from these questions, the problems most frequently examined by the committee refer to the right to strike and to bargain collectively, the dissolution or suspension of organizations, and measures of antiunion discrimination.

The committee's action has often led, directly or indirectly, to the release of trade unionists from prison or their return from exile. Its activities also have a preventive impact. The mere presentation of complaints often leads governments to resolve a trade union problem or to refrain from measures that violate principles of freedom of association, in order to avoid the case being aired publicly at the international level.

At the same time, governments are interested in cooperating with the committee in order to defend themselves against accusations made against them and to demonstrate in certain cases that they are unfounded, or to explain the reasons that have led them to take certain measures. The way in which the procedure has functioned for more than forty years demonstrates that governments have understood it in this way, and in the great majority of cases they cooperate with the committee.

The Fact-Finding and Conciliation Commission

The commission is composed of independent personalities appointed by the Governing Body. The commission may convene between three and five of its members to examine a complaint. Complaints may be submitted to it by the Governing Body under the procedure described earlier, by the conference (on the recommendation of its Credentials Committee), or by a government that complains against another government. Only governments and organizations of employers or of workers may submit complaints.

If the United Nations receives a complaint against one of its members that is not a member of the ILO, the complaint will be transmitted to the commission if the UN Economic and Social Council (ECOSOC) considers it appropriate to do so and if it has obtained the prior consent of the government concerned. If the ILO receives the complaint, the Governing Body will first submit it to ECOSOC so that the same procedure may be followed. It is interesting to note that in three cases, complaints concerned nonmember states of the ILO (Lesotho in 1975, the United States in 1979—it had briefly withdrawn from the ILO but returned in 1980—and South Africa in 1992).

Complaints Systems

The ILO constitution provides two systems for complaints of violations of ratified conventions. Representations are covered in articles 24 and 25. This procedure may only be initiated by an organization of employers or of workers that alleges that a country has not taken measures to ensure the satisfactory observance of a convention it has ratified. The Governing Body decides, on receiving a representation, whether to forward it to the government concerned and invite the government to make a statement on it. If the representation is sent to the government, and the government does not make a statement "within a reasonable time," or if the Governing Body does not consider the statement to be satisfactory, it may publish the representation and the statement, if any, received in reply to it. This procedure was used only rarely until the end of the 1970s, but since that time representations have been received far more frequently.[22]

If the representation alleges violation of a convention on freedom of association, it is usually transmitted to the Governing Body Committee on Freedom of Association, which examines them in accordance with its normal procedures. However, the rules of article 24 apply as concerns the kind of complainant (more restrictive than the rules of that committee for other complaints, as will be seen below).

The procedure also provides that the Governing Body may decide at any time that the representation shall be examined under the complaints procedure laid down by articles 26 et seq. of the Constitution.

Articles 26 et seq. of the constitution lay down the procedures for the complaints procedure. This procedure was not used successfully until 1961, but in this case as well frequency of submission of complaints has increased.

A complaint may be submitted by one country against another alleging that the latter has not taken measures for the effective observance of a convention, if both countries have ratified the convention. The Governing Body may also follow this procedure "on its own motion," in the words of article 26, or on a complaint from a conference delegate (the method used most frequently in recent years). The Governing Body may communicate the complaint to the government against which the allegations are made, so that it may make any comments it wishes. If the Governing Body does not consider this communication necessary, or if it does not receive a satisfactory answer within a reasonable time, it may appoint a commission of inquiry to consider the complaint and to report on it.

This procedure does not require the consent of the government concerned and may take place even when the government of the country against which the allegations are made decides not to participate in it.

The commission of inquiry examines the case, often holding hearings and making on-the-spot visits. It submits a report in which it sets out its findings, makes recommendations on the steps that should be adopted to meet the complaint, and indicates the time limits within which these measures should be taken (art. 28).

The report is communicated to the Governing Body and to the governments concerned, and is published. The governments concerned should indicate, within three months, whether or not they accept the recommendations of the commission of inquiry and, in case they do not, whether they desire to submit the case to the International Court of Justice. The court may confirm, modify, or annul the conclusions or recommendations of a commission of inquiry, and the court's decision is not subject to appeal. This, however, has never happened.

If a country does not comply with the recommendations or conclusions of the court within a defined period of time, article 33 of the constitution provides that the Governing Body may propose to the conference the measures it considers necessary to secure compliance. Until recently this provision was entirely theoretical, but in an exciting new development it is now being applied to Myanmar (Burma) for the first time. The commission of inquiry appointed for this case found in 1998 that—as was already well known—there is massive and systematic forced labor in the country, violating the Forced Labor Convention, 1930 (Convention 29). When the government refused to accept that this was true and failed to take measures to correct it, the Governing Body began to consider the application of article 33 in 1999, and in June 2000 the conference adopted a set of measures which were to go into force on 30 November 2000 unless the Governing Body declared itself satisfied that the measures taken complied with the recommendations of the commission of inquiry. However, the Governing Body did not find that the government had complied, and the measures went into force. One of the measures involved the question of the implementation of the commission of inquiry's recommendations and of the application of Convention 29 by Myanmar, which should be discussed at future sessions of the International Labor Conference, at a sitting of the Committee on the Application of Standards specially set aside for the purpose. Other measures adopted by the Governing Body recommend that the organization's constituents—governments, employers, and workers—"review, in the light of the conclusions of the Commission of Inquiry, the relations that they may have with [Myanmar] and take appropriate measures to ensure that the said Member cannot take advantage of such relations to perpetuate or extend the system of forced or compulsory labor." Further, the Governing Body calls on international organizations to "reconsider, within their terms of reference and in the light of the conclusions of the Commission of Inquiry, any cooperation they may be engaged in with the Member concerned and, if appropriate, to cease as soon as possible any activity that could have the effect of directly or indirectly abetting the practice of forced or compulsory labor." Finally, the Governing Body invited "the Director-General to request the Economic and Social Council (ECOSOC) to place an item on the agenda of its July 2001 session concerning the failure of Myanmar to implement the recommendations contained in the report of the Commission of Inquiry and seeking the adoption of recommendations directed by ECOSOC or by the General Assembly, or by both."

The Governing Body and conference have continued to examine the application of Convention 29 in Myanmar since then, and as of the time this paper was completed in the first half of 2002, the office had made several visits to the country to attempt to ascertain whether forced labor was continuing and to assess the measures taken. The Governing Body and conference have been informed that while some measures appeared to have been taken, they remained insufficient, and action by the ILO continues in parallel with an initiative by the UN secretary-general on more general problems in the country. Nevertheless, at its March 2002 session, the Governing Body was informed that an agreement had been concluded between the ILO and the government to station a liaison officer in the country to assist in the elimination of forced labor, the latest in a series of small but significant steps the government has taken under ILO pressure.

After a complaint procedure is completed, the government may inform the Governing Body that it has taken the measures necessary to apply the recommendations of the commission of inquiry or the court's decision and may request that another commission of inquiry be convened to verify these assertions. If this report is favorable, the Governing Body may recommend to the conference that it cease whatever measures were taken under its earlier proposals. Normally the results of commissions of inquiry are simply followed up through the regular supervisory procedures for the application of ratified conventions.

Does the ILO System Work?

The ILO has been seriously remiss in not paying sufficient attention to analyzing how well this system works, in terms of the effect its supervision has, and we are now carrying out such detailed analyses.[23] Why did we not do so before? In large part this was because for many years the system itself was its own justification, especially during the Cold War. It was set up and maintained as a bulwark against the Communist system, especially for its insistence that freedom of association required the possibility of trade union pluralism and that such fundamental rights as freedom from discrimination applied also to political opinion.

Because of this attitude, no one was asking how well it worked. In this atmosphere, the ILO got lazy. It continued to fight against violations of rights in the same way it always had, but was slow to respond to a changing world. But concerns with budgets, allied with a renewed concern for greater integration among the UN system organizations, have changed this. The ILO started looking at its effect, in a series of discussions carried out in the ILO Governing Body beginning in November 2000. These have resulted in an affirmation of the basic validity of the system, but also in some changes to concentrate on the most important problems, to reinforce connections between the supervision of the application of standards and their implementation at the national level, and in a few other adjustments.

From the viewpoint of a practitioner, I can say that it works—not always, but certainly more frequently than any other international supervisory system. I base this on having spent more than twenty-five years working in this area, at the ILO headquarters in Geneva, and in what we call "the field," that is, on the ground working directly with the constituents.

First, as a source for law: most countries in the world—and the United States and China are the two big exceptions—have ratified most of the fundamental instruments. They form a common basis of law throughout the world and are rarely challenged openly these days. Myanmar is the only state challenging the forced labor paradigm, and they are simply denying that they are practicing forced labor instead of trying to justify the practice. On child labor, the boom in commitment to the elimination of this terrible practice—and the money being made available to the ILO and others to fight it—is incredible, with the 1999 Convention 182 gathering ratifications at a record rate, and the International Program for the Elimination of Child Labor being given so much money that it is often difficult to spend it wisely, as fast as the donors want. Is child labor going away? Not yet, not everywhere, but it is being fought, and hard. Discrimination is still rife everywhere in the world, far too many of the world's trouble spots are fueled by racial and ethnic hatred, and sex discrimination is too deeply ingrained for it to disappear quickly. But laws and mechanisms are gradually being put into place, with the ILO's help.

Freedom of association is the other principal question for the ILO. As the recent Human Rights Watch study[24] demonstrates very well, this is a difficult subject and there are problems with its implementation everywhere. The United States has found that it cannot ratify the international standards on the subject—as it has said in its communications to the ILO, it is committed to the principles of conventions 87 and 98, but is unable to ratify them because of some technical differences. I am not evaluating that statement here, but it is not the opinion of everyone that these differences with international law are minor.

Nevertheless, there is constant vigilance by the ILO, and the Committee on Freedom of Association has been able to document hundreds of releases of trade unionists from prison and returns from exile among its accomplishments. The ILO has established a body of law and a reference point for freedom of association throughout the world, and there have been some significant gains, such as Indonesia and Korea, in recent years.

And the work we are doing in promoting the declaration and its underlying standards is having a real effect, even if this is as yet too small. There is nevertheless every sign that this trend will continue to accelerate. The growing number of ratifications is the first encouraging sign, and the improvements noted by the Committee of Experts at each session, though still not nearly sufficient, are a second.

On the basis of the signs the ILO is getting we are conducting studies and training sessions around the world on labor standards and human rights. We have concrete projects building on the financial support especially of the United States and some others, for eliminating forced and bonded labor in Nepal—for a major effort in the trafficking of women and child in the Mekong Delta (the only major human rights project in which China is cooperating)—for setting up mechanisms in Brazil and Namibia under which workers can make effective complaints of discrimination and have a way to protect themselves. The very large amount of work, with United States and other funding, on eliminating child labor throughout the world, through the IPEC program, is one of the brightest spots in international human rights work. On others, my own office has been carrying out a series of meetings around China to discuss ratifying the Discrimination (Employment and Occupation) Convention, 1958 (Convention 111), and I hope they don't beat the United States to it. In early 2001 the ILO visited Iran to conduct the only international seminar on international human rights held there since 1979, and our work with that country continues. There are many other instances in which countries are asking the ILO to come and help improve workers' rights.

The conference at which this paper was presented was characterized by a discussion of ILO's dental characteristics: does the ILO have teeth? Could it get teeth? Should we let someone else have teeth for our mouth? It is an interesting discussion, and one that has been going on for a while. But in fact no international organization is likely in the near future to adopt a sanctions-based approach to violations of labor standards, unless it be in such a severe case as Myanmar. The ILO will just have to keep "gumming" violators and letting them feel the effects more gradually, with the support of our partners in the United States and elsewhere.

CHAPTER 4

Risks and Rights

*The Case for Occupational Safety and
Health as a Core Worker Right*

Emily A. Spieler

> "My foreman said, 'You be sure you don't get that mule where
> no rock can fall on him.' I asked, 'What about me?' He said,
> 'We can always hire another man, you have to buy another
> mule.'"
>
> —A story sometimes told by older coal miners
> in the United States.

> A law student in West Virginia suggested that health and
> safety was the most important arena for continued employ-
> ment regulation in the United States in the twenty-first cen-
> tury. "Why?" I asked her. "Because you can always quit . . .
> but you need two legs to walk out on," she answered.

This book rests on two principles: first, that critical workers' rights
must be viewed as human rights; and second, an obvious corollary,
that all workers are due at least some minimal level of protection from
unfettered managerial control. This assertion of rights in the labor context unabashedly challenges the arguments of neoclassical economists

---

Regarding the epigraphs, I have heard the story about mules and men told frequently by coal
miners in southern West Virginia. This is the version told by Nimrod Workman, coal miner
and singer, in *Harlan Co. USA* (directed by Barbara Kopple), a documentary film about the
United Mine Workers of America strike in Brookside, Kentucky, in 1978; and it was told again
by Cecil Roberts, Jr., President of the United Mineworkers of America, to a large audience at
Charleston, West Virginia, on May 24, 2001.

The law student I quote here attended my seminar, Current Issues in Employment, in the
Fall of 2000 at West Virginia University College of Law. It was this comment that started me
thinking about the issues I explore in this chapter.

that the market efficiently resolves workplace issues and maximizes social welfare.

Various arguments underlie this reliance on rights. First, labor advocates question the belief that the "free" market delivers the best results for workers. In fact, a well-functioning market has unacceptable distributional consequences; the unequal economic power of workers and companies at specific enterprises can lead to unconscionably repressive conditions; default rules can be 'sticky' as well as misleading; and informational asymmetries and segmented labor markets mean that many workers lack real choice, an essential element in a well-functioning market. Second, the extension of human rights to the private sector is critical, as the increasingly complex web of governmental and private arrangements means that private entities function internationally in ways that mirror governmental functioning. Pure reliance on an unregulated market permits the persistence of human rights abuses in workplaces that are the equivalent of direct political oppression by governments.

This essay specifically explores the application of human rights concepts to occupational safety and health risks, starting with the premise that health and safety is a critical element of workplace justice.[1] Hazards at work pose risks to both the physical and economic health of workers. Although occupational injury and fatality rates have declined in the United States, a significant number of people are still killed or injured. An estimated 65,000 workers die each year from work-related illnesses and injuries, a total of more than 180 deaths each day.[2] Of these, approximately 6,000 workers die from traumatic work injuries, an annual rate of about 5.3 per 100,000 workers.[3] In 1999, the last year for which data are available, there were 1.7 million reported injuries and illnesses in private industry that required workers to take time off from work, and more than 1 million additional cases of workers who remained at work, but with restricted work activities, during that same year.[4] Official record keepers acknowledge that at least an additional 25 percent of these injuries occur but are not reported to government authorities.[5] Uncounted numbers of injured workers end up without employment as a result of their injuries; the social and economic costs associated with these events are huge.[6]

Not surprisingly, the occupational fatality and injury rates in advanced industrial countries are substantially lower than the rates in less developed parts of the world.[7] The U.S. fatality rate compares favorably to the death rates in Latin America and the Caribbean (13.5 deaths per 100,000 workers), the Republic of Korea (34 per 100,000), or Thailand (19 per 100,000 workers).[8] The International Labour Organization (ILO) has estimated that 1.1 million people per year die worldwide from occupational diseases, a number surpassing the average annual number of deaths from road accidents (999,000) and war (502,000).[9] There are reports as well that the number of workplace injuries is increasing with industrialization at alarming rates in developing countries.[10]

Although serious hazards are less common in developed countries with stronger economies and legal regimes, workers and commentators suggest that the protections are nevertheless not adequate. In recent years, workers have died in fires because escape doors were intentionally locked in countries as economically and politically diverse as Thailand, China, and the United States. In the United States, workers report that the Occupational Safety and Health Act (OSHA) is inadequate, that hazards are sometimes intentionally created or tolerated by management, and that these hazards and resulting injuries often go unreported. Injured workers paint a dismal picture of every aspect of the workers' compensation system. Workers feel that their employers expend their resources mounting successful political campaigns against workers' compensation and OSHA—to the detriment of workers.

In approaching the question of health and safety as a human right, I grapple with three separate issues in this essay.

First, I address the following question: where does workplace health and safety fit within the evolving international discussion regarding human rights at work—and where should it fit? In answering this question, I start by describing and critiquing the current emerging consensus regarding human rights in the workplace. This new consensus elevates specific core labor rights to human rights, but excludes working conditions from these key elevated rights. I then explore whether it is appropriate to exclude health and safety from among these core labor rights. In this section I describe the history of inclusion of health and safety in international human rights discussions and then examine the arguments for and against exclusion or continued inclusion.

To address my second major issue, I begin the challenging task of defining the "right" to health and safety. This is a difficult problem, worthy of serious and continuing debate and discussion. This section only begins to explore this topic and invites further development by others.

Finally, in the third part of this chapter, I address the assumption that relatively low occupational injury and illness rates reflect a fully realized right to healthy and safe working conditions for workers in the United States. I echo the concerns of others that, while health and safety conditions on average may be far better in the United States than in poorer countries, there are cracks in the U.S. legal regime as well as inefficiencies in the labor market that allow serious risks to persist in many workplaces.

In the end, those of us who believe that labor rights are human rights must be prepared to confront the neoclassical economic argument that assertions of rights damage not only the aggregate wealth of a society but also the well-being of workers. In responding to these arguments, we are forced to consider three questions. First, does the current system of laws, norms, and markets in fact maximize aggregate wealth? Second, does this current system achieve a distribution of wealth that meets our normative views about equality and fairness? Both of these questions are explored in this chapter. Finally, can practices, norms, or laws be changed by assertions of rights?

This last question demands that we consider the real-world utility of this entire discussion. It is my hope that the exploration of the application of rights to risks may provide an important rhetorical foundation to confront abusive working conditions in both developed and developing countries. Without a clear statement that workers have a human right to safe workplaces, international and national discussions can continue without any concern for the persistence of sometimes astonishingly abusive conditions (while we wait for proof of the hypothesis that the market will improve the working conditions of the most oppressed workers). One can imagine meetings at which serious and concerned people, including trade unionists, agree to put aside stories of extreme abuse on the basis that these issues are not within enumerated international concerns. But if there is acceptance that workers have some right to safety at work, national laws and international agreements (as well as changed social expectations that develop) will begin to transform abstract theory into enforceable rights. In contrast, the currently dominant rhetoric of the market masks, or is used to justify, fundamental inequalities of the employment relationship, supports the perpetuation of working conditions that are abusive, and obscures the need for basic principles or standards to correct for inequalities within the labor market.

Health and Safety in International Human Rights Discourse

A long history of inclusion of health and safety in international and national laws, declarations, and treaties reflects deep concern about hazardous working conditions resulting from industrialization. Recently, however, pressure has mounted to increase reliance on market forces in order to encourage economic development. This has occurred at the same time that the battle over inclusion of labor and environmental standards in international treaties has grown. In response, a new articulation of labor rights has emerged, separating general labor rights, including all working conditions, from core human rights at work. In the following sections, I discuss the exclusion of working conditions from these core rights, briefly describe the roots in international law for the inclusion of health and safety in core rights, and explore the appropriateness of the current exclusion.

The Exclusion of Health and Safety from Core Labor Rights

As the dominance of neoclassical market theory has grown, international consensus appears to be relegating economic and social rights, and particularly those involving working conditions, to a lower tier of importance in human rights discourse. There is an inevitable political tension between those who would expand social and economic rights, including workplace and health rights, and those who resist this expansion based on ideological reliance on market solutions for human problems.

In 1998, after a number of years of debate, the ILO adopted the Declaration on Fundamental Principles and Rights at Work.[11] Faced with a growing and arguably unwieldy and unenforceable list of ILO conventions, as well as international resistance to principles regarding working conditions, the ILO and member states chose to name four rights as "basic" or "core" worker rights: freedom of association and the right to collective bargaining; elimination of forced or compulsory labor; abolition of child labor; and elimination of discrimination in employment.[12] These core rights have now been characterized as human rights, as opposed to labor rights. Other organizations, including the Organization for Economic Cooperation and Development (OECD), the International Monetary Fund (IMF), and the World Bank followed the ILO's lead and accepted that these core rights constitute the critical labor rights for international discussion.[13] It is important to be clear that this emerging consensus does *not* mean that the four core rights will automatically be included in trade agreements or be made enforceable through either governmental or nongovernmental means.[14] Rather, this consensus suggests that, to the extent that any labor rights are to be recognized and enforced, it is these core rights that merit consideration. Working conditions, including wages, hours, and safety, are excluded from these core rights.

The decision to relegate working conditions to a second tier of rights is both understandable and troubling.[15] It is understandable because the decision makes strategic and political sense and is grounded in commonly accepted economic arguments. All four of the ILO's core principles focus on the formation of the labor market and not on the establishment of any minimum standards within the employment contract. These identified "core" rights authorize managerial or corporate control of workplace decision-making, subject only to equality principles (i.e., all workers must be treated equally), protection of young people, and the right to bargain individually or collectively. The individual right to bargain is rooted, as it is in U.S. law, in the prohibition on forced labor that establishes the right of the individual to quit—the equivalent, in U.S. terms, of the employment-at-will doctrine.[16] These core rights avoid any assertion of a right to a minimum level of protection within the employment relationship itself, and therefore set no expectations regarding working conditions, including health and safety. Instead, the actual conditions of work are left to employers, as controlled by local economic conditions and the local legal system, much as they were in the now developed world at the turn of the last century.

The apparent underlying assumptions are that working conditions, including occupational safety, are context driven, difficult to define, and contingent on local levels of economic development and productivity. Thus, improved working conditions and better distributional outcomes are best achieved in a market environment in which the four core rights can be exercised.[17] In fact, this argument may be stronger in the arena of health and safety, for which scientific and engineering expertise are essential in both quantifying risk and proposing interventive strategies. Moreover, advocates characterize these four rights as sufficiently concrete and self-defining to be easily understandable and enforceable.

Advocates for the limitation to these four core rights also assert that this approach of limited market-forming rights means that poorer regions will retain critical competitive advantage through lower labor costs, thus nurturing potential for economic growth and allowing for maximum flexibility in the specific labor market conditions in any given region. The costs involved in guaranteeing wages and working conditions might have adverse effects by reducing the number of jobs and by creating downward pressure on wages (as employers treat newly imposed standards as exogenous wage increases). In particular, health and safety often requires application of capital resources and, according to some economists, the market (rather than regulatory intervention) produces more optimal levels of investment in health and safety.[18] As the economy strengthens, workers can exert pressure through association, through choice in the labor market, and through exercise of political rights; as workers gain in both productivity and strength, the more contingent components of the labor contract—including wages and health and safety conditions—will improve.

Poorer countries see an assertion of rights regarding working conditions as intrusive and potentially damaging to fledgling economies (which need to retain their comparative advantage in some industries for a sustained period of time if they are to become developed). Spokespersons for these poor countries doubt the motivation of those in developed countries who argue in favor of broader labor rights, seeing these assertions as protectionist and paternalistic, forcing workers to accept the costs of improved working conditions in a depressed labor market. At the same time, developing countries are anxious to encourage economic development and expansion of employment opportunities to assist in fighting all aspects of poverty. They fear that minimum standards for working conditions will discourage investment by limiting the comparative competitive edge based upon lower labor costs.

Moreover, the selection of these four rights represents broad consensus among private parties, developing states, and the developed world. Parties across the political spectrum, including a wide range of international business organizations[19] as well as trade unions, support this articulation of core rights. At the same time, large employers and multi-national corporations benefit from the lack of any enforcement of minimum standards in the developing economies. Thus, these core rights support corporate flexibility, garnering the support of business and political conservatives.

Current dominant political ideology suggests that improved working conditions are best secured through the operation of market forces. Consensus concerning specific minimum standards was unlikely to emerge in the tripartite ILO discussions that involve developed and undeveloped states, businesses, and trade unions. To expand the list of core rights to include working conditions would also re-create the fundamental "laundry list" problem of the ILO conventions and related labor standards. While not denying the existence of deplorable working conditions, the apparent assumption is that wages and working conditions will improve with economic development and the emergence of viable trade unions: that is, their boat will rise with the economic tide as the economies develop. And while this compromise may abandon vulnerable workers in developing countries to abhorrent conditions, trade unionists value the strong international consensus around basic organizing principles.

It is true that the power of this broad endorsement of core labor principles as rights should not be underestimated, particularly if enforcement mechanisms can be established and these rights can be successfully incorporated into trade agreements. But this creation of a hierarchy of labor rights is also deeply troubling. Elimination of other labor rights involving working conditions encourages regulatory competition as countries compete to decrease labor costs in order to attract business, thus encouraging a race to the bottom. The drive for consensus also leads to a continuing search for the least common denominator: only the most serious abuses of even these four core rights become recognized as serious enough to merit the status of human rights violations.[20] Further, this approach relegates subminimum wages, excessive hours, and sometimes brutally dangerous conditions to a lower level of importance in human rights discourse: it ratifies the view that labor is a commodity that is fully subject to market forces, no matter how abusive the resulting working conditions. These core market-forming rights essentially endorse the traditional American common law default rules governing employment, presumptively giving managerial control over all aspects of the employment relationship to the employer. It may be true that conditions are often better in facilities owned by multinational corporations than in facilities owned and operated by local entrepreneurs. Nevertheless, in the context of the current world economy, inadequate working conditions are sometimes supported (directly, covertly, or indirectly) by multinational corporations. The lack of insistence on some minimal level of worker rights is disquieting: it serves the interests of powerful private parties, but enables and justifies significant oppression of workers in undeveloped labor markets where unions are (and may remain) weak. This concern is especially justified when one considers the particular problems posed by health and safety hazards.

Does Health and Safety Belong among Core Labor Rights?

The powerful arguments in favor of exclusion of health and safety from core rights (whether called "human rights" or "labor rights") must be addressed carefully. While some advocates of these positions may be boldly attempting to enable international labor exploitation, many people who support the new core rights are in fact concerned about the best way to achieve advancement for people in developing countries. In the following sections, I describe the roots of health and safety rights in international dialogue and address directly the concerns of those who take the welfare of workers seriously.

THE BASIS IN INTERNATIONAL LAW FOR VIEWING HEALTH AND SAFETY AS A CORE RIGHT

The right to health and safety has been dually rooted in rights to workplace fairness and to preservation of physical health. Until the recent development of the four core principles, working conditions, including health and safety, were consistently included in both national and international declarations. The more general right to health is increasingly recognized as a necessary component of social and economic rights that guarantee physical security. Occupational safety and health brings these two concerns together.

In fact, occupational safety and health was the subject of one of the very first international treaties. In 1906, a multilateral treaty banned the production and importation of white phosphorus matches as part of an international effort to suppress this manufacturing method because it caused a "gruesome occupational disease."[21] According to recent commentary, the rationale for international cooperation was that even though the production of phosphorus matches was dangerous to workers, no country would confront this problem alone because phosphorus substitutes were more expensive. Acting collectively, however, concerned "nations could protect workers in each country and move jointly to strengthen labor standards."[22]

Recognizing the social problems caused by industrialization, the Treaty of Versailles in 1919 required those who signed to endeavor "to secure and maintain fair and humane conditions of labor" and established the ILO to promote and improve working conditions.[23] The ILO constitution, written at a time of rapid industrialization in many parts of the world, noted in its preamble: "Conditions of labour exist involving such injustice, hardship and privation to large numbers of people as to produce unrest so great that the peace and harmony of the world are imperilled; and an improvement of those conditions is urgently required; as, for example, by . . . the protection of the worker against sickness, disease and injury arising out of his employment."[24]

At the urging of trade unions, the 1944 Declaration of Philadelphia proclaimed that "labour is not a commodity" and further recognized "the solemn obligation" of the International Labour Organization to advance a world program that would achieve "adequate protection for the life and health of workers in all occupations."[25] The human rights status of workers' rights was again affirmed in the Universal Declaration of Human Rights in 1948: "Everyone has the right to work, to free choice of employment, to just and favourable conditions of work and to protection against unemployment."[26] Recognizing that "these rights derive from the inherent dignity of the human person," the International Covenant on Economic, Social, and Cultural Rights states, more specifically, "The States Parties to the present Covenant recognize the right of everyone to the enjoyment of just and favourable conditions of work which ensure, in particular: . . . (b) Safe and healthy working conditions."[27] This covenant, entered into in 1976, articulates the most comprehensive protection of labor rights that exists in international law.

Drawing from the foundation established by the Universal Declaration and the International Covenant, the ILO has adopted specific standards governing occupational health and safety. Guiding principles are set out in standards such as the Occupational Safety and Health Convention, which aims "to prevent accidents and injury to health arising out of, linked with or occurring in the course of work, by minimizing, so far as is reasonably practicable, the causes of hazards inherent in the working environment."[28] This convention also calls for inspection systems, provision of protective clothing, and protection for workers who remove themselves from work situations that they believe are too dangerous to health or life. In addition, more specific conventions regulate economic sectors (such as construction and mining) and designated risks (such as chemicals and asbestos) or require specific measures of protection (such as medical examinations).

Despite the recent narrowing of ILO core rights and the current failure to condition world trade on compliance with labor standards, regional treaties and trade agreements acknowledge the central importance of workers' rights, including the right to humane and safe working conditions. For example, in 1984 the U.S. Congress amended the General System of Preferences program to include whether a country "has taken or is taking steps to afford to workers . . . internationally recognized worker rights." Among these rights were "acceptable conditions of work with respect to minimum wages, hours of work, and occupational safety and health."[29] The North American Agreement on Labor Cooperation, a complementary side agreement to the North American Free Trade Agreement, specifically targets both occupational safety and health and compensation for work-related injuries among eleven enumerated labor rights.[30] European treaties set out very strong requirements for working conditions, including health and safety, as well as social benefits.[31] In fact, workplace health and safety is one of the few areas of labor rights susceptible to Europe-wide regulation through directives adopted by a qualified majority vote.[32]

The right to safe working conditions is also strongly supported by the more general right to health that appears in numerous international rights covenants, including the United Nations Charter and the Universal Declaration of Human Rights.[33] The 1946 constitution of the World Health Organization recognized that the "enjoyment of the highest attainable standard of health" is a fundamental right of every human being.[34] The International Covenant on Economic, Social, and Cultural Rights includes the most explicit guarantee of the right to health, including occupational health. It states:

(1) The States Parties to the present Covenant recognize the right of everyone to the enjoyment of the highest attainable standard of physical and mental health.
(2) The steps to be taken . . . to achieve the full realization of this right shall include those necessary for: . . . the improvement of all aspects of environmental and industrial hygiene [and] the prevention, treatment and control of . . . occupational . . . diseases.[35]

A growing health and human rights movement in the last decade is rooted in the principle that "promoting and protecting human rights is inextricably linked with promoting and protecting health."[36] The broad right to health is viewed as encompassing the social and economic roots of poor health status and is not limited to the provision of personal health care services. Building on rights to public health, other commentators have suggested that rights to workplace safety and health may be rooted in this general right to health.[37] The recent development of a literature on the right to health challenges the relegation of occupational safety and health to a lower tier of importance in labor rights discussions. In view of the fact that workplace risks are a significant source of morbidity, mortality, and disability, the right to health cannot be achieved without a reduction of risks in the workplace.

ARGUMENTS FOR RETENTION OF HEALTH AND SAFETY AS A CORE LABOR RIGHT

The recent exclusion of health and safety from core labor rights is based on critical assumptions regarding the ability of the market, over time, to create adequate improvements in health and safety conditions (or provide wages that compensate for the persistence of hazards). Thus, according to this view, workers in poorer countries will benefit from the superior bargaining power provided by the four core rights and will achieve improved health and safety conditions as both their bargaining power and the economies of their home countries grow.

But this rhetorically and politically attractive worldview fails to address significant issues. First, arguing within the market paradigm, the market in fact may not be adequate to resolve health and safety issues in an economically efficient manner. Second, market based arguments fail to address critical noneconomic issues. Those who rely on the market are therefore wrong on two counts: they are wrong because their own market-based principles do not support their conclusions; and they are wrong because nonmarket-based arguments are persuasive, at least to those of us who do not adhere doggedly to purist neoclassical economic theory. In fact, relegation of health and safety to market solutions leaves workers vulnerable to unacceptable abuses.

The Market and Health and Safety.　In general, confidence in market solutions is predicated on a belief that the market functions in a manner that produces a level of optimality. (Of course, law can and does both shape and correct for market imperfections.) Labor economists often acknowledge imperfections in the market that affect the optimality of the market-based contracts. These imperfections can include problems of asymmetric information (workers lack information that employers have and therefore cannot exercise real choice); market segmentation caused by prejudice and stigma; monopsony or oligopsony (one or very few employers control the market); and so on.

Classical economists will argue that the labor market adjusts for health and safety risks, primarily by providing compensating wage differentials to workers willing to assume higher risk. But there is substantial reason to believe that the market fails, even in developed countries, to consistently provide workers with higher wages for increased risk.[38] Workers may either not know about or comprehend the risks (an information failure)[39] or they may fail to "bargain" for increased pay because of limited mobility in the labor market (a reflection of inadequate competition in the market).[40] It is certainly quite clear that many workers in hazardous jobs do not receive fully compensating wage differentials, and that, to the extent higher wages are ever available, they do not compensate for long-term latent risks, as opposed to traumatic injuries.

Workers lack both the necessary information and, equally important, the ability to process complex information relating to risks. There is strong evidence that people are unable to assess risks and probabilities accurately.[41] It is the access to usable information that is part of the presumptive underbelly of compensating wage differentials and the efficiency of the market to resolve issues of risk. Although there may be widespread agreement among economists that voluntary "well-informed consent is sufficient to justify risk exposures," there is substantial question regarding the extent to which workers voluntarily consent to risks at work.[42] The information may be difficult to obtain or not available in useful form.[43] But even with usable information, those workers who lack choices in the labor market cannot effectively influence working conditions because they are not choosing among jobs with greater or lesser safety. Because of segmentation and other inequalities that may exist even in an "efficient" labor market, some workers will be unable to refuse risks and will not be compensated for accepting them, even if the risks are known. Rights or regulation in this arena are designed to prohibit "exchanges born of desperation."[44]

Moreover, health and safety is a local public good: when health and safety conditions in a workplace are improved, they are improved for all workers who might otherwise be at risk. The marginal benefit for some other workers (or perhaps the workplace as a whole) is therefore always higher than that for the individual marginal worker.[45] Individual choices may fail to promote safety for the group and the individuals within it because individual workers may be unwilling to modify wage demands enough to make investment in health and safety for the group worthwhile. If this is true, the "bargains" reached by individual workers will not be efficient, and the market will not provide adequate incentives to employers to improve health and safety.

At the same time, wage losses suffered by workers who are injured are large and disabled workers are effectively excluded from jobs.[46] If "hazard pay" does not fully compensate all workers for the future probabilistic losses associated with injury and illness, then the costs of deaths and injuries are externalized from firms and placed on workers themselves, their families, and the general community. Employers' incentives to control workers' risks may therefore be limited, particularly in environments in which state-mandated injury compensation is either unavailable or inadequate and workers lack mobility or choice.[47] In fact, recent declines in reported injuries in the United States suggest that the market may not act to correct hazards until there is a significant labor shortage. Conversely, slack labor markets with high unemployment quite clearly undercut wage differentials for hazardous work.

Developing countries by definition have slack labor markets and high unemployment. Labor markets in these countries are more inefficient and may have dominant purchasers of labor that monopolize local labor markets and make the availability of options considerably more questionable. When combined with the often-consolidated nature of political power, employers have both legal and de facto control over working conditions in these weakly developed labor markets. It is the lower labor costs associated with these markets that give these countries their competitive edge; it is this competitive edge that the limitation of labor rights to the four core rights seeks to preserve. Abusive working conditions that result in injuries mean that workers are unable to compete in the labor market and are without alternative means of support. This becomes a circular problem: the ability of workers to seek improved conditions is contingent on their ability to quit, to withhold their labor, to bargain (individually or collectively), and to seek alternative employment; the ability to seek alternative employment is contingent on the continued health of the worker. In order for workers to have sufficient means to withhold labor or quit jobs in order to bargain for improved wages and benefits, their health must be protected. Serious injury or death permanently obliterates the ability of workers to compete in the envisioned improved labor market. Temporary poverty caused by low wages is dramatically different from permanent disablement resulting in inability to earn any wages. The market formation principles of the core labor rights are abrogated by a decision to leave protection against excessive risks at work to the presumed eventual success of the labor market. In the meantime, injury costs are transferred to the community, limiting the effectiveness of safety incentives.

Nonmarket Arguments regarding Health and Safety. Despite the fact that current dominant ideology suggests that risks to workers are best addressed through market-based solutions, market-based discussions do not address key issues in health and safety.

First, the model of workers as efficient rational self-interested maximizers is seriously flawed. As the current expanding literature on social norms, behavioral economics, and values suggests, people make decisions for a variety of reasons, not all of them rational or economically efficient.[48] The willingness to stay in a dangerous job that offers lousy wages may be the result of economic coercion (i.e., lack of choice) or a desire to stay in a particular geographic locale because of proximity to family or community (i.e., a social norm) or it may be the result of fear. That is, a higher wage (or safer) job may not be available or it may not meet other noneconomic needs. Acceptance of risks, even if the risks are known, may be the result of deeply held noneconomic values. The acceptance of risks on these bases will not produce compensating wage differentials in the manner suggested by classical economists.

Second, even when it functions efficiently, the market provides aggregate not individual solutions. Even in theory, markets only produce efficiency (in an economic sense), not justice or equality. In particular, the labor market fails to provide adequate solutions for especially vulnerable or relatively powerless workers. Aggregate assessments of the success of the market therefore may mask serious distributional injustices.[49] These injustices are shown by inequalities of wealth, but they are also shown by inequalities of risk. To the extent we assume that the market will change working conditions, we accept that workers who are more vulnerable to coercion in the labor market will work in less favorable, perhaps even inhuman, conditions. For workers who do not have work alternatives, the theoretical notions of "hazard pay" and other economic corrections for hazardous work are complete fantasy. In the case of health and safety, inequalities appear when one compares conditions in workplaces in China to those in the United States, but they also appear within the United States where relatively privileged workers (who are more likely to be native-born, European American, and unionized) may encounter less risk and better working conditions than relatively less privileged workers (who are more likely to be female, immigrants, Hispanic, African American, poorly educated, and nonunion). Rights-based theory confronts the problems of inequality in a segmented labor market by asserting an entitlement to a common floor, based on ideas of justice and humanity.[50]

These inequalities are exacerbated by the fact that very few workers in either developing countries or the United States are unionized. Employers fight collective bargaining rights vigorously everywhere; even with its designation as a core labor right, it is safe to assume that many workers will not achieve unionization. Although classical economists may oppose unionism as creating monopsonist market imperfections, the inclusion of trade union rights within the core labor rights suggests an acceptance of a need to correct market injustices through worker combinations. But if successful organizing and collective bargaining are difficult to achieve, then the inequalities of the market doom some workers to persistently dangerous conditions.

Third, the stories about extreme work hazards—such as deaths in fires when doors are locked—are not really about local conditions and economic bargains. As noted above, the right to be free from forced labor—that is, the right to quit—is only useful to those who are alive, who can walk out, and who can continue to compete effectively in the labor market for other jobs. The four selected core labor rights directly reflect basic political rights: freedom of speech, association, and right to petition (associational and bargaining rights); equality (nondiscrimination); prohibitions on involuntary servitude (no forced labor). The right to life and the right to be free from arbitrary physical abuse are also fundamental rights; these have been inexplicably excluded from the core principles for work. In view of the egregious health and safety hazards in some workplaces, it can be argued that postponing the improvement of health and safety until market forces can effect change is analogous to postponing the release of political prisoners who may die in prison until a despotic government is replaced through democratic elections. It is in fact the right to life that we are talking about when we talk about work safety.

Although neoclassical economists would certainly disagree, it can be persuasively argued that human life is incommensurable. Attempts to put value on life involve normative decision-making in the guise of science. The right to life is deeply embedded in every human rights declaration, and it is presumed in these declarations that individuals' lives must be protected from those who wield unequal power. This is precisely the issue in occupational safety and health.

In addressing a Safety Summit at the McDonough School of Business on March 30, 2001, Paul O'Neill, the controversial U.S. secretary of treasury and former CEO of Alcoa, suggested that safety is a *precondition* for work:

> A truly great organization requires that people be aligned around important values and they understand what they are. And no matter where you are in the world, they're the same. So that you have a construct that you can use as a basis for keeping your organization together no matter what the economic conditions are and no matter what the competitive conditions are, there's always a binder that holds

human beings together. . . . . Safety is not a priority. Safety is a precondition.

He continued:

When I started doing this [Alcoa's safety program], I called in the top financial staff and said to them, "If any of you ever calculate how much money we save as a consequence of being excellent in safety and health, you're fired. And the reason you're fired is because we're not going to be able to accomplish the zero [injuries] that I intend for us to accomplish if the people think this is another management scheme to make money or save money. *This needs to be about human value*" (emphasis added).[51]

O'Neill is no liberal, but this interjection of human value into a discussion of corporate policy is a recognition of the incommensurability of life.[52]

O'Neill's remarks reflect in part the theme of best practices, including safety practices, that is the current rhetorical, and perhaps actual, approach of progressive managers of large firms.[53] But his remarks also reflect a long history of philosophical recognition of the value of physical security and safety that resists quantification. As Arthur Okun has suggested, "The case for a right to survival is compelling. . . . The principle that the market should not legislate life and death is a cliché."[54] It is this recognition of the incommensurability of life that underlies what has been termed the "safety principle" that puts physical security ahead of economic compensation.[55] This same principle can be extended to safety at work, leading various authors to conclude that there are "levels of safety that reasonable workers would not wish to relinquish."[56] As Professor Gross has noted, the right to physical security is indispensable to the enjoyment of all rights and therefore protection of health is central to all labor rights.[57]

Finally, under the legal doctrines of the United States and many developing countries, the rules governing the employment contract are tipped toward employer prerogatives. When combined with the rates of high unemployment and other aspects of the economies of poorer countries, this is particular cause for concern. Without specific legal intervention into the employment contract by legislative bodies or courts, the employer has complete right to control the workplace. This means that the current legal regime (as well as the economic regime) in many developing countries permits the employer to control all aspects of the employment relationship, subject only to restrictions imposed by a not-yet-developed labor market. The construction of a right changes our default and normative assumptions about the legal regulation of work.[58] This changed assumption is an alternative to the view that the worker who continues to work has accepted risks at work and that it is the right to quit that tempers the employer's ability to require work in risky environments.

The development of the core labor rights suggests that it is appropriate to rely on the market in both developing and developed countries: optimally safe working conditions will follow from economic growth that occurs, restricted only by the operation of the four core rights (to the extent these rights are enforced). Yet the application of both market principles and nonmarket rights principles to occupational safety and health suggests that the abandonment of health and safety until the economic boat rises may be politically and morally indefensible.

What Does It Mean to Say That Health and Safety Is a "Right"?

Given that there are persuasive arguments against relegating occupational safety and health to secondary status in international and national discussions of labor rights, the issue of definition of the right must be confronted. At the outset, it is important to acknowledge three points. First, the idea that the four core rights included in the 1998 declaration are self-defining and universal, and therefore distinguishable from working conditions, is nonsense: these four core rights also require definition, are intrinsically ambiguous, and are context-dependent. This is particularly obvious with regard to child labor rules, but it is perhaps more complex with regard to rights to organize and bargain. For example, does the United States abrogate international human rights standards by its limitations on the right to strike or to engage in secondary boycotts? This appears to be the position of a recent Human Rights Watch report critiquing associational rights in the United States.[59]

Second, like the core rights, the right to health and safety is not self-enforcing. Rights require both adequate local definition and mechanisms for enforcement. In the labor rights arena, this is a difficult and troublesome problem: national laws are inadequate; the ILO lacks enforcement powers; and there is an apparent unwillingness of international organizations to create enforcement mechanisms for even the core rights. This is a universal problem, not one specific to health and safety, and is beyond the scope of this chapter.

Third, the current ILO health and safety conventions, as well as regulations of the U.S. Occupational Safety and Health Administration, do not always provide a useful basis for defining a core health and safety right. These standards are often rightly criticized: they set sometimes excessively specific or rigid requirements for elimination of specific hazards, fail to be either technology-forcing or adequately flexible to respond to new data regarding health risks, and omit some important hazards. Although many specific standards may be appropriate, they cannot form the basis for a broadly defined human right to nonabusive working conditions.

There has been remarkably little written that is useful in defining a human right to workplace health and safety. Of course, one might boldly (and simplistically) assert the proposition that health and safety should be viewed as a human right, and leave it at that. That is precisely the approach to the other core rights that has been adopted by the ILO. A danger with this approach is that any undefined labor right has a tendency to migrate to an unsatisfactory least common denominator. The alternative approach is to begin the challenging process of further definition of the right to health and safety, starting with three separate but essential components: the right to information; the right to be free from retaliation for raising safety concerns or refusing imminently dangerous work; and the right to work in an environment reasonably free from predictable, preventable, serious risks.

The Right to Information

Among those who advocate for health and safety rights, there is broad support for the right of workers to have access to information regarding hazards. Information transfer underlies the classical economic analyses regarding workplace hazards. The worker's ability to assess risks, bargain over wages, or accept the risks must be derived from the fact that the worker has adequate information to assess the risk. Lack of information, on the other hand, means that workers obligate themselves to hazardous work without having the necessary knowledge that would underlie a fair bargain, a decision to refuse the work, or exercise of any legal rights to health and safety.

While acknowledging the centrality of workplace risks, Gary Fields suggests that the right to health and safety can be limited to a right to information only: "No person has the right to expose another to unsafe or unhealthy working conditions without the fullest possible information." According to Fields, "This would allow for people knowingly to enter risky or unsafe occupations, which often they are forced to do by economic necessity. This is enough of a violation of human decency. It is indecent for employers to withhold this information from employees until irreversible harm has been done."[60]

Beyond the idea of simple "indecency," this approach assumes that the failure to transfer information is the key impediment to a successful market solution for excessive risk. The assumption is that if a worker knows of the risks, she or he can make effective choices: the worker can consent to exposure to the risk, or bargain for a compensating wage differential or refuse the employment. The labor market will thereby create optimal incentives for safety and compensation for injury.

It is true that the right to information is a key component of health and safety rights. But it is not sufficient, for the reasons suggested above: that knowledge of risks is ineffectively communicated to applicants for jobs; that information provided may not be adequate to lead to informed decisions; that some workers accept risks out of desperation and the acceptance of such risks is neither consensual nor compensated; that people's ability to process information and to consent to risk is problematic; that bargains reached by individuals for a local public good will not be optimal for the group; and so on.

The right to information—accessible and comprehensible information—is therefore necessary but not sufficient to the right to healthy and safe working conditions.

The Right to Be Free from Retaliation for Raising Safety Concerns or for Refusing to Perform Work That Poses Imminent Danger

The risks in a workplace are largely within the control of the employer. If employees know of the risks but cannot raise their concerns and questions, then they have no power to act to modify the risks or the employment agreement. The right to be free from retaliation—for raising concerns or refusing imminently dangerous work—is the second key component to employees' right to achieve improved health and safety conditions at work. It is a necessary component of the core associational right to organize and bargain collectively, which presumes that workers should have the choice to "stay and fight" rather than to quit. It is true that workers can always leave, exercising their core right to be free from forced labor (and thereby change the market by encouraging employers either to improve conditions or change working conditions in order to retain workers). Of course, this solution rejects the core nature of associational rights and also presumes that workers who are subjected to the most egregious conditions have sufficient labor market mobility to move to another job. Since the inequities of the market may prevent this from occurring, the right to be free from retaliation—that is, to be free from job loss when raising concerns regarding working conditions—is an essential component to a right to health and safety.

The Right to Work in an Environment That Is Free of Predictable, Preventable, and Serious Hazards

If the market is inadequate to address gross abuses, then the persistence of risks in workplaces is based on nonconsensual exposures and the right to health and safety is not adequately addressed through information transfer and associational/organizing rights. It must include some basic element that recognizes a right to work in an environment that is not so dangerous as to offend human rights standards. It is unquestionably here that the task of defining the right to health and safety becomes most challenging.

Recognition that there needs to be a line over which employers cannot conscionably cross is a common theme in both the academic literature that addresses rights to physical security as well as the response of the popular press to workplace disasters.[61] Some have simply suggested that workers have a nonwaivable right to be free from excessively dangerous conditions or from grave danger. Susan Rose-Ackerman (in 1988) and Cass Sunstein (in 2001) have each suggested a two-tier approach: workers have a nonwaivable right to "levels of safety that reasonable workers would not wish to relinquish" and waivable but presumptive rights to further protections.[62] Sunstein terms the former "truly dangerous conditions," suggesting that this would also respond to "potential problems with inadequately informed waivers."[63]

Of course, to say "excessive" or "grave danger" or "truly dangerous" is no more helpful than to say "safe."[64] It begs for definition.

In approaching this definitional quagmire, one must first acknowledge that degrees of risk vary based on a variety of factors: employers' desire to provide safety; employers' knowledge of risks and preventive strategies; employers' economic ability and willingness to implement these strategies; the general state of knowledge with regard to risk and prevention; the availability of technology to provide safe workplaces; the way in which individual workers perceive risk; and the willingness of workers to accept the level of risk that they perceive. People voluntarily take risks as a regular matter in their daily lives, and there is no reason to think that workplaces will ever be risk-free.

There is a spectrum of health and safety risks, ranging from deliberate employer malfeasance involving intentionally caused hazardous work situations (such as locked escape doors in workplaces in which fires occur); to nonfeasance involving the failure to act to prevent injuries that are the result of easily preventable and predictable events (such as the failure to provide hard hats in dangerous work zones); to less clearly definable nonfeasance where detection of hazards is difficult or prevention is expensive; to situations in which there is little direct culpability because of the need to expand information and develop new technologies that might reduce workplace risks (such as the need to understand and prevent occupationally caused asthma). There is a world of difference between risks that are the result of the current state of technology and risks that are the result of an employer's bad acts.

Along this spectrum, I suggest that *human rights* violations occur when employers' deliberate and intentional actions expose workers to preventable, predictable, and serious hazards.[65] The fundamental right to be free from these hazards should be guaranteed.

Two areas of litigation in the United States provide useful insights: tort litigation over workplace injuries and imposition of fines for violations under the Occupational Safety and Health Act. In both of these arenas, agencies and courts have been required to distinguish between "normal" workplace risks and excessive risks.

Workers' compensation provides broad liability protection to employers: employers pay premiums and in return are guaranteed that employees cannot sue under the common law for damages in tort. This bargain holds even if a higher level of vigilance by the employer could have prevented the injury, as well as if the employee's own actions contributed to the occurrence of the injury. Some state courts have, however, developed limited exceptions to the exclusive nature of the workers' compensation remedy.

The most common exception involves what I will call "first-order malfeasance": the injury is directly and subjectively intended.[66] In the workers' compensation arena, the common illustration of this principle is when the employer deliberately hits an employee in order to injure her. In the current discussion of international human rights abuses, the equivalent scenario occurs when an employer deliberately punishes workers by subjecting them to heat, beatings, lack of water, and so on.[67] This may occur while workers are physically prevented from leaving the workplace or it may be in the context of general economic coercion. In either case, workers are subjected to outrageous abuse without adequate recourse due to limitations on their ability to quit and find alternative employment. In essence, the workers are prisoners facing human rights abuses, although they may not meet the standard of "forced labor."

To continue the same terminology, "second-order malfeasance" occurs when the employer creates dangerous conditions, knowing that workers are likely to be seriously injured, and the employer does so without regard for the serious and life threatening risks to workers. Until recently, most states in the United States shielded employers from liability for injuries resulting from these risks. In the past twenty years, however, an increasing number of states have held employers to be liable in tort for injuries when the employer knew that the injury was "substantially certain" to occur and intended the act that caused the injury.[68] In these situations, the workers may lack sufficient information to know about the risks, or they lack the ability to process this information, or they may be unable to quit as a result of economic or physical coercion. Examples of this type of malfeasance include the following: locking the exit doors (usually to prevent pilfering) and disabling fire extinguishers so that fires are lethal, as occurred in Bangkok in 1993 when 200 Thai women died,[69] in Hamlet, North Carolina, in 1992 where 25 African American women died (described more fully later in this chapter), and in the Triangle Shirtwaist fire of 1911 in which 145 young immigrant women died;[70] deliberately removing guards from machinery[71] or exposing workers to deadly chemicals;[72] sending underground miners under unsupported top; removing water sprays from tunneling equipment so that workers are exposed to deadly levels of silica dust;[73] and so on.

Similarly, the Occupational Safety and Health Act distinguishes between nonserious and repeated or willful violations and makes provision for larger penalties for these violations.[74] OSHA also specifically acknowledges that some situations, which involve imminent danger of harm, justify immediate injunctive relief. Again, the regulatory scheme suggests that it is possible to distinguish nonfeasance (however culpable) from malfeasance, in which the employer knowingly allows hazards to persist.[75] While employers can be cited for serious violations based on a constructive (should have known) standard,[76] willful and repeated violations involve a "flaunting" of the law based on actual knowledge of wrongdoing.[77] For a repeated violation, the employer must have been previously cited for a substantially similar violation and a final order must have issued from the Occupational Safety and Health Review Commission for the prior violation.[78] The standard for willfulness is stringent, similar to the standard for avoiding workers' compensation immunity: the employer must have committed the violation of that act "voluntarily with intentional disregard or demonstrated plain indifference to the Act."[79] One federal appellate court decision set out an extraordinarily tough standard for willful violations: "willfulness connotes defiance or such reckless disregard of consequences as to be equivalent of a knowing, conscious, and deliberate flaunting of the Act."[80] Other federal courts have adopted a standard for willfulness that does not require as clear a showing of venial motive.[81]

Common law tort law, of course, always recognizes that these differences exist: awards of punitive damages result from a jury determination that a defendant's knowing malfeasance caused a plaintiff's injury. These types of cases can also result in criminal prosecutions.[82] David Rosner suggests that criminalization of workers' deaths is an important "step in the transformation of our thinking about the nature of industrial accidents and deaths" in which workplace deaths are seen as preventable and predictable events, rather than unpredictable accidents.[83]

The injuries and deaths that result from malfeasance are not "accidents" nor are they injuries that occur because of lax enforcement of standards. Rather, they are the result of deliberate practices that see workers' lives as expendable. The reaction to the Bangkok fire is telling. According to the *Bangkok Post,* "This is no time to be bleating about damage to the economy or frightening away foreign investment. No aspect of our economy should be based on a disregard for human life, exploitation or greed."[84]

Acts of clear malfeasance by employers are never justifiable based on local economic or political conditions. While many demands for safety and health may be economically and technologically contingent, the right to be free from risks created by malfeasance should be seen as inviolate. There is no justification for excluding these abusive working conditions from core human rights simply because more extensive protections are difficult to define.

In contrast to this type of malfeasance, employers may allow dangerous conditions to exist, but not act specifically and intentionally to create the risks. Interventions may exist that would decrease deaths and injuries, but they are not used; the employer may be aware of the risks, but chooses not to act. Often, these conditions reflect the general practices in an industry, abhorrent as these may be; as industry practices change or the labor market tightens, employers may act to improve health and safety conditions. In the United States, these kinds of violations do not justify OSHA citations for willful or repeated violations, nor do they justify escaping the no-fault workers' compensation system. While posing serious risks to workers, these situations may involve nonfeasance, rather than clear malfeasance, and therefore may be more open to debate in the human rights arena. The spectrum of culpability for these injuries is highly variable. The economic and technological feasibility for elimination of these risks may vary from one country to another. The imposition of specific standards developed in an advanced country may be economically inefficient or simply infeasible in less developed countries.

The right to be free from employer *malfeasance* should be considered absolute and essential, but it is not sufficient to fully clothe the human right to health and safety: it is the least common denominator, the most basic articulation of the right. Some degree of nonfeasance will always violate the basic right, but its scope will vary based on local conditions.

There is precedent in human rights discussions to recognize the particular conditions of a region.[85] As conditions improve, the breadth of the right expands: labor rights ratchet upward, involving a progressive realization of rights within available resources.[86] In more developed countries, the right to safe workplaces and to compensation for injuries should be broader than in poorer countries. The fact that "considerations of cost, feasibility, capacity and so on are always part of the equation" simply means that cost is a relevant factor; this "should not preclude a consensus in the international community that workplace health and safety should be part of core labor standards."[87]

The fact that implementation of a right may in part be locally contingent undeniably creates uncomfortable ambiguity in the definition of rights. It encourages the search for a least common denominator that is a universal *standard* for violation of the right: no child under six should be working; no worker should be locked into a workplace without regard to fire hazards. But there is a difference between the development of local standards for the implementation of a right and the fundamental nature of the right itself.

There is a universal principle: that no worker should work in conditions that involve knowing exposure to preventable, predictable, serious risks. The extent to which a particular risk can be prevented may be dependent on available resources. Risks resulting from employer *malfeasance* always violate the human right to health and safety, while predictable and preventable risks resulting from employer *nonfeasance* vary based on local economic and technological conditions. In developed countries like the United States, nonfeasance in the prevention of predictable serious risks in the workplace may constitute a human rights violation; equivalent nonfeasance in an economy in which resources are more limited may not constitute such a violation. Only to this extent is the right to health and safety dependent on local conditions.

Local conditions do not always justify variations in the level of workplace safety, however. When specific economic relations suggest that there is full capability of providing a level of safety consistent with more developed areas of the world, the right to safety must be maximized. Multinational corporations build facilities in poor countries hoping to benefit from lower wages or from access to natural resources or available markets. The level of tolerable risk in these workplaces should not sink to the level permitted by the lower level of economic development of the surrounding market. Corporate "best practices" appropriately do not suggest substantially reduced levels of health and safety protections based on differing labor markets. While competitiveness in the market may depend on the lower levels of wages and benefits that are paid in the host country, it does not generally depend on levels of workplace risk. Facilities that are owned by multinational corporations and exported to areas of lower development should serve to ratchet up the level of safety available in the local market; this is a principle endorsed by Paul O'Neill when he served as CEO of Alcoa. Local firms that benefit from contracts with firms from the developed world should also be expected to strive for working conditions that are superior to those provided by local firms that do not benefit directly from the input of foreign capital. Thus, while local conditions may affect the right to safety, international capital should serve to continuously improve the expected levels of safety provided in poorer countries.

Health and Safety in the United States

The United States walks a political tightrope between a legal regime ostensibly designed to protect workers and strong support for a market-based economy. The legal rules appear to support strong minimum protections and associational rights for workers. Legal rights nominally include all three components of the human right to safety and health enumerated above. At the same time, free market enthusiasts effectively oppose regulatory interventions on behalf of workers. Regulatory standards are expected to be highly protective; regulatory enforcement is lax.

This duality can be seen in the data and the stories of workers. On the one hand, strong regulatory language, shifts to safer industries, and declining injury rates suggest that health and safety hazards are no longer a worrisome problem in American workplaces. On the other hand, persistent injury rates in some sectors, ineffective enforcement of rules, and workers' descriptions of harrowing working conditions (as well as inadequate and unfair compensation systems) contradict this optimistic picture. The resulting tension reflects a system that is facially protective of workers but that may often fail as a practical matter to provide critical tools for limiting workplace risks and compensating injured workers. In the end, given the level of economic development, there is a serious question as to whether the right to health and safety is fully realized in the United States.

U.S. Health and Safety Efforts Appear Strong

All three components of the core right to health and safety—the rights to information, to be free from retaliation, to workplaces free from predictable, preventable, serious risk—are directly addressed in the U.S. federal regulatory scheme for health and safety. The flagship laws include the Occupational Safety and Health Act of 1970[88] and the Mine Safety and Health Act of 1977.[89] The hortatory language of OSHA is clear and ambitious: to "assure so far as possible every working man and woman in the Nation safe and healthful working conditions."[90] The secretary of labor is charged by the act with setting health standards that will assure ("insofar as practicable") that "no employee will suffer material impairment of health or functional capacity even if such employee has regular exposure to the hazard . . . for the period of his working life."[91] Under the regulatory scheme, standards issued by the Department of Labor regulate a wide range of health and safety hazards.[92] Employers are statutorily required to comply with these standards as well as to conform to the "general duty" to provide a workplace "free from recognized hazards that are causing or are likely to cause death or serious physical harm to his employees."[93]

The Occupational Safety and Health Administration, and state agencies enforcing approved state plans, are responsible for enforcement of the act. These regulatory agencies are authorized to conduct investigations and on-site inspections of workplaces and to institute enforcement proceedings for violations of OSHA standards or of the general duty clause.[94] The law authorizes modest civil fines and criminal penalties.[95] Since 1986, OSHA has imposed increased penalties for egregious violations when employers' past activities suggest bad faith or indifference to worker safety.

The statute and regulations guarantee to workers and unions the right to participate in the standard setting process;[96] to request health hazard evaluations to investigate health problems of unknown origin[97] and regulatory inspections;[98] to participate when an inspection occurs;[99] to appeal the period that OSHA allows an employer to correct a violation;[100] and to seek party status in adjudications when employers appeal citations issued after an inspection.[101] Reporting of illnesses and injuries is required; employees have the right to inspect their employer's logs.[102] Under the hazard communication rule, workers in the manufacturing industries are guaranteed specific access to chemical hazard information.[103] Employees also have a right to obtain medical records and exposure data if they are exposed to toxic substances or harmful physical agents.[104]

Section 11(c) nominally protects employees from retaliation for exercising rights under the law.[105] Both the Occupational Safety and Health Act and the regulations prohibit retaliation for exercising statutory rights. The regulations specifically extend this protection to include complaints to employers regarding health and safety concerns as well as a right to refuse to perform imminently dangerous work.[106]

Combined with this strong federal regulatory scheme for health and safety, workers have three additional and essential legal rights: rights to organize for improvement of working conditions under the National Labor Relations Act (NLRA);[107] rights to injury compensation under workers' compensation laws; and rights to employment if they become disabled as a result of injury under the Americans with Disabilities Act[108] and state antidiscrimination laws. Judicial decisions have placed health and safety firmly within the bounds of mandatory subjects of collective bargaining between unions and employers.[109] As in other areas, the enactment of federal minimum standards legislation like OSHA did not remove the obligation of employers to bargain with unions regarding health and safety issues.[110] The federal health and safety rules thus create a minimum floor for health and safety protection; NLRA rights expand and reinforce the federal regulatory guarantees. Unions have rights to obtain information regarding hazards that are far broader than that provided under OSHA.[111] In addition, unions' safety professionals have access to the work premises as part of the union's representational function.[112] The right to raise health and safety concerns to employers and others is considered to be protected concerted activity under sections 7 and 8(a)(1) of the NLRA.[113] The right to refuse dangerous work is clearly included within rights to engage in concerted activity, to strike, and to refuse dangerous work.[114] Arbitrators of disputes under collective bargaining agreements view discipline for engaging in health and safety activities as improper, at least nominally, although the grievant must show that the hazard justified the disobedience.[115]

State-mandated workers' compensation programs provide medical benefits and wage replacement for workers who are injured at work, without regard to fault. Most states also prohibit discharge in retaliation for filing a workers' compensation claim.[116] Some argue that workers' compensation also provides effective safety incentives, although others vigorously dispute this assertion.[117] In addition, as noted above, in a limited number of instances in a few states, workers may also be able to bring lawsuits against employers who allow excessively dangerous conditions to exist that are substantially certain to result in serious injuries.

The Americans with Disabilities Act requires employers to provide reasonable accommodation to qualified employees with permanent disabilities, including workers who have been disabled as a result of injuries or illnesses caused by work.[118] Discharge due to disability arising from work injuries is therefore theoretically prohibited if the injured worker can perform the essential functions of the job, with or without reasonable accommodation. Employers should therefore have an incentive to eliminate risks that will cause disabilities as well as to introduce technologies that will lessen the burden of disability.

Regulation of health and safety thus sits on a four-legged stool in the United States: OSHA (and other regulatory laws); the NLRA; workers' compensation (and tort liability); and antidiscrimination provisions for the disabled. Together, these four types of regulation combine to provide the three key health and safety rights described above. A superficial review of this legal regime at least suggests that the right to health and safety at work is fully realized in the United States.

The legal regime is additionally strengthened by the strong economic trends over the last decade in the United States. Although wealth inequality widened, unemployment declined and wages, even wages at the bottom, rose.[119] While reported injury rates rose from 1983 to 1992, there was a remarkable decline thereafter, falling from 8.9 per 100,000 workers in 1992 to 7.4 in 1996 to 6.7 in 1999, a decline of 25 percent.[120] This decline is not simply a reflection of shifts to safer industries: the decreases are reported across all industries, including the most dangerous jobs in the most dangerous industries.

The reasons for this sudden decrease in reported injuries after several decades of increasing rates are now the subject of considerable debate. Because of serious problems in the collection of data, some researchers believe that injuries are simply not being reported, and that the rate of nonreporting of injuries may be increasing.[121] Others believe that the decline is real and attribute it to a variety of factors: new management practices, capital investment due to the booming economy, a tight labor market, rising wages that have made workers "willing to forgo some extra pay in exchange for safer working conditions,"[122] or the effects of high workers' compensation costs in the preceding period. Few believe that the regulatory regime produced these recent declines: the legal rules have not changed substantially since 1980; during the last decade, employers' workers' compensation costs declined dramatically;[123] and the OSHA budget for enforcement also declined in real dollars.[124] Whatever the cause, the picture that emerges is one of an expanding economy with a progressive legal regime creating broad and effective protection for workers.

U.S. Health and Safety Rights Are Weaker Than They Appear

But this picture of aggregate improvements in health and safety risks and a strong regulatory environment is contradicted by the stories that many workers tell. Workers are convinced that both the promises for health and safety and for reasonable and timely compensation after an injury have been broken. As noted in the introduction, injuries and illnesses continue to be prevalent in U.S. workplaces. Workers report stories of health and safety abuses and suggest that they feel unable to act because of fear of retaliation.[125]

The story of the fire at Imperial Foods, although admittedly extreme and atypical, illustrates the problems. Imperial Foods was a poultry processing plant in Hamlet, North Carolina. In 1992, a fire killed twenty-five workers and injured another fifty-six. The workers died because the doors to the plant were kept locked and the workers could not escape when the fire spread. The jobs were dirty, dangerous, and low paid. The workers were predominantly African American women. There was no trade union at the plant. According to the local religious minister, workers said they did not raise complaints about safety because they did not want to lose their jobs. Although there had been two previous fires, the factory had never been inspected by any agency responsible for workplace safety. Government inspectors found that this third and deadly fire was the result of the plain failure of the company to provide a safe working environment: the company appeared to have recklessly violated many health and safety regulations. In an attempt to cast blame onto the workers, one state official, a member of the North Carolina Occupational Safety and Health Advisory Council, was quoted as saying, "I imagine they stole chickens just as fast as they could go. . . . If there had been more honest employees, those doors probably wouldn't have been locked."[126] The circumstances of this fire are startlingly similar to the fire in the Bangkok toy factory that killed two hundred mostly women workers that same year: in both, prior fires had occurred and been ignored; in both, workers died because the doors were locked; in both, the employer deliberately ignored simple safety requirements.

Workers' compensation insurance was provided to Imperial Foods through the residual market of the insurance industry, thus blunting or eliminating any potential safety incentives that may sometimes be provided by workers' compensation. High-risk employers can buy insurance in this market when regular insurance companies are unwilling to provide them with insurance voluntarily because of the excessive financial risk. This residual market is structured so that safer employers subsidize the insurance rates of the high-risk employers, in order to keep the insurance rates affordable for these high-risk employers.[127]

In the case of Imperial Foods, the prior failure to inspect and enforce the safety laws was primarily the result of inadequate agency resources. Workers did not come forward because they had no job security, no union, were vulnerable to retaliation, and lacked alternative job possibilities. The events in Hamlet demonstrate the persistence of monopsony in southern rural towns. Moreover, the company could obtain mandatory insurance for injury risks because of subsidies from other employers.

The Imperial Foods story is emblematic. Other stories abound. Like the workers at Imperial Foods, workers in the apparel industry face deplorable conditions. A 1994 government report found that sweatshops are widespread in the American garment sector, noting that "in general, the description of today's sweatshops differs little from that at the turn of the [last] century."[128] Workers are given inadequate breaks, low pay, and no benefits. There is widespread noncompliance with labor and health and safety laws. Attempts to unionize are rare and are generally unsuccessful. Immigrant workers worry that they will lose their work visas if they lose their jobs. But even U.S. citizens are reluctant to risk job loss in order to assert rights under the laws. Despite the fact that some recent studies suggest that at-will employees may overestimate their level of legal protection, workers nevertheless may fear retaliation and be unable or unwilling to raise concerns regarding working conditions to their employers.[129]

Mechanization and speedup have made both traumatic and repetitive motion injuries common in both the apparel and the poultry processing and meatpacking industries.[130] Ergonomic injuries were the leading cause of lost workdays in 1999, the last year for which data are available.[131] Applications for workers' compensation benefits for these injuries are often unsuccessful due to particular aspects of state laws. Attempts by the Occupational Safety and Health Administration to regulate ergonomic hazards have so far been unsuccessful. For several years, at the urging of industry, Congress passed laws specifically instructing the agency not to issue any rules regarding these hazards. When this ban was lifted, the agency issued a rule in November 2000; one of the first actions of the new Bush administration was to invoke the previously unused Congressional Review Act, which allows for expedited disapproval of regulatory actions, to throw out the new rule and prohibit issuance of a similar one.[132] As of this writing, there have been promises to issue a new ergonomics rule, but no proposed regulation has been forthcoming from the Department of Labor. At the same time, the U.S. Supreme Court has demonstrated a reluctance to characterize a worker with serious repetitive stress injuries as disabled, and therefore protected by the Americans with Disabilities Act.[133]

Working conditions in the agricultural industry are also dangerous and often abusive. Migrant workers are paid low wages, provided with substandard housing, and receive little health and safety protection. Again, most are racial minorities or immigrants and are particularly vulnerable to oppression by their employers. Occupationally caused injuries and illnesses are common. Although the industry has the second highest rate of occupational injury (second only to mining), agricultural employers received less than 3 percent of the Occupational Safety and Health Administration's inspections between 1993 and 1998, according to a recent Human Rights Watch report.[134] Only twelve states require employers to provide workers' compensation coverage for agricultural workers.[135] The National Labor Relations Act does not cover agricultural workers, so that in many states they lack the legal protection necessary to organize unions. Workers in this dangerous industry are both outside an efficiently competitive labor market and also fall through the cracks of the regulatory regime.

Examples of dismal working conditions and denial of workers' rights are unfortunately not rare occurrences. Aggregate statistics hide serious and persistent abuses that some workers must endure. Without question, the language of the Occupational Safety and Health Act is strong. But in a country allegedly dedicated to the rule of law, the law does not deliver what it promises. In fact, there are serious holes in the U.S. legal approach toward elimination of dangerous working conditions. The least powerful workers may exist outside the apparently protective regulatory regime.

A number of factors contribute to the inconsistent adequacy of health and safety rights in the United States.[136] First, a more detailed review of the legal regime reveals serious limitations in the three core elements of the right to health and safety. The right of workers to obtain and understand information regarding workplace hazards is limited. Future employees have no entitlement to information. Employers are not obligated to disclose most information without a specific request from an employee. Informational rights under OSHA are limited. Unions often focus their attention more on workers' compensation than on identifying and preventing risks. The ability to understand complex information regarding toxic exposures is circumscribed by employees' inadequate access to helpful professionals. Only a few international unions provide this kind of assistance.

The right to be free from retaliation is also inadequate, particularly for nonunion employees. The anti-retaliation provisions of OSHA are in reality close to worthless: complaints must be filed within thirty days; OSHA lacks administrative adjudicative or enforcement powers; lawsuits must be filed by the Solicitor of Labor in federal district court; decisions by the solicitor not to pursue complaints are discretionary and nonreviewable; workers have no private right to file actions. Thus, the adjudication of the complaint rests on the discretion and good will of an understaffed office of government attorneys. Complaints are rarely pursued and the remedy, assuming an action is filed and won, is limited to back pay for the affected employee. Many workers are unaware of these rights, including the short time period for the filing of a complaint.

Thus, federal law gives little incentive to employers to conform to anti-retaliatory requirements. Partly in reaction to the inadequate rights under OSHA, some state courts have expanded common law rights to allow workers to challenge retaliatory discharges involving safety complaints.[137] But low-wage and other less privileged workers are not generally able to pursue these common law remedies successfully.[138] Although arbitrators and the NLRB will uphold the right of workers to pursue safety concerns, most unions have not negotiated for a specific right to refuse unsafe work and most have negotiated away the right to strike over safety issues during the term of a contract.[139]

Workers' rights under OSHA to seek enforcement and penalties for violations of regulations are also extremely limited. The effectiveness of OSHA depends on the agency's administrative enforcement of the act. But OSHA is astonishingly underfunded and therefore unable to enforce existing substantive regulations aggressively. The agency's budget was not increased from 1982 to 1999; it lost $100 million to inflation over this time period and employed two hundred fewer people in 1999 than in 1971.[140] According to the AFL-CIO, OSHA could inspect each American workplace covered by the law only once each century at its current rate of funding;[141] it has never had more than two thousand inspectors for 6 million sites.[142] Not surprisingly, most workplaces are never inspected. Moreover, remedies for violations of rules are weak. As a result, despite the political hype that surrounds health and safety regulation, the risk (and the cost) associated with noncompliance for employers is quite low.

Regulations are slow to issue: the OSHA rulemaking process is excessively complex, time-consuming, and "ossified."[143] OSHA has promulgated only two contested regulations since 1992. Few rules have been completed in less than three years, and most rules have taken between four and seven years to complete. Well-organized and financed political opposition to the agency has curtailed its ability to achieve its goals. Congress has interceded to stop the development of regulations in particularly difficult areas: the example of the ergonomics rule is a case in point. Some argue that the very strength of the law creates political gridlock: the strong hortatory language of the preamble and the prohibition on cost benefit analysis in the development of health standards result in both increased political opposition and agency paralysis.[144] Others argue, just as vigorously, that cost benefit analyses promote gridlock and fail to address critical distributional issues.

Perhaps not surprisingly, OSHA appears to be more effective in unionized workplaces.[145] Workers in unions have two critical advantages: they are covered by collective bargaining agreements that provide them with useful protection against retaliatory discharge; and they are more knowledgeable about health and safety laws. In addition to primary rights under the NLRA and collective bargaining agreements, workers are protected by unionized status in ways that reinforce their ability to exercise these other rights: unionized workers are more likely to request information, seek and participate in inspections, or exercise other rights to participate in OSHA proceedings. The rights guaranteed by the labor laws for organizing and bargaining are major weapons in the fight for better working conditions, both directly and indirectly.

But a look beneath the surface reveals that the protections of the National Labor Relations Act are also sometimes more theoretical than real. Only about 9 percent of the private sector work force in the United States is now organized into unions. The barriers to successful union organizing are described in painful detail in the human rights report issued by Human Rights Watch in 2000 that focuses on workers' freedom of association in the United States under international human rights standards.[146] Almost the entire remaining 91 percent of the private sector U.S. workforce works without contractual protection as "at-will" employees—guaranteed only the right to quit and protected by minimum standards only to the extent that these standards are adequately enforced in all sectors. Perhaps not surprisingly, these unorganized workers may be reluctant to exercise theoretical rights to a safe working environment. The weakness of the trade unions means that labor is a relatively weak political force; the lack of legislative support for both budgetary expansion and regulatory initiative reflects this weakness.

Workers' compensation laws may also not be very effective as a safety incentive, particularly for smaller employers.[147] As eligibility requirements for benefits have been tightened and reported injuries have declined over the last decade, employers' costs have fallen dramatically while employers have remained shielded from tort liability for all but injuries caused by first-order malfeasance in the majority of states.[148] Thus, employers internalize less of the costs of workplace injuries and have declining incentives to prevent injuries. In some states, sectors of workers who are particularly vulnerable to social deprivation and injuries, including agricultural and household workers, are entirely excluded from coverage. Workers who file for benefits find themselves increasingly stigmatized; the result is that large numbers of workers with legitimate injuries may not file for benefits at all.[149] The workers' compensation system itself is riddled with problems that raise questions about the adequacy and fairness of the delivery of benefits to workers. Moreover, weak legal job retention provisions in state law and the antagonism of the federal courts to a strong reading of the Americans with Disabilities Act mean that employers continue to be able to replace workers who are partially disabled, even if they could continue to perform the essential functions of their jobs with accommodation.[150]

Underneath the theoretical protections provided by OSHA, the NLRA, the ADA, and workers' compensation lie two persistent and serious problems: the employment-at-will doctrine and the immunity that workers' compensation provides to employers against liability for injuries. Together these two doctrines provide remarkable protection to employers. Fear of retaliation leads many workers to make rational decisions not to risk their jobs in order to fight for better working conditions. Declining workers' compensation costs and protection from tort liability for negligently caused injuries means that employers are insulated from the costs of workplace injuries. The result is a system that fails to provide consistent protection for anyone, but particularly for low-wage, minority, immigrant, and nonunion workers.

Conclusion

The emerging international consensus to view health and safety as a secondary labor right is deeply troubling. In fact, the toleration of high levels of workplace risk permits a continuation of abusive conditions that in many ways mirror abuses that are viewed as human rights violations in the political sphere. Workplace risks need to be recognized and evaluated based on an understanding that workers must have a right to information, a right to be free from retaliation, and a right to working environments that are free from recognized and preventable risks.

This right may vary somewhat depending on the specific conditions and the level of economic development of a country. In developed countries like the United States and other OECD countries, a fully realized right to safety at work should not be open to question. Yet, in the United States, a strong legal regime and economic strength mask serious problems for some workers. While health and safety abuses in the United States are less common and generally less severe than in many developing countries, there are nevertheless important lessons to be drawn from the continuing occupational safety and health problems that confront workers.

First, apparent successes reported in aggregate data and averages may mask significant distributional injustices. Even in developed countries, there is not uniform enforcement of important labor rights, including health and safety, for all workers in all sectors of the economy. Both aspirational laws (like OSHA) and data reports sometimes hide significant problems for distinct populations of workers. Sectors of the labor force that are vulnerable to discrimination and low wages, particularly racial minorities and immigrants, are also vulnerable to bad, even deplorable or criminal, working conditions that pose serious and immediate risks of bodily harm. Workers in the apparel industry, for example, are at serious risk whether they work in China or in the United States. The human right to working conditions that are free from preventable and predictable risks is important to workers in both developed and developing countries.

Second, because of the continuing vulnerability of these populations, there is a strong link between improving occupational safety and health and enforcing other fundamental labor rights. In particular, the health and safety of these vulnerable populations suffers when there is also a failure to provide effective enforcement of other rights: rights against discrimination for minorities and immigrants; rights to free speech at work, to association, to engage in concerted activity, and to organize trade unions; and any evolving rights to job security and social benefits. Failure of a country to support these other rights will result in occupational hazards, injuries at work, and possible destitution for vulnerable populations. This does not mean that the right to safety and health is simply contingent on these other rights. But as the legal and social norms at work change to allow for expanded demands of workers, there is no question that working conditions will also improve.

Third, complete dependence on the economic market to correct abusive working conditions would be misguided. During the 1990s, unemployment in the United States was at historical lows and wages rose for even the lowest paid workers. Nevertheless, some workers continued to face unacceptable health risks at work. This is a function of a number of factors. These include the fact that the labor laws do not provide adequate protections and that the current system of compensation allows firms to externalize the costs of injuries and illnesses, leaving workers, their families, and other social programs to pay for these costs. The failure of the economic market to provide adequate protections to all workers also highlights the problem with the four core labor rights that are currently endorsed in international law.

Fourth, and perhaps most obviously, the existence of aspirational laws does not guarantee effective enforcement. Workers in countries with theoretically strong legal protections are still subjected to continuing abuses. The abuses of workers in both poor and wealthy countries are persistent, troubling, and worthy of investigation and exposure.

CHAPTER 5

A Pragmatic Assessment from the Employers' Perspective

Edward E. Potter

For many, human rights are most often thought of in the context of various United Nations' declarations and covenants. Although UN instruments contain a limited number of human rights provisions relating to the workplace,[1] the principal multilateral forum for addressing human rights in the workplace is the International Labour Organization (ILO). Significantly, in terms of present-day debates over the linking of worker rights and trade in the World Trade Organization, the ILO was not born exclusively as a human rights institution but rather also as a multilateral organization to take labor conditions as a factor out of international competition.[2]

Since its inception, the ILO has adopted 185 conventions and 193 recommendations. The latter have no binding force and are advisory. As multilateral treaties, conventions create no international legal obligation unless they are ratified and have no leveling effect on labor standards unless all nations ratify them. ILO conventions are intended to establish minimum labor standards and, today, cover virtually every aspect of conditions of employment. ILO standards range from basic matters such as freedom of association and worst forms of child labor to more technical issues such as wage setting, social security, and chemical safety.

ILO Declaration on Fundamental Principles and Rights at Work

Since its formation in 1919, the ILO has adopted eight fundamental human rights conventions:

- Convention 29 concerning forced labor (1930)

• Convention 87 concerning freedom of association and protection of the right to organize (1948)
• Convention 98 concerning the right to organize and collective bargaining (1949)
• Convention 100 concerning equal remuneration (1951)
• Convention 105 concerning abolition of forced labor (1956)
• Convention 111 concerning discrimination (1958)
• Convention 138 concerning minimum age (1973)
• Convention 182 concerning worst forms of child labor (1999).

Although there is general agreement that these conventions are fundamental, they have not been ratified by all ILO members. The practical effect is that about half of the world's workers are not covered by these conventions. To address this gap and recognizing that the ILO "is the competent body to set and deal with these standards,"[3] the ILO initiated internal discussions among its tripartite constituents in 1994 that led to adoption of the Declaration on Fundamental Principles and Rights at Work in 1998. The declaration is based on the general principles found in the ILO constitution and the ILO's 1944 Declaration of Philadelphia that are the subject of the fundamental conventions, and not the conventions themselves.[4]

The principles are:

• Freedom of association and the effective recognition of the right of collective bargaining.
• The elimination of all forms of forced or compulsory labor.
• The effective abolition of child labor.
• The elimination of discrimination in respect to employment and occupation.

The declaration makes all 175 ILO members accountable for making sincere efforts to achieve the policies and objectives of four categories of fundamental rights regardless of whether the member nation has ratified any of eight fundamental ILO conventions.

The question is: are the eight fundamental ILO conventions or the four principles of the ILO Declaration considered to be human rights that have implications for U.S. law?

What Is a Human Right?

The Third Restatement of the Foreign Relations Law of the United States defines "human rights" as referring to:

> freedom, immunities, and benefits which, according to widely accepted contemporary values, every human being should enjoy in the society in which he or she lives.[5]

What experience has demonstrated to me, however, is that what constitutes a "human right" is in the eye of the beholder. Regardless of what country, culture, or heritage a person comes from, most individuals will agree that, if stated generally, and if the right addresses a serious infringement of the human condition or seriously offends common values, certain rights can constitute human rights either by international agreement or by custom. The international consensus on whether something is a human right quickly breaks down, however, if the right is not viewed as being basic or broadly viewed as being serious, or if it is defined in too detailed a manner. If the international consensus breaks down, then the matter is no longer a human right in the sense that it has legal and policy implications. This was amply demonstrated by the fervor of the four-year negotiations that led to adoption of the 1998 ILO declaration.

It is this conundrum that makes this topic interesting and difficult. My guess is there is not a consensus even among Americans with a common heritage and values of what constitutes workplace human rights because we will begin to disagree once we move away from the general principles or objectives. If it turns out that my hunch is wrong, there remain, however, substantial obstacles before the human rights on which we agree would have implications for U.S. labor law and policy.

U.S. Domestic Experience with Human Rights

As a starting point, we need to look first at the U.S. experience concerning the impact of human rights law on domestic law generally. Certain things must be kept in mind:

(1) the U.S. experience thus far is very limited and has not gone very far in integrating human rights law into domestic law; for example, before 1988, the United States had not ratified any major human rights treaty;

(2) the Bill of Rights to the U.S. Constitution and a variety of issue-specific statutes already provide a very broad basis of protection for human rights in U.S. domestic law to which Congress and the courts have been very respectful; and

(3) the U.S. Constitution and constitutional doctrine have unique features, including the doctrine of self-executing treaties and special doctrines concerning the appropriate division of powers between federal and state governments and among the various branches of the federal government.

There are four bases under which a human right could have implications for domestic policy: if it (1) is a matter of customary international law; or (2) involves general principles of law common to the major legal systems of the world; (3) is a ratified human rights treaty; or (4) is encompassed as a side agreement or within the terms of a trade agreement.[6]

Labor Rights as Customary International Law

Labor rights as human rights might be found under customary international law, in other words, preemptory norms of international law (*jus cogens*) such as the principles of the United Nations Charter prohibiting the use of force. In the labor rights area, preemptory norms of international law that relate to the workplace include:

- slavery or slave trade;
- murder or causing the disappearance of individuals;
- torture or other cruel, inhuman, or degrading; treatment or punishment;
- prolonged arbitrary detention;
- systematic racial discrimination.[7]

While the list is not closed and some rights might achieve this status in the future, what is notable is that the areas that are considered to be important workplace human rights at the international level—the right to join a trade union, nondiscrimination in all of its forms, and worst forms of child labor—currently are not considered to be preemptory norms of customary international law in the United States.

There is another category in which a nation state violates customary international human law if it "practices, encourages, or condones . . . (g) a consistent pattern of gross violations of internationally recognized human rights."[8] This catchall category potentially includes other categories of human rights that are not violations of customary law if committed singly or sporadically. In other words, they

> become violations of customary law if the state is guilty of a "consistent pattern of gross violations" as state policy. A violation is gross if it is particularly shocking because of the importance of the right or the gravity of the violation.[9]

What is evident is that for a labor right to become customary international law, it must involve a severe and gross violation of a human right that is common in all legal systems.[10] Equally evident is that customary international labor law cannot involve matters of legal detail. In a large sense, this category is very similar to the scope and purpose of the ILO Declaration on Fundamental Principles and Rights at Work.

In any event, U.S. courts have been quite reluctant to incorporate customary international law into U.S. law. As established by the Supreme Court in its 1900 decision in *The Paquete Habana*, 175 U.S. 677 (1900), U.S. courts will treat rules of customary international law as part of "the law of the land" and will apply these rules as appropriate in cases coming before them, at least in the absence of contrary legislation or executive policy. Experience has been sparse regarding direct incorporation of customary human rights policy into U.S. domestic law. While rare, such decisions appear to be based on the grounds that domestic law required such a result, rather than on an invocation and incorporation of international human rights standards,[11] or involve widely abhorred practices such as torture outside the United States.[12] Such cases have not involved, to date, domestic workplace human rights issues. Consequently, at the present time, it is doubtful that workplace human rights issues would be considered to be customary international law by the courts.

Labor Rights as General Principles

United States courts have not dealt with the question of human rights in the context of general principles of law common to the major legal systems of the world. But the International Court of Justice has concluded that declarations of principle impart a strong expectation that member nations will abide by it.[13]

Although it may take years for it to occur, U.S. courts might eventually view the 1998 ILO Declaration on Fundamental Principles and Rights at Work as an articulation of principles of policy common to the major legal systems. These are not issues of legal detail, however. The declaration represents a solemn commitment of the 175 ILO member nations to seek to achieve the goals and objectives, but not the detailed legal requirements, which are the subject of the fundamental ILO conventions.

Similar to the basis for customary international law, the 1998 ILO declaration and its follow-up procedures will bring the full weight of the ILO's authority, technical assistance, and censure to address persistent failures to protect fundamental worker rights such as pervasive bonded child labor, impediments to union registration, slave labor, and systemic discrimination. Because it draws its legal authority from the ILO constitution and not the eight fundamental ILO conventions, the declaration is not intended or designed to address isolated incidents or technical legal violations.

Indeed, anyone who has participated in or witnessed the ILO supervisory machinery with respect to ratified conventions can readily see that at the international level the enforcement of international obligations under ratified treaties is only effective with respect to the most basic, egregious failures such as incarceration of trade union leaders and the severe restrictions on the formation of unions, but is ineffective on how particular labor law regimes actually work. This is because the international consensus on what the treaty means breaks down with respect to the specific legal requirements.

The Treaty Route

On the surface, therefore, it may seem that the most direct way to integrate human rights into U.S. domestic law is through the ratification of treaties. Unlike most other nation states in which treaties are essentially contracts between nations that are not intended to create domestic law obligations without implementing legislation, the U.S. Constitution provides that treaties are the "supreme law of the land" under Article 6,

§ 2.[14] Consequently, unqualified ratification of multilateral treaties such as UN and ILO conventions by the United States creates international obligations that are incorporated into domestic law, superseding prior inconsistent federal and state statutes.[15] In such circumstances, the courts are under a duty to give judicial effect to the treaty provisions.[16]

For anyone who has been close to or followed U.S. ratification of a UN or ILO convention, one comes to appreciate that the process is totally geared to making sure that the treaty will not, in and of itself, directly affect federal or state law, or interfere with U.S. prerogatives in any way. This is true regardless of who is in the White House or which party controls the Senate.

Thus, frequently, the executive branch, the courts, or the Senate circumscribe a treaty's domestic effect. With respect to both the executive branch and the Senate, we have the historical residue of the proposed Bricker Amendment to the U.S. Constitution in the 1950s, which would have permitted treaties to make domestic law only through legislation passed by both the House of Representatives and the Senate. To avoid this possibility and in the aftermath of the Bricker Amendment that failed by one vote in the Senate, it has been the consistent policy of the State Department since the 1950s to submit treaties for Senate advice and consent that include: (1) a statement in the law and practice report and in a proposed declaration that the treaty is non-self-executing; (2) reservations within the ratification instrument where U.S. law and practice are different from that required by the treaty; and/or (3) proposed implementing legislation to be enacted before the treaty is deposited with either the ILO or UN to cure differences between the treaty's requirements and current law. In the case of ILO conventions where reservations are not permitted, the United States has been the only ILO member nation to clarify its ratifications with understandings and declarations.

The U.S. ratifications of the International Covenant on Civil and Political Rights in 1992 and ILO Convention 105, concerning the abolition of forced labor in 1990, illustrate this discussion.[17] They are typical of what occurs. Both were ratified with non-self-executing declarations, that is, that the treaty creates no new domestic rights and that no new domestic legislation is contemplated. The covenant contained several reservations limiting the United States' international commitment on free speech, torture, capital punishment, treatment of juveniles, and reductions of penalty.[18] The covenant had four understandings and ILO Convention 105 had two. The understandings to Convention 105 clarified that the treaty did not limit the contempt power of courts in circumstances where strikers are jailed for engaging in an illegal strike and that the United States did not consider the determinations of the ILO Committee of Experts—the designated fact finding body within the ILO to assess compliance with a ratified convention—to be binding on the United States.

The covenant also contained other declarations, including one concerning restrictions on rights in exceptional circumstances and legislative history that makes clear that both the administration and the Senate understood and concluded that "the rights of association embodied in Article 22 of the Covenant are general rights of association similar to those contained in the First Amendment and that nothing in the Covenant would require the United States to alter or amend any labor legislation."[19] In particular, the administration and the Senate went out of their way to make clear that the covenant did not contemplate specific protections of trade union rights found in the UN Covenant on Economic, Social and Cultural Rights and ILO Convention 87 concerning freedom of association and the right to organize.[20]

The Courts and Human Rights

Thus, based on current U.S. practice, courts are substantially constrained in finding new human rights under a ratified human rights treaty. Even if the executive branch or Senate did not qualify ratification of human rights treaties on a non-self-executing basis or with reservations or understandings, courts by judicial construction have considered a treaty to be effective as domestic law only if it is self-executing or implemented by congressional legislation. In determining whether a treaty or its provisions are self-executing, the courts have generally looked at the intent of the parties, the precision and detail of the language, and whether there is a separation of powers problem, that is, whether the subject matter relates to powers of the executive or legislative branches rather than the judiciary.[21]

There are, however, no precise rules for determining whether a treating is self-executing and, consequently, there is no certain method for making this determination.[22] But as long as both Democratic and Republican administrations and the Senate continue to declare that human rights treaties are non-self-executing, courts are quite likely to follow because the intent of the negotiators of multilateral treaties is likely to be unclear. In particular, because other signatory countries do not have the same constitutional and legal doctrines for implementing international treaties as the United States, other countries may not envision UN and ILO treaties as being self-executing because their constitutions and laws do not contain a provision comparable to the supremacy clause of the U.S. Constitution.[23]

In fact, cases where a court has held a human rights type obligation in a treaty to be self-executing, and thus directly applicable without the need for implementing legislation, are quite exceptional.[24] All the cases with respect to the human rights provisions of the UN Charter or other multilateral treaties have gone the other way.[25]

Human Rights and Trade

Although we have had little experience to date, another means by which human rights workplace standards potentially could affect U.S. domestic policy is through their unilateral, bilateral, and multilateral linkages with trade.

U.S. Unilateral Approaches

The United States has been a principal proponent of unilateral imposition of human rights conditions on imports beginning with restrictions on goods made by convict labor in 1890. Since 1930, the U.S. Trade Act prohibits imports produced by forced labor. Goods produced using abusive child labor were added in 1998. Such unilateral applications of human rights standards by the United States clearly could affect the domestic laws of some exporting nations if they want to trade with the United States.

In 1983, a "carrot" approach to workplace human rights was taken. The U.S. Generalized System of Preferences (GSP) was amended to include the requirement that developing countries take steps to realize "internationally recognized worker rights." These rights have since been included in nearly a dozen trade-related laws, including the African

Growth and Opportunity Act of 2000. "Internationally recognized worker rights" are defined as including the right of association, the right to organize, and collective bargaining; establishment of minimum age, minimum wage, hours of work, and the right to occupational health and safety; and a ban on forced labor. None of these statutes define these worker rights but the legislative history to the GSP and related statutes make clear that ILO standards are intended to be the applicable benchmarks. These rights, which include economic cost items in addition to basic human rights, have provided one basis for developing countries to claim that the linkage of human rights to trade is intended to compromise adversely their low-wage comparative advantage. Clearly, this is a flawed perspective on the part of developing countries because the trade preference granted by the United States is a unilateral, discretionary grant and is not contractual as would be the case under the World Trade Organization rules-based regime.

Since 1983, only a handful of countries have lost trade preferences under the GSP and these have involved situations involving serious worker rights problems or other political considerations in relatively economically weak countries in South America and Africa. Across Democratic and Republican administrations, there has been a reluctance to withdraw GSP preferences for worker rights violations with more significant trading partners. A notable exception was U.S. denial of GSP preferences on seven Indonesian products in 1997 and 1998 because of Indonesia's insufficient progress in promoting worker rights, in particular, freedom of association. However, this action took place only after a decade of AFL-CIO complaints under the GSP program.

In 1988, a "stick" alternative to "internationally recognized worker rights" was taken. Section 301 of the Trade Act of 1974 was amended to make another country's actions, policies, and practices "unreasonable" if they involved a "persistent pattern of conduct" that denied "internationally recognized worker rights" as defined under the GSP. Significantly, no Section 301 action has ever been brought by the U.S. trade representative or pursued by the AFL-CIO or other nongovernmental organization against another nation for pervasive violations of worker rights.

Although "carrot and stick" approaches do not directly affect U.S. domestic policy, they have the potential to do so over the long term if, through economic and political suasion, the U.S. were to impose human rights legal requirements that vary from existing U.S. labor standards. In view of the size of the U.S. economy and consumer market, it is unlikely in the short term that unilateral human rights approaches by other countries would be viable or effective in altering U.S. domestic policy under a unilateral trade preference or sanction regime.

Bilateral Trade Treaties

The United States has over 270 bilateral trade agreements with developing countries. Beginning with the fall of the Berlin Wall at the end of the 1980s, the United States began including hortatory language in the preamble of these agreements urging that the country concerned take steps to achieve internationally recognized worker rights. During the second term of the Clinton administration, the United States began to link trade arrangements with worker rights practices with some limited potential consequences on U.S. labor policy.

CAMBODIA TEXTILE AGREEMENT

In January 1999, the U.S.-Cambodia textile agreement became the first bilateral textile trade agreement containing a substantive labor provision. It provides for an annual quota increase of 14 percent if the United States finds that Cambodia is in "substantial compliance" with its labor laws and internationally recognized core labor standards. In December 1999, the U.S. Government found that Cambodia was not in "substantial compliance" with its labor laws and, therefore, not entitled to the 14 percent increase. However, the U.S. Government did acknowledge that progress had been made by Cambodia and offered a 5 percent increase, effective as soon as an ILO independent monitoring program was established.

In May 2000, the Cambodian government, the Garment Manufacturers Association of Cambodia, and the ILO reached a monitoring agreement. The ILO program will provide for factory visits by ILO monitors, who will collect information about factory compliance with internationally recognized core labor standards and Cambodian labor law. The program will produce quarterly public reports, the results of which the U.S. Government will consider when making its annual decision regarding whether to grant Cambodia a 14 percent quota increase. The ILO monitoring program will run for three years at a cost of $1.4 million. The U.S. will provide $1 million, while the Cambodian Government and Garment Manufacturers Association will provide $200,000 each. It is hard to see the U.S. agreeing to such an ILO monitoring program with respect to U.S. worker rights practices.

U.S.–JORDAN FREE TRADE AGREEMENT

A bilateral trade agreement with greater potential to affect domestic policy is the U.S.–Jordan Free Trade Agreement that took effect in December 2001. Negotiated in October 2000, this agreement is the United States' fourth bilateral free trade agreement. The agreement set a precedent by being the first worldwide that incorporated labor provisions within the trade agreement itself rather than in a side agreement. In substantive terms, the United States and Jordan reaffirm their commitments under the 1998 ILO Declaration and "strive to ensure that the Declaration's principles" and "internationally recognized worker rights"[26] are "recognized and protected by domestic law."[27] The agreement prohibits derogation of labor laws to encourage trade and failure to effectively enforce labor law in a manner affecting trade that are subject to unrestricted punitive sanctions.

Although the chances that either Jordan or the United States would impose trade sanctions for failure to meet labor commitments are remote, the substance of those commitments are vague and the intent and scope to the derogation and effective enforcement provisions are unclear with potential implications for U.S. domestic law if included in other trade agreements. Trade actions against the United States might be possible on the following bases: (1) The United States has not and cannot ratify one of the ILO's forced labor conventions and both ILO conventions on freedom of association and collective bargaining because of differences in U.S. law; (2) amendments to the Fair Labor Standards Act that provide for greater hours of work flexibility, for example, could be viewed as derogation of existing labor and employment law for trade purposes; and (3) decisions by the federal or state administrative agencies and courts that appear to deviate from current precedent could be viewed as constituting lack of effective enforcement or derogation for trade purposes. In sum, a social clause in bilateral or regional trade agreements could make an already cumbersome public policy process of protecting workplace human rights in this country even more cumbersome through the external threat of trade sanctions for alleged violations of workplace human rights in the United States with limited prospects that the trade agreement itself would affect domestic law.

The U.S.–Jordan trade agreement also has implications for the multilateral system. Although bilateral agreements offer opportunities to address issues that cannot be reached through multilateral agreements, provisions on nontrade, domestic governance issues make achievement of regional and multilateral trade liberalization more difficult. Specifically on trade and labor, World Trade Organization (WTO) director general Mike Moore said in March 2001 that "WTO members will never agree to trade sanctions to enforce labor standards. It is a line in the sand that developing countries will not cross. They fear that such provisions could be abused for protectionist purposes."[28]

Multilateral Approaches and the WTO

Most often when trade regimes are discussed with the potential of affecting the domestic labor policies of any country, it is in the context of the multilateral trade system. Although little known, every administration since 1953 has had the negotiating objective of bringing labor issues under the multilateral trading system. The Clinton administration proposal to establish a working party to study the relationship of worker rights and trade was rejected in April 1994 by developing countries because they viewed the proposal as the first step to undercutting their comparative advantage. Developing countries constitute almost 80 percent of the votes in the WTO.

The WTO, as was the General Agreement on Tariffs and Trade (GATT) before it, is a "rule-making body" that oversees and enforces international trade agreements voluntarily negotiated by its 140 members. As such, the WTO is a multilateral system of trade rules that are based on contractual obligations that developing countries have little incentive to set aside. Under its current charter, the WTO has no provision for collective condemnation and application of trade sanctions against its members. In view of the opposition of developing countries, amending WTO rules to permit one country to impose sanctions against another for noncommercial reasons would undermine the balance of rights in the current agreement and would be rejected by many developed and developing countries as an invasion of sovereignty.[29]

The U.S. business community also has been opposed to the labor linkage in the WTO. As stated by former OECD ambassador Abraham Katz on behalf of the U.S. business community in January 1999:

> If, by any chance, additional provisions [on labor and the environment] were added, the actions of individual contracting parties would wreak havoc with the MFN [most favored nation] system and cause innumerable disputes. To amend the WTO to change the fundamental nature of the organization would be next to impossible. On the trade and labor front, developing countries are highly suspicious of the attitudes of the U.S. and some other Western governments, which have continued to push without success the idea of bringing labor issues into the WTO. They believe that these governments are more concerned about protecting their markets from low-priced competition than about observance of labor standards. As in the case of the WTO Committee on Trade and the Environment, they demonstrated a similar suspicion of Western motives. They strongly resist the notion of giving a trade body the right to judge a country's adherence to that which they consider to be matters of domestic governance.[30]

Notwithstanding the opposition of developing countries and the U.S. business community, the Clinton administration continued to pursue a working parity on worker rights issues in the WTO. This resulted in a statement by the WTO trade ministers at the conclusion of their December 1996 ministerial conference in Singapore that:

> We renew our commitment to the observance of international recognized core labor standards. The International Labour Organization (ILO) is the competent body to set and deal with these standards, and we reaffirm our support for its work in promoting them. We believe that economic growth and development fostered by increased trade and further trade liberalization contribute to the promotion of these standards. We reject the use of labor standards for protectionist purposes, and agree that the comparative advantage of countries, particularly low-wage, developing countries, must in no way be put into question.[31]

As a result of the WTO Singapore Declaration, on June 18, 1998, the ILO adopted its Declaration on Fundamental Principles and Rights at Work and Follow-up discussed earlier. The declaration's follow-up procedures, involving an annual follow-up concerning nonratified fundamental ILO conventions and a global report on one of the four principles of the declaration on a four-year reporting cycle, now constitute the only worldwide forum for addressing workplace human rights issues that encompasses nearly all countries.

The declaration and its follow-up bring the full weight of the ILO's authority, opinion, censure, and technical assistance to address persistent failures to protect fundamental worker rights. The ILO has more impact than it is given credit for. The publicity that accompanies ILO efforts in Cambodia and Bangladesh, for example, provides a powerful incentive to governments and private companies that engage in egregious workplace human rights violations to clean up their acts. As experience under the ILO's supervisory system shows over and over again, countries do not want to be in the spotlight for poor labor practices because of the adverse consequences on foreign direct investment in their country and potential limits that may be put on their exports by developed countries. By the same token, companies do not want to run the risk of consumer resistance to their products because of problems in the labor area. In this process, the United States is not exempt but, to date, the AFL-CIO has not sought to use the declaration's follow-up procedures as a tool to bring international political pressure on the United States to remedy deficiencies under the National Labor Relations Act or any other U.S. employment law.

North American Agreement on Labor Cooperation

In 1993, Mexico, Canada, and the United States reached agreement on the North America Free Trade Agreement (NAFTA). At the time, it was a precedent-setting regional trade agreement. Labor issues were not included in its terms, but were addressed in a side agreement—the North American Agreement on Labor Cooperation (NAALC). It was the first time that worker rights issues were to be addressed in the context of any trade agreement. The NAALC emphasizes both cooperative activities and dispute resolution with respect to eleven labor principles.

The three countries are committed to promote the principles, subject to each country's domestic law. As such, the principles do not establish common minimum standards for domestic law among the three nations. Rather, they indicate broad areas of concern where the three countries have developed, each in its own way, laws, regulations, procedures, and practices that protect the rights and interests of their respective work forces. The working assumption is that there is no problem with the substance of each country's laws. The principal focus of both the cooperative activities and the dispute-resolution procedures is whether each country is effectively enforcing its labor and employment laws.

Under the dispute-resolution procedures, only trade-related issues involving child labor, occupational safety and health, and minimum wage can exhaust all the steps of the dispute-resolution procedure including arbitration and fines. Freedom of association is limited to ministerial consultations. After eight years, there have been twenty-four submissions alleging lack of effective enforcement. No submission has resulted in action beyond ministerial consultations, highlighting the reluctance of sovereign governments in the same region from interfering in domestic policy of another country.[32] Follow-up from the ministerial consultations has involved further cooperative activities designed to understand each country's employment law systems and to educate on more effective enforcement procedures and practices, primarily involving Mexico. Of the seven submissions involving lack of effective enforcement of U.S. labor and employment law, none to date has resulted in a change in U.S. law and practice.

Conclusion

Experience with linking workplace human rights and trade is very much in its infancy. Since 1993, the U.S. government has been at the forefront. Because of its large domestic market, the United States has substantial leverage on developing countries when it takes unilateral action through import restrictions or by withdrawing trade preferences. Even when acting unilaterally with developing countries, however, the United States has only sought to remedy the most serious infringements of workplace human rights and not the more detailed requirements of the fundamental ILO standards. As experience under the NAALC shows, the United States treads lightly on the domestic labor policies of Canada and Mexico. Over time (well beyond my lifetime), bilateral trade agreements modeled on the U.S.–Jordan Trade Agreement offer the possibility of affecting U.S. domestic labor and employment law by applying derogation and effective enforcement standards to U.S. domestic labor policies. But the odds of U.S. workplace human rights being affected by such agreements is remote because the situation would need to involve a very egregious human rights violation and a trading partner with substantial economic leverage over the United States.

In hindsight, the 1999 Seattle WTO ministerial meeting appears to have been a high-water mark for consideration of linking worker rights with trade on a multilateral basis. At the present time and for the foreseeable future, there appears to be no opportunity to link worker rights and trade on a multilateral basis after the February 2001 Doha WTO ministerial meeting. The challenge now is to maintain the momentum of the 1998 ILO Declaration on Fundamental Principles and Rights at Work to promote higher levels of workplace human rights and capacity building efforts in developing countries. This is a positive, forward-looking approach that emphasizes cooperation.

The most direct way for human rights to have implications for U.S. labor policy is through the ratification of treaties. In 1984, I wrote a short booklet on what ratification of ILO conventions 87 and 98 would mean for U.S. law and practice, assuming they could be ratified on an unqualified basis.[33] Sixteen years later, except for the flipping and flopping of the Supreme Court on federal-state jurisdiction with respect to public-sector workers, the implications identified in that book remain valid. Unqualified ratification of one or both of those conventions would redirect U.S. labor policy significantly. To mention just a few, the conventions would broaden the right to strike but give representation rights to minority unions. They would revoke or modify substantial portions of the Landrum-Griffin Act, but would remove limits on disaffiliations of local unions from international unions.

Similarly, as presently applied, unqualified ratification of the ILO's 1930 forced labor treaty (Convention 29) would prohibit states and the federal government from privatizing the operation of prisons, something now occurring in a dozen states and proposed in the first Clinton administration budget. And, ratification of the ILO's treaty on equal pay for work of equal value (Convention 100) would redirect equal pay for equal work to equal pay for comparable work in this country.

Because all of these questions are complicated issues, it is unlikely that these conventions would be ratified until the legal differences are resolved legislatively and politically. To the extent that they are (in terms of enactment of relevant legislation by both the House of Representatives and the Senate and, where necessary, at the state level), human rights will have implications for U.S. labor policy. In other contexts, such as in trade agreements and under the ILO declaration, human rights will have a more peripheral impact, addressing one or more policy aspects of U.S. labor and employment law over a period of many years. With more than half of the world's population living on a dollar a day or less, the best use of our energy and talents may be to work to make fundamental workplace rights customary human rights around the world.

CHAPTER 6

U.S. Labor Law Serves Us Well

Thomas B. Moorhead

I think our law serves us better than any of the so-called international norms loose in the world.

Human Rights Watch, a nongovernment organization, or NGO, has recently issued a study of U.S. labor laws and finds them sadly lacking in the sense that Human Rights Watch perceives that our laws by and large conflict with international labor rights standards. When they do, this is considered a "bad thing." The Human Rights Watch, however, is guilty of assuming what it is setting out to prove. There is no explanation of the basis of these norms or whether they are truly generally accepted international labor norms. There is also no discussion of whether or not they are good for the individual.

From my work internationally, I am aware that many European and other non-American observers believe that our labor laws somehow create a Darwinian workplace. Let's review the facts.

The United States has enjoyed an extended period of increasing prosperity, which has evolved and expanded under four U.S. presidents. We began deregulation during the Carter administration, followed by major tax cuts, an active support of venture capital along with an increased emphasis on deregulation and initiatives in aid of the creation of small and medium enterprises during the Reagan administration and the reinforcement of these developments during the Bush and Clinton years.

Today our unemployment rate is under 4 percent. There are, of course, many reasons for this, but one of them has to be the balance our labor laws maintain between workers and management. What gives us

In the preparation of this paper, I am indebted to the insights and work of Duncan Campbell of the ILO; Edward E. Potter, president of the Employment Policy Foundation; and Stewart Sullivan, corporate vice president (retired) of Pfizer, Inc. The views presented in this chapter are the personal views of the author, and do not represent the official views of the U.S. Department of Labor.

our strength is our diversity, our flexibility, adaptability to change, and emphasis on the rights of the individual *and* the rights of the majority. Our labor and employment laws have frequently addressed social issues well ahead of the international community in the areas of equal opportunity, workplace safety, and the rights of the disabled to jobs. Our labor law allows individual employees to make up their own minds while guaranteeing free speech, union rights, and secret ballots.

If we look closely at individual labor norms, we will find that European labor law is the usual frame of reference in the development of international labor standards. This is certainly true at the International Labour Organization where a standard setting discussion centers around a report and draft convention and recommendation prepared by the ILO office with a decidedly European bent. United States labor laws, on the contrary, are grounded in the principle of individual employee rights to organize and bargain collectively. ILO conventions are directed at establishing institutional rights and privileges for organizations. We are criticized as a country because we have not ratified ILO Convention 87 (Concerning Freedom of Association and Protection of the Right to Organize). Convention 87, however, creates no express protections for the individual employee—any individual rights are derivative of the rights of organizations and it is the rights of the organization not the individual that are paramount under Convention 87. Conversely, under U.S. law, union rights are derived from the rights offered employees.

Union density in the United States is currently under 10 percent of the private-sector work force. If one were to believe the Human Rights Watch Report, this is mainly due to employer hostility to unions. Granted some hostility exists, but I do not think anyone can seriously argue that such hostility is the main factor in explaining low union membership. I have not heard that argument advanced in France where fewer than 10 percent of the employees are represented by unions. Individualism and the rights of the individual tend to receive greater emphasis in American culture and American law than in European countries, and this is likely to have something to do with the average American's propensity not to join unions.

As an aside, I am bemused at the naiveté in one part of the Human Rights Watch Report where as evidence of management hostility to unions they cited a study by professors Freeman and Rogers that a majority of managers would oppose any unionization effort in their workplace, and at least one-third of them said it could hurt their advancement in the company if employees they managed formed a union. Of course, it is going to hurt their advancement. If I have learned one thing in over thirty years of dealing with unions, it is that managements, not unions, organize a workplace. More precisely, bad management causes workers to organize, so, of course, it will reflect badly on those managers. In hundreds of conversations I have had with local union leaders over the years, it was never wages or benefits that got employees interested in a union; it was their treatment by management.

Each society in adopting its laws has to make a choice on how to balance two policy aims: equality of opportunity and equality of outcomes. In the United States, our laws tend more toward equality of opportunity whereas in many European countries it swings towards equality of outcomes. What are the consequences of this? Collective rights and entitlements receive a greater emphasis in Europe and hence in international labor standards. Bargaining is more centralized as a collective matter, and I am not aware that the individual worker gets to vote, as he or she does in the United States, on the collective contracts entered into by the unions in the various commercial sectors with the large employer federations. All of this adds up to greater labor market inflexibility in Europe with the outcome being a lower rate of job creation, higher unemployment, and higher long-term unemployment.

The "rights" (and I believe they are "human rights") that U.S. workers enjoy include:

• the right to exclusive representation by a union once it is certified as the bargaining agent. I am reminded of a situation in a plant in Belgium where perhaps 70 percent of the workers were represented by the national Christian union and 30 percent by the national Socialist union. After collective bargaining led to an impasse, the union could not get the two-thirds vote necessary to authorize a strike, so they took the company to Labor Court in Brussels. The Labor Court found management's last offer fair so management imposed it. When it came time to bargain the following year, the Christians refused saying management would just do what it wanted anyway. The Socialists wanted to bargain but management said they did not represent a majority of the workers and refused. It was the end of collective bargaining in that plant. That would not have happened under the U.S. system.

- The right to have an individual grievance processed to arbitration (almost all U.S. union contracts contain such a clause), which is enforceable in court. The worker may, of course, represent himself but is entitled to have the union represent him and at no fee. United States law also imposes on a union the duty of fair representation; an individual employee can sue a union that does not diligently pursue a grievance. Contrast this with France where an aggrieved worker would have to take management to Labor Court. Although a union delegate can represent the worker (who would need a special authorization to act), this is not the usual case. In most cases, the employee has to hire and pay for an attorney. In my view, the U.S. worker is better off.

- An employee in the United States has the right to object if money he pays as dues or assessments to the union is used for anything other than proper union business. This so-called Beck right is a very individual one. In Germany, by contrast, union members turn 1 percent of their pay over to the union. There is no individual Beck right in Germany. Which is the more "Human Right"?

Are there generally accepted international labor standards and can they be compatible with U.S. labor law? The answer is "yes" to both questions. A generally accepted international labor standard is a high impact standard that seeks to address fundamental workplace issues on which there can be a broad consensus on applicable policies or principles. The recently adopted ILO Convention 182 on the Worst Forms of Child Labor is such a standard. It has been ratified by the United States and is fully compatible with U.S. law and practice. The ILO Declaration on Fundamental Principles and Rights at Work is another source of generally recognized international labor standards. United States employers were in the forefront of those advocating its adoption, and Ed Potter, who has a paper in this volume, was the employer vice chairman for the discussion and adoption of the declaration.

Now freedom of association is one of the standards embodied in the declaration. Our law provides for it but not within the confines of Convention 87. For example, Convention 87, if adopted in the United States, would overrule the Landrum-Griffin Act, which is concerned with the internal practices of unions and whose major purpose is to protect union members from improper union conduct. Title I of the Landrum-Griffin Act creates a bill of rights for members of labor organizations. It provides for certain fundamental rights for union members such as freedom of speech and assembly, the right to vote in union elections, the right to run for union office, the right to be treated fairly with respect to the imposition of dues and fees, and the right to bring suit against the labor organization. These are basic human rights by my definition. Eliminating them does not advance human rights in the workplace at all.

One has to keep in mind, in referencing ILO conventions and recommendations as the source for generally accepted international labor standards, how they are adopted. Recently there has been a trend toward highly detailed instruments that are simply unratifiable once adopted. (The Worst Forms of Child Labor was an exception.) In many cases, the employers have abstained and governments cynically support worker aspirations when they have absolutely no intention of following up at home by submitting the convention to the ratification process. Between 1970 and 1996, 80 percent of the governments who voted for a convention have not ratified it. Three examples should suffice. In the debate on the adoption of the Homework Convention the government of India stated it could not ratify the convention "in the next fifty years" but it was a good idea so they would vote for it. More recently, the Australian government announced during the debate on the adoption of the Revised Maternity Protection Convention that it was completely unratifiable in their country, nevertheless they voted for it. I am sure a forthcoming election in that country had something to do with their vote. Our own government is no better. Sandra Polaski, as one of two U.S. government delegates, cast our country's vote for the same convention. I doubt if she could give us a timetable for its submission to the Senate for ratification.

The low level of ratifications of ILO conventions should also give us pause in determining whether or not a generally accepted international labor standard exists. Over two-thirds of the ILO membership have ratified fewer than 25 percent of the outstanding conventions (only six countries have ratified more than 50 percent of the conventions). The point of all this is that we have to be very careful in what we assume are generally accepted international labor standards. The few that fit the definition I have mentioned will be generally compatible with U.S. labor law.

Finally, I am appalled that Human Rights Watch would consider the secondary boycott a universal human right. In their report, they correctly point out that U.S. labor law bans the practice of using labor power to damage an uninvolved business and possibly cost innocent workers their jobs. Human Rights Watch is guilty of an egregious use of the term *human right*.

It is important to remind ourselves that in Freedom House's annual summary of political rights, civil liberties, and freedom status conducted since 1972, no country has ranked higher than the United States. By comparison several of the European countries, which some would like us to mold our laws on, rank just a shade or two below the United States in political rights, civil liberties, and freedom status. It seems that discussions of these worker rights and human rights issues should also focus on trade union globalization; union influence; the impact of these worker rights proposals on trade, investment, and the free movement of goods; and ensuring responsible union behavior, especially multinational union behavior.

It is to the benefit and well-being of all—a nation, an employee, an employer, a prospective employee, and where they exist, employee representatives—to develop and maintain a cooperative, positive, flexible, innovative, productive, profitable, nondiscriminatory, nonexploitive, safe, healthy, and open working environment that recognizes and builds on diversity. There is no one way for this to be achieved. All should contribute to this end. United States labor laws do. They work for us and could be used profitably by other countries as well.

CHAPTER 7

Voice for All

*Why the Right to Refrain from
Collective Bargaining Is No Right at All*

Roy J. Adams

The essential argument presented and defended in this paper is that conventional behavior of unorganized American employers, legitimized by American labor policy, offends international human rights standards. The corporate policy of union avoidance (and thus of collective bargaining avoidance), which is the norm among unorganized employers, is equivalent to the use of forced and child labor and overt discrimination on the basis of race, creed, sex, and color. The persistence of arbitrary authority in industry is an illegitimate vestige of long discredited nondemocratic institutions whose elimination ought to be given top priority.

In the first section below I review the development of the international workers' rights consensus.

In the second section, I consider two theories of the standard against which collective bargaining policy may be evaluated in light of the international consensus. Choice theory holds that a nation is in compliance with international standards if its working people are not forbidden to engage in collective bargaining. Voice theory sets a higher standard. It insists that, in order to comply with international obligations, states must be proactive in protecting employee rights. Indeed, to comply with both the letter and spirit of international standards they must ensure that all workers have in place an independent collective voice through which their employment interests may be represented.

In section three, I consider the deficiencies of choice theory as it has taken shape within American labor policy. In particular, by obfuscating

I would like to thank all of the following people for their comments on earlier versions of this paper: Bernie Adell, Chris Albertyn, David Cingranelli, Noam Chomsky, Sheldon Friedman, Jim Gross, Allen Hyde, Brian Langille, Ron McCallum, George Ogle, Joe Rose, Clyde Summers, Lee Swepston, and Gilles Trudeau. The final result is, of course, entirely my responsibility.

freedom of association and the right to bargain collectively rather than treating them as distinct and equal rights, U.S. policy denies a collective voice at work to a majority of the American work force. Contrary to numerous international human rights agreements that the United States has voluntarily entered into, American labor policy perpetuates arbitrary authority in industry.

The International Consensus

During the 1990s, a strong international consensus emerged which affirms as fundamental human rights a set of core labor rights. Parties from all parts of the political spectrum support this consensus. Among the international organizations affirming support for the human rights character of core labor standards are the Organization for Economic Cooperation and Development, the World Trade Organization, the International Labour Organization, and most recently the United Nations in the form of a global compact forged with labor, business and nongovernment organizations. Notable employer organizations signing on are the International Chamber of Commerce, the International Organization of Employers, a large and growing number of major multinational corporations, and the U.S. Council for International Business, the primary representative of American business interests abroad.[1]

The major consensus document is the International Labour Organization's 1998 Declaration on Fundamental Principles and Rights at Work.[2] Founded in 1919, the ILO is the UN agency focused on labor issues. It has a tripartite character with representation from organized labor, business, and states. The primary function of the ILO is to establish global standards with respect to labor issues by adopting conventions which, when ratified by member states, usually (but not always) become law in those states. But, in addition to putting into practice the conventions they have adopted, all ILO members have certain constitutional duties. The Declaration on Fundamental Principles makes those constitutional responsibilities explicit. It obliges all ILO members to "respect, to promote and to realize in good faith" five core rights that are deemed to be fundamental human rights.[3] They are:

1. Freedom of association
2. Effective recognition of the right to collective bargaining

3. The elimination of all forms of forced or compulsory labor
4. The effective abolition of child labor
5. The elimination of discrimination in respect of employment or occupation

The ILO considers that the 1998 declaration has the effect of "committing the Organization's 174 member States to respect the principles inherent in seven core labor standards and promoting their universal application."[4] With respect to labor relations policy, the key agreements are Convention 87 concerning freedom of association and protection of the right to organize and Convention 98, which establishes principles with respect to the right to organize and bargain collectively. The United States is one of the few countries in the world that has ratified neither convention.[5] As documented by Edward Potter, the reason for this failure is that many aspects of American law and policy fail to rise to the level of ILO principles.[6] By signing the declaration, the United States has agreed to bring its policy in line with the principles contained in conventions 87 and 98.[7]

In the employment context, freedom of association, as defined by the ILO, means that "workers and employers, without distinction whatsoever, shall have the right to establish and, subject only to the rules of the organization concerned, to join organizations of their own choosing without previous authorization." ILO principles further hold that such organizations have the right to draw up their own constitutions and rules, elect their own representatives, organize their administration and activities, and formulate their own programs. These organizations should not be liable to be dissolved or suspended by outside authority.[8]

Collective bargaining is defined by the ILO as "all negotiations which take place between an employer, a group of employers, or one or more employers' organizations on the one hand and one or more workers' organizations on the other for determining working conditions and terms of employment, for regulating relations between employers and workers and for regulating relations between employers and their organizations and a workers' organization or workers' organizations." Although collective bargaining is commonly understood to include negotiations between trade unions and employers, the ILO definition extends to cases where, in the absence of a union, delegates may represent workers if they are "duly elected and authorised by them in accordance with national laws and regulations."[9]

Generically, then, the right to collective bargaining means that working people have a fundamental human right to codetermine their conditions of work and to select representatives of their own choosing in order to negotiate those terms on their behalf.

In affirming these rights to be human rights, the Fundamental Declaration brings them under the umbrella of the broader international human rights consensus.[10] Among the basic standards of that consensus is the principle that "human rights and fundamental freedoms are the birthright of all human beings; their protection and promotion is the first responsibility of Governments." That consensus also holds that "all human rights are universal, indivisible and interdependent and interrelated." Each of them, according to the Vienna Declaration of the World Summit on Human Rights, which was endorsed by nearly all of the world's nations, must be treated "on the same footing, and with the same emphasis."[11]

Assessing Compliance with International Obligations

Although these stipulations seem, at first glance, to make the issue clear, in practice there are two starkly different theories of the steps necessary to comply with the international human rights consensus regarding freedom of association and the right to collective bargaining.

The first theory, on which U.S. labor policy is based, holds that the obligation is to provide employees with a choice. According to the terms of the U.S. National Labor Relations Act (also known as the Wagner Act), covered workers may choose to establish a collective bargaining relationship but they are also explicitly granted the right to refrain from doing so. Section 7 of the act states that "employees shall have the right to self-organization, to form, join or assist labor organizations, to bargain collectively through representatives of their own choosing, and to engage in other mutual aid or protection." It also says that employees have "the right to refrain from any or all of such activities." American workers have the freedom to associate and the freedom not to associate. They also have the right to bargain collectively and the explicit right not to bargain collectively.

This concept of the government's responsibility—to provide workers with a choice—seems to be accepted by all parties to the employment relationship in the United States, including most trade unionists and other advocates for collective bargaining. Policy debates center on how to make choice effective.[12] There is essentially no debate about whether choice is the appropriate standard with respect to these rights.

The almost total acceptance of a right not to associate in the United States is consistent with the stipulation in the Universal Declaration of Human Rights that although "everyone has the right to freedom of . . . association" no one "may be compelled to belong to an association." As Sheldon Leader points out, a law requiring everyone to belong to a state-designated labor organization is as much a violation of freedom of association as a law forbidding unionization.[13]

Although the International Labour Organization has refused to take a position on union security provisions in collective agreements, many nations, having embraced what might be referred to as a strong version of freedom of association, have passed laws forbidding trade unions to negotiate mandatory union membership clauses.[14] United States policy on this particular issue is equivocal. Although mandatory dues payment may be required of all workers in designated bargaining units under the National Labor Relations Act, the courts have forbidden the union to discipline covered workers who refuse to comply with all of the requirements of membership. In essence, although mandatory union membership clauses are theoretically permitted, American workers may refuse to fulfill membership obligations.[15] De facto, these regulations ensure freedom to associate and freedom not to associate.

Internationally, however, a different logic is commonly applied to collective bargaining. Indeed the most popular theory would seem to be that all working people have a fundamental human right to participate in the making of their conditions of work. They have a right to be consulted by their employer about employment decisions that are critical to them. As Colin Crouch[16] puts it, among the "fundamental citizenship rights" of all contemporary workers are "collective rights to representation by autonomous organizations in relations between employees and their employers." The government responsibility under this theory is not to put employees in a position where they must choose between representation and deferral to authority unaccountable to the governed. It is, instead, to ensure that all employees have a voice at work.

Thus, among the aims the European Community adopted in 1974 were "progressively to involve workers or their representatives in the life of undertakings in the Community" and "to develop the involvement of management and labour in the economic and social decisions of the Community."[17] Towards fulfilling that commitment, via the process known as social dialogue, trade unions and employer organizations have the legal right to consider and make recommendations about social legislation before the community votes to adopt or reject. Also, consistent with that commitment, in 1994 the European Union adopted a European Works Council directive, which requires European corporations to provide information to and consult with elected employee representatives before going ahead with decisions of importance to employees.[18]

At the national level most continental European countries, while fostering the freedom of workers to join or not to join trade unions, have put in place mechanisms ranging from conventional collective bargaining through statutory works councils to worker representatives on corporate boards of directors, that provide nearly all working people with a voice at work. As a result, although union membership density varies significantly from country to country, collective agreements in most continental European countries cover between 70–90 percent of the labor force. In the United States, however, where employee representation is contingent on the exercise of freedom of association not only by individuals but rather by a majority of employees in bargaining units designated by the National Labor Relations Board, the large majority of working people are excluded from enterprise decision-making (see table 7.1 below).

In short, in Europe the hypothetical right to desist from participating in enterprise decision-making is not considered to be legitimate. The objective is to ensure that there are institutions in place that allow all working people to influence their conditions of work.

In the United States, however, freedom of association and the right to collective bargaining have been, without much reflection, treated as unitary phenomena and, as much as anything, that mental laziness has been responsible for the denial of representation to most American working people. In order to establish a bargaining relationship, American workers must exercise their freedom of association.[19] However, American society strongly supports both a right not to associate and freedom of speech.[20] Apparently motivated by a desire to maintain complete control over employment decision-making, American employers have seized on these rights to pursue policies designed to deny employees a voice at work. Freedom of speech has been used to defend employer involvement in union formation and the process of establishing a bargaining relationship. According to many observers, the result of employer opposition has been the denial of the right to bargain in practice despite its theoretical existence on paper. Thus, according to Block, Beck, and Kruger:

> Although the employer may act legally, the result of pyramiding legal activities one on top of another is an outcome that was surely not intended by the Act. The NLRA was enacted to provide employees with a free and uncoerced choice regarding whether to be represented by a union and to provide the employees in a unit in which a union was chosen the right to bargain collectively. The law can be used, however, to achieve precisely the opposite result.[21]
>
> Ironically, then, a system that was designed to provide a choice of representation to employees seems only to provide employers with a choice—a choice as to the type of employee relations system they will create.[22]

The evidence suggests that most unorganized workers in the United States fear reprisals for getting involved in an organizing campaign and evidence on the actual practice of victimization indicates that their fears are fully warranted. In their sample of American workers, Freeman and Rogers found that, of those who had been involved in a unionization campaign "two-thirds said that management had opposed the organizing campaign in ways that ranged from information campaigns to threats against or harassment of union supporters."[23] Human Rights Watch found a "growing incidence of workers' rights violations."[24] Although U.S. policies formally

> comport with international human rights norms, [the] reality of NLRA enforcement falls far short of its goals. Many workers who try to form and join trade unions to bargain with their employers are spied on, harassed, pressured, threatened, suspended, fired, deported or otherwise victimized in reprisal for their exercise of the right to freedom of association.[25]

Freeman and Rogers also interviewed a sample of managers who reported that "if the employees they managed formed a union" it would "hurt their career a great deal." They note that under U.S. law "a manager who refuses to oppose a union can be summarily dismissed."[26]

Although collective bargaining is commonly thought of in North America as an adversarial process of negotiation between employers and state-certified unions leading to written agreements containing management's rights clauses, formal grievance procedures, and many other specific attributes, that nexus is only one variant of collective bargaining. As indicated by the ILO definition above, the term *collective bargaining* refers to a wide range of practices that include but are not limited to the specifics of typical American practice. Generically, the term includes any set of discussions between employers and representatives selected by employees to discuss employment issues with a view toward reaching mutual agreement on those issues. This broad definition includes, for example, negotiations that take place between worker representatives and employer appointees within the context of works councils established statutorily in many countries. These institutions cover practically the entire work force in several European nations.[27] The ILO's conception of collective bargaining also includes the negotiations taking place within the statutorily established wages councils that were a basic part of British industrial relations for most of the twentieth century.[28] It includes the discussions that take place within legally required joint health and safety committees in Canada.[29] It includes cases where employers and autonomous employee representatives develop their own relationship outside the confines of the Wagner Act's legal framework in Canada and the United States.[30]

Despite evidence that they are intensely antiunion in the context of the legal framework of the Wagner Act, a substantial percentage of American managers recognize the appropriateness and value to the firm of employee representation. In a recent study, Lipset and Meltz found that, despite the injunction against employer-dominated company unions, about 20 percent of American workers are covered by employee representation plans unilaterally established by their employers.[31] In their sample, Freeman and Rogers found that "much of management favours a more substantial employee voice in joint committees." Moreover, "nearly one-half of managers said that they favored employees electing their own representatives to such committees."[32]

A major stumbling block in moving this area of agreement into conformity with international standards is the reluctance of top corporate decision makers to relinquish their hold on power. If those employers identified in the Meltz and Lipset study as having representation schemes were to allow participating employees to select their own leaders and develop their own agendas, these relationships would probably qualify under both U.S. and international law as legitimate collective bargaining arrangements and thus would add significantly to the collective bargaining participation rate in the United States.[33] Unfortunately, as Rogers and Freeman found, American managers generally "oppose programs that would keep them from making the final decisions about workplace governance."[34]

Why Choice Is an Inappropriate Standard

On considering the evidence reviewed briefly above, most trade unionists and intellectuals supportive of collective bargaining in the United States argue that if employees had real free choice the collective bargaining rate in the United States would be much higher. Most are critical of the government for failing to end the rampant illegality aimed at repressing the urge to organize and bargain collectively. Their objective is a policy in which employee choice would be truly unfettered. The argument made here is entirely different. I suggest that choice is the wrong standard altogether. Employees should not be compelled to choose between bargaining and no representation. Workers ought to have the effective right to join or form unions of their own choosing but, over and above that right, the obligation of government, consistent with the theory embraced by the European Union, is to ensure that all workers, whether or not they have taken the initiative to form independent organizations, have in place representative institutions through which they are able to influence their conditions of work. When examined closely the case for choice as the standard for compliance with the human right to bargain makes little sense.

Since only about 10 percent of the private sector work force in the United States is covered by collective agreements, American choice theory would have us believe that most American workers prefer not to bargain collectively, which is to say that they have no desire to influence the many collective aspects of work critical to their well being. They prefer not to be consulted about the company's wage budget, about the nature of the wage payment system, about the work organization system, about the amount and nature of training provided by the firm, about the framework in place for ensuring a safe and healthy workplace, about the implementation of equal employment opportunity. They prefer to have management unilaterally establish policies on these issues without their advice and consent.

On its face, this notion is preposterous. Employees may prefer to forgo the confrontational version of collective bargaining available to them under the NLRA, but no sane and self-respecting adult would prefer to be entirely excluded from employment decision-making. In a democratic society, how can anyone legitimately accept, without discussion, whatever the employer might put in place when the option of being consulted is available? Why would anyone with a modicum of human dignity prefer a passive and subordinate status within the enterprise society? They wouldn't and the available evidence indicates that they don't. In their recent survey, Freeman and Rogers found that, although many workers weren't keen on the adversarial brand of bargaining available under the NLRA, nearly all of those responding wanted some form of voice at work. Some 88 percent of those surveyed indicated that they wanted to be represented in the making of the rules of work.[35]

Despite the survey evidence that American workers want a representative voice, the argument is frequently made that the American people are individualistic, and although they may want to have a say about their employment conditions, they prefer to negotiate individual contracts. However that may be, those who prefer to participate in the full range of organizational governance via individual negotiations are seeking the impossible. Some employment issues are individually negotiable and a case might be made that (contrary to the requirements of the NLRA which grants exclusive bargaining status to the bargaining agent) employees should be provided with the opportunity to bargain individually over them. For many years industrial relations experts have argued that individual negotiations favor the employer whose bargaining power obviously exceeds that of most individual employees. Nevertheless, it is not unreasonable to maintain that, if employees choose to do so, the state should not forbid them to bargain individually over issues that are amenable to individual bargaining despite the apparent imbalance of power.

But many critical conditions of work are collective in nature and cannot be negotiated by each employee separately. With respect to issues such as the overall wage budget, the wage structure, the training system, the health and safety system, the promotion scheme, the implementation of human rights and employment standards legislation, to name only a few relevant issues, the only choices are collective decision-making or imposition. How the firm handles these issues, the amount of resources it devotes to them, and decisions to make major changes to them are all inherently of concern to employees. In firms of any size, however, individual bargaining over them is infeasible.

Another argument commonly made in the United States against aggressive promotion of collective bargaining by government is that it would be economically damaging to companies now operating under unconstrained managerial discretion. Such arguments helped, for example, to defeat labor law reform in the 1970s.[36] A considerable amount of research in the United States has attempted to test the hypothesis that collective bargaining is bad for business. Among economists a debate on the issue continues to rage without a definitive winner. Indeed, a considerable amount of evidence points to positive economic benefits of collective bargaining.[37]

Whatever the outcome of the economic debate, from a human rights perspective, these arguments are irrelevant because according to the international consensus fundamental human rights "trump" other considerations. Some economists have argued theoretically that economies would be more efficient if workers were permitted to sell themselves into slavery. Whatever the potential economic benefits, slavery is repugnant to democratic values and thus beyond the realm of consideration.[38]

If fundamental human rights are indivisible, and if collective bargaining is a human right as the international consensus affirms it to be, then the persistence of arbitrary authority in industry should arouse indignation no less intense than the continued existence of forced labor in countries such as Burma and child prostitution in countries such as Thailand.[39]

The evidence suggests that, despite the human rights character of collective bargaining, about 90 percent of American private-sector workers are excluded from collective employment decision-making. Their conditions of work, which are critical to their well-being and life chances, are imposed without their advice and consent. Some of those employees would like to be represented under NLRA rules but are precluded from doing so because of deficiencies in U.S. law and its administration. Many others want, but are denied, representation in a format different from that available under the NLRA because employers refuse, in contempt for international standards, to enter willingly into such relationships, and the state, contrary to its international obligations, has not provided employees with statutory options. Despite this sorry state of affairs, defenders of the status quo insist that choice must remain the standard for establishing a bargaining relationship because to deny choice would be offensive to democratic principles.

Superficially, that argument might be appealing but on closer examination it falls apart. In the modern democratic state there are some choices that result in conditions so morally repugnant that they cannot be allowed. Of the five core labor rights standards endorsed unanimously by government, business, and labor delegates to the ILO's annual conference as fundamental human rights, theoretical negative rights are clearly not permitted with respect to three of them. We do not, for example, permit people to sell themselves into slavery. We do not allow states to choose apartheid, and we do not allow children to choose to prostitute themselves or enter into other forms of exploitative labor arrangements. From a human rights perspective the alternative to voice for employees—deferral to authority unaccountable to the governed—is as obnoxious as any of these possibilities and its continued existence is shameful. Not only should it not be available to be chosen, but like slavery, child labor, and discrimination, the elimination of arbitrary authority in industry should be the urgent objective.

One way of looking at the situation is that the choice with respect to this issue was made long ago. Collective bargaining is commonly characterized as the preferred method to introduce democratic principles into industry. Once a nation opts for democracy it need not, and should not have to, continually remake that decision with respect to its practice in its various institutions. Placing before the American people an option for the establishment of a hereditary count of Westchester, duke of New York, or king of America is absurd. The issue to be decided is not whether there ought to be democracy but rather what form democratic participation ought to take. Debate about the relative merits of Wagner-Act-style negotiations, statutory works councils, and independent extralegal relations voluntarily established by employers and representatives freely chosen by their employees is legitimate and appropriate. In a democratic nation, however, no representation as a option should be accorded no legitimacy.

Implications for Labor Policy

With respect to the proper interpretation of the international consensus, theory has dramatic practical implications for labor policy. If the negative right not to bargain were rejected then a number of steps would logically follow. For example, closing what the ILO calls "the representation gap," would become the central objective of American policy.[40] Adopting such a policy would mean a sharp break with policy approaches that have been deeply ingrained for decades. Among the most sacred of principles is that of "balance," which holds that the government has a responsibility to treat the interests of business and the trade union movement equally. To favor one over the other is considered to be inappropriate.[41] The problem with this theory is that it focuses on the interests of business and existing trade unions. In doing so, it neglects the interests of employees in a voice at work. As the recent Human Rights Watch report insists, workers deserve to be considered "autonomous actors" to whom unions and collective bargaining are "tools" for the "exercise of basic rights." They should not be conceived of as "objects of unions' or employers' institutional interests."[42]

Although a policy of aggressively and purposively attacking the representation gap may seem extreme given American conventions, such a policy has recent precedent. Unapologetically closing the gap was precisely the policy objective adopted in France in the early 1980s.[43] The initiatives that the French took led to a significant expansion of collective bargaining coverage. Today more than 90 percent of French workers are covered by collective agreements.[44] More recently, in the wake of the ILO's Fundamental Declaration, the labor ministers of the Americas, including the responsible American secretary, promised to "extend the coverage of collective bargaining to the greatest possible number of sectors of the economy." More explicitly, the Chilean government publicly promised to put in place policies that would result in the doubling of the collective bargaining coverage rate in that country.[45]

On accepting the same objective, an American president, desiring to bring American conventions into line with international standards, might immediately urge employers voluntarily to agree to meet with representatives freely and independently chosen by the employees in order to discuss any issues of mutual concern. Even in its current state, American labor policy does not forbid the voluntary establishment of flexible bargaining relationships tailor-made to the preferences of the parties. The research by Meltz and Lipset[46] and by Freeman and Rogers[47] indicates that many American employers see the value in such arrangements even though they are apparently reluctant to surrender control of them. A strong moral stance by the president in favor of collective bargaining could be based not only on international human rights law but also on the United States constitution.[48] Because of the authority of the office, such a presidential initiative would make it difficult for employers to continue publicly and openly to pursue union avoidance strategies. There would, of course, be opposition. But forceful coupling of collective bargaining rights with the deeply rooted rights to be free from forced and child labor and discrimination in employment would be a powerful force for exposing that opposition as illegitimate and immoral.

A president, faithful to the letter and spirit of international obligations that the United States has voluntarily accepted, might also send legislation to Congress requiring the establishment of employee representative councils.[49] Typically, representatives to these bodies are elected by all relevant employees whether union members or not. The councils commonly have responsibility for codetermining a range of issues identified in law. In Germany, for example, representative councils established by statute are responsible for a wide range of issues, including training policy, safety and health policy, the implementation of employment legislation, and the implementation of collective agreements negotiated on a multiemployer basis by trade unions. Companies may not lay off workers without council consent subject to an arbitration procedure in which the employer must demonstrate necessity. Subject to arbitration, the council also may veto individual dismissals.[50]

Trade unions in Germany may and generally do run candidates for council election. As a result, the large majority of councilors are active trade unionists. Although German unions were initially opposed to these institutions, fearing that they would undermine independent labor organization, they have learned to live with them and now consider them to be the union's institution within the workplace.

I realize that the labor movement in America is wary of these institutions and fears that they might develop into weak, employer-dominated substitutes for genuine independent representation. These fears are not unreasonable, and they need to be effectively addressed. But there has been a lot of international experience with representative councils, and unions abroad have found ways to coexist compatibly with them. Where they exist, labor movements today generally approve of them.[51] With the good will of all parties to the employment relationship and with the international experience as a resource, developing an acceptable American model should not be an insurmountable problem.

It would be appropriate, for example, for trade unions to set up local union branches in enterprises in which they do not have majority support. The object of these local organizations would be to represent member interests as best they could without the support provided by the Wagner Act model to certified unions. The jurisprudence of the ILO's Freedom of Association Committee makes it clear that employers offend international standards when they refuse, as they commonly do in the United States under NLRA conventions, to recognize and meet with minority unions with a view toward satisfactorily resolving whatever issues they raise.

With respect to the representative councils, independent unions could run candidates for council office. Indeed, in line with the international experience, the law might make it easier for unions to nominate candidates than for candidates to get on the ballot independently. If able to capture the council, the local union would be able to use its statutory powers to advance member interests. Canadian unions need not rely solely on their natural bargaining power to improve the health and safety conditions for their members. They also have the advantage of statutes that require employers jointly to develop and administer health and safety rules with them.

For this scenario to occur, it would be necessary to have more effective protection of workers from victimization for involvement in union activity. If councils were established by statute, employer opposition to union membership would be expected to diminish at any rate. Having to deal with an employee representation agency with statutory powers, there would be less to gain by dissuading employees from taking out union membership. Moreover, were the office of the president to forcefully condemn bargaining avoidance as a violation of human rights it would be difficult for employers to engage in practices now accepted as the norm. A combined effort by human rights and labor organizations to protest the immorality of these actions in cases where employers attempted to persist with them (much as the civil rights, women's rights, and gay rights movements have done) would make such practices costly.

The Practicality Issue

At this point the objection is frequently raised that my proposals are impractical and thus of no more than esoteric interest. Clearly, the realists say, they are beyond the realm of the possible. Most of these realists accept the current normative milieu as a given and do not consider the option of changing it. But as the civil rights, women's rights, and gay rights movements have demonstrated during the past half-century, social values and behavior are not immutable. They can be changed.

Winning wide support for the rejection of the illegitimate "right" of employees to defer to arbitrary authority should not be unattainable if pursued with vigor by labor and human rights groups. From a democratic perspective, the persistence of a system of workplace governance in which the governed have no representation is insupportable and the evidence clearly indicates that American workers do not approve of the current situation in which their conditions are imposed on them without their advice and consent. The evidence also suggests that many American managers, in fact, see the value in incorporating employees in employment decision-making.

A campaign which insists that freedom of association and the right to bargain collectively are separate but equal rights subject to careful consideration on their own, that collective bargaining consists of a range of activities that include but are not limited to conventional adversarial bargaining, and that all workers have a human right to a voice at work rather than a false right to submit to unaccountable authority ought to have a good chance of winning widespread support. Such a campaign should permit the uniting of the American labor and human rights communities in a movement whose prospects for achieving reform are at least as good as were those of the civil rights movement in the 1940s.

On the other hand, experience over the past several decades in the United States indicates that minor alteration of the Wagner Act model is unlikely to succeed under current political and social assumptions. Attempts at reform since the mid-1970s have repeatedly been defeated. Most recently an attempt to outlaw the technique of hiring permanent strike-breakers, behavior that is contrary to international labor standards, was defeated in the U.S. Senate by a filibuster.[52]

Moreover, if one looks at American labor policy from an international perspective, it seems obvious that the proposals on the table for tinkering with the Wagner Act model such as those put forth by the Dunlop Commission[53] or those more recently suggested by Human Rights Watch,[54] even if they were attainable, would not materialize the human right of all workers to a voice at work. Canada imported the American labor policy model in the 1940s. Over the years it was revised to include most of the reform options proposed for the United States. At least some Canadian jurisdictions have introduced policies such as speedy certification votes, card check certification, first contract arbitration, and stiff and rapid sanctions against law breaking employers. No Canadian jurisdiction permits permanent strike replacements and a few forbid the employer to hire strike replacements at all.

The results of this more labor-friendly version of the Wagner Act model have been less than dramatic.[55] Instead of nine in ten private-sector workers having no voice at work, eight of ten equivalent workers are excluded in Canada.[56] From the institutional perspective of unions who might consider themselves to be purveyors of a service to prospective employee clients, a doubling of market penetration might be a significant achievement. If the human right to voice for all employees is the object, however, there is no reason to expect that adoption of the Canadian version of the Wagner Act model will achieve that end in the United States.

Conclusion

In conclusion, the United States has promised on the world stage to honor international workers' human rights standards but it is not fulfilling its obligations. In order to deliver on its promise the United States needs to alter its labor policy fundamentally. The object ought to be the elimination of arbitrary authority in industry. The policy tools to achieve that end are readily available. Without a major change in course, the large majority of American workers are likely to continue to be denied, against their will, what most of the world has affirmed to be a

Table 7.1
Union Density and Collective Bargaining Coverage Estimates,
Early 1990s[a]

Country	Union Membership Density (% unionized)	Proportion of Employees Covered by Collective Agreements (%)
France	8–12	70–80
Germany	39–45	90
Netherlands	35–40	75–80
Austria	45–50	90+
Switzerland	28–35	65
Sweden	80–95	90+
United States	15–17	18–22

Source: Roy J. Adams, "Industrial Relations under Liberal Democracy," in
North America in Comparative Perspective (Columbia: University of South
Carolina Press, 1995): table 4.1
[a]Slightly more up-to-date estimates of union density and bargaining
coverage in these countries and others is provided in the appendices to the
ILO's World Labour Report of 1997. International Labour Office, *Industrial
Relations, Democracy and Social Stability* (Geneva, 1997). However, some of the
data reported by the ILO are problematic. For example, contrary to all other
existing estimates the ILO reports that the bargaining coverage rate in the
United States is only 11.2% while union density is 14.2%. Other studies of the
US have generally found that bargaining coverage is about 2–3% higher than
union density. Kumar for example, reports a unionization rate of 16.1% and a
bargaining coverage rate of 18.3%. Pradeep Kumar, *From Uniformity to
Divergence: Industrial Relations in Canada and the United States* (Kingston,
Ontario: IRC Press, 1993). For the purpose of the argument made here this
controversy is largely beside the point.

birthright of all human beings. Without exception, all workers have a
right to participate collectively in making employment decisions that
shape their lives. They have a fundamental human right to bargain collectively.

CHAPTER 8

"An Injury to One . . ."

Transnational Labor Solidarity and
the Role of Domestic Law

James Atleson

"**S**ympathy strikes . . . are becoming increasingly frequent because of the move towards the concentration of enterprises, the globalization of the economy and the delocalization of work centres. While pointing out that a number of distinctions need to be drawn here . . . the [ILO Freedom of Association] Committee considers that a general prohibition on sympathy strikes could lead to abuse and that workers should be able to take such action, provided the initial strike they are supporting is itself lawful."[1] The notion that all citizens of the world possess basic rights has gained currency in recent years, and it is reasonable to argue that the workplace, the location in which people spend most of their lives, should not be exempted. Indeed, various international conventions and documents set forth specific workplace rights, and unions may be able to expand or enforce those rights by their own efforts. Labor unions are beginning to think about how they can take part in the world market and engage in actions that aid fellow workers elsewhere in the world.

The concept of worker solidarity is fundamental to the law of many nations. In the United States, for instance, the concept of solidarity is embodied in the National Labor Relations Act's definition of "employee," expressly extending beyond the boundaries of any individual employer: "The term 'employee' shall include any employee, and shall not be limited to the employees of a particular employer."[2] If worker solidarity is important to advance shared goals within one country, the

The author would like to thank Ellen Dannin for her careful comments on an earlier version of this paper, Alan Hyde, Patrick Macklem, Makoto Ishida, and Guy Mundlak for their suggestions, and Fred Konefsky for his unfailing support of this and all other projects. Jason Bowman and Kevin Hsi provided valuable research assistance. Versions of this effort were presented in a number of forums, including the 1999 Intell Conference, Cape Town, South Africa; the 1998 Law and Society Conference, Chicago, Illinois; and the 1999 Labor Law Group Conference, Scottsdale, Arizona.

increasingly global nature of work and the mobility of capital suggest that it is essential that worker solidarity exist across national boundaries. After all, the expansion of transnational corporations makes it likely that in some instances worker solidarity across national boundaries could well involve workers employed by the same employer.

Labor lawyers and unions, at least in the United States, have thus far not stressed international labor rights, and international human rights groups have generally not focused on labor rights, at least collective rights.[3] Recently, however, a sense of the internationalism unions talked about in the late nineteenth and early twentieth centuries has returned,[4] although most of it has focused on attaching some recognition of minimum standards to trade pacts.

In recent years, the subject of international trade has tended to dominate any assertion or discussion of international labor rights. The creation of new trading blocks and, especially, the World Trade Organization (WTO), has moved the possible linkage of worker rights and trade to the front page. Nevertheless, there are serious doubts whether trade agreements can be a likely, let alone an effective, vehicle for the promotion of international labor rights.[5]

The WTO could consider and adopt some kind of social clause, but this scenario seems doubtful. Although the effort to use the WTO to establish international labor standards is continuing, and may seem hopeful, adoption of a "social clause" in this body dominated by "free traders" and populated by third world governments, unions, and employers who perceive such efforts as limitations on their economic success, seems unlikely.[6] Although no nation may be an island, labor is deemed localized. Moreover, efforts to interfere with the "free market" are routinely attacked as paternalistic or inconsistent with deeply held views. The current acceptance of these views by many policymakers tends to create difficulty in raising claims based on human dignity, democratic values, justice, and worker rights.

The ILO can be looked to for highly relevant standards, although "it does not claim to provide, in any true sense, a transnational forum with a mandate to evaluate the conduct of individual companies and unions."[7] ILO standards are promoted by investigations and reports, and, thus, public pressure and embarrassment serve as enforcement mechanisms.[8]

The procedures of multistate arrangements such as the NAFTA labor side agreement, the North American Agreement on Labor Cooperation, although perhaps useful for publicizing disputes and the lack of enforcement of domestic labor law, will be unlikely to "promote or regulate 'normal' ongoing collective relationships in the transnational sphere." Some multistate arrangements, particularly the European Union, have attempted to legislate in employment areas, although other than safety issues and works councils, it has not yet dealt with collective labor relations.

Despite the history of attempts to set international standards for labor and employment, legal regimes are nevertheless intensely local in character. As Professor Harry Arthurs of Osgoode Hall Law School has stated, "Across the global economy, and even within its most advanced regional economic systems, all collective labour relations regimes are essentially local regimes, even when they involve transnational corporations."[9] As Lord Wedderburn, one of the foremost labor scholars, noted, "One is struck by the contrast between the facility of the internationalization of capital and the obstacles that obstruct international trade union action. Capital is not tied, but each trade union movement is tied to the particular social history of the country in which it operates."[10] Thus, labor law is basically national just as labor is still primarily based nationally. Yet, Lord Wedderburn's comments in 1973 are still valid:

> The true correlative to an international agreement securing to capital the right to move and, therefore, organize across the boundaries of national states would be an agreement securing to collective organizations of workpeople the right to take common action in negotiating, bargaining with and, if need be, striking against the multinational enterprises. . . . It is not free movement of labor but free international trade union action which is the true counterpart to free movement of capital.[11]

ILO conventions include powerful statements concerning the right of freedom of assembly, the right to join unions and engage in collective bargaining, and the prohibition of child and forced labor and race and sex discrimination.[12] Most American labor lawyers, I am fairly certain, have not read, or perhaps even heard of, the ILO's standards, let alone the relevant UN documents such as the Universal Declaration of Human Rights; the International Covenant on Civil and Political Rights; and the International Covenant on Economic, Social, and Cultural Rights. This would no doubt not apply to lawyers who are generally much more attuned to international and comparative developments. Outside the United States, international documents and, indeed, decisions of foreign courts, are often known and even cited in briefs. Harold Dunning, formerly chief of workers' relations in the ILO, has said that it "would be all but impossible to find any trade union office in the world where Convention No. 87 is not only well known but also held in high esteem."[13] It would be difficult, however, to make the same assumption about unions in the United States.

Even if these documents were more widely known, it is less than certain they would have any impact on promoting worker rights. United States lawyers, for instance, do not have a great deal of experience in citing or using international or comparative law sources. It is also sobering that even lawyers who regularly engage in transnational legal practice have little faith in the value of international legal norms. Many believe that the ILO, while useful in setting standards, can be ignored because it has little ability to enforce those standards. Yet, the labor standards in ILO documents have provided the values that have guided the supporters of labor rights and that have been employed in regional trade agreements such as the labor side agreement to NAFTA as well as in numerous corporate codes.

Nevertheless, trade agreements and ILO standards provide thin reeds for the advancement of labor. In addition, the very forces of globalization may make it unlikely that domestic law can be relied on to advance worker rights and conditions when domestic law has been under assault by economic forces as well as organizations such as the IMF and World Bank.[14] Nations cannot be insulated from global forces, and the labor law system of all nations will be affected by forces outside national control and, perhaps, outside the control of the participants.[15] As Christopher Arup has noted,

> the nation state finds its regulatory options limited when it seeks to be either a host or home country site for globally coordinated production. For example, as a host site, it may become reluctant to insist upon high labour standards within its own territory, for fear of making local products uncompetitive and risking disinvestment and capital switching to more sympathetic regulatory environments by cost conscious employers. As a home base for multinationals which source production offshore, it may be reluctant to extend the reach of high labour standards

beyond its territory, for fear of losing the commercial advantages of local domiciling and headquartering.[16]

This suggests that labor may have to rely on the possibility of self-help, directed internationally. Attempts to forge international relationships among workers or to take action across borders will clearly involve national labor law systems. Yet, domestic legal regimes often create serious problems for unions who wish to promote international standards or the notion that labor rights should be treated as human rights. The "hollowed-out state" turns out to be not so hollow after all. Just as many argue that states, far from ceasing to effectively function in the global world, actually legislate the rules and structure of the global economy, states regulate the freedom of workers within their borders to exert economic pressure.

This, then, is a look at law from the ground up. Formal labor law, as other types of regulation, often looks different at the level it is to be applied, sometimes having greater effect than a sober reflection of the actual sanctions would suggest, sometimes having less effect than legislators hoped. Moreover, the ability to engage in acts of transnational labor solidarity is obviously limited to workers, primarily organized, who are in a position to exert economic pressure. Depending on the nature of the work involved and the relative strength of the parties, sympathy actions may be highly effective or virtually impossible. In this sense, this essay deals with a limited group of workers. Yet, transnational activity is clearly occurring, and its incidence seems to be increasing. Moreover, as will be subsequently noted, certain unions have gained importance in the global economy. Thus, whatever the formal legal rules may be, unions are acting internationally to counteract capital. International solidarity, therefore, may be a lever to advance the values set out in ILO documents.

The multinational corporate structure creates problems both of public and private democratic governance. Unions as well as nations find themselves dealing increasingly with corporations that "can more easily weather economic struggles, conceal information, and transfer, or more credibly threaten to transfer, work to other locales or, indeed, other countries, than could their predecessor counterparts."[17] For unions, which are organized nationally, the likelihood that corporate decisions are made elsewhere, by the home-based parent company, makes it difficult to exercise countervailing influence or power. Moreover, unions know that bargaining as well as investment decisions are made in the light of the success of subsidiaries in other countries. To take one example, the U.S. autoworkers are aware that negotiations with General Motors are related to conditions at Vauxhall in the United Kingdom, Opel in Germany, Holden in Australia, Saab in Sweden, as well as GM plants in Latin and South America.[18]

In short, many industrial disputes have an international dimension. Not only do employers, especially in the United States, often threaten to move abroad, but firms themselves are often foreign companies. According to Jay Mazor, non-U.S. companies employ one-third of the members of the United Food and Commercial Workers Union in the United States. Approximately two-thirds of AFL-CIO unions are engaged in some kind of international activity.[19]

The growing imbalance of union-management power has been accentuated by new production strategies, automation, and communication advances.[20] Not only does capital flow easily across national borders, but borders are increasingly irrelevant to the marketing and production of goods. Specialized production methods lessen the effectiveness of union pressure. For instance, in 1987 Olivetti, the Italian based corporation, produced electric typewriters in its domestic factories, calculators in Mexico and Italy, and computers in Argentina. Labor conflict in any one country would not affect continued production in other locations.

As early as 1969, unions have coordinated action against multinational corporations in the countries in which the firms operated.[21] Trade unions in Europe in some of the industries affected by the expansion of multinational firms, especially chemicals and metal trades, began to "advocate coordinated action by unions in different countries in which these corporations had operations."[22] The idea of bargaining with multinational corporations gave new life to the international trade secretariats (ITSs), international confederations of unions in the same industry that had played a less significant role when unions had been primarily concerned with Cold War issues.[23] The secretariats provide data for bargaining purposes and also coordinate communication and assistance among affiliates. Such assistance might involve unions in the same industry but who work in different nations or unions in the same transnational corporation. Certain secretariats, especially the International Metalworkers' Federation, have tried to coordinate bargaining across borders.[24] Moreover, the passage of the labor side agreement to NAFTA has spurred collaborative efforts by U.S. and Mexican unions.[25]

The most comprehensive organization is the International Confederation of Free Trade Unions (ICFTU) based in Brussels. The ICFTU was created in 1949 by national unions that withdrew from the World Federation of Trade Unions because of the influence of unions in the eastern block. The ICFTU, therefore, is a creation of the Cold War, although it can be considered a descendent of nineteenth-century international union organizations. The organization's membership does not consist of national unions, but, rather, of national union centers or confederations. Currently, there are 215 national union centers in 145 nations and territories, with approximately 125 million individual workers represented.[26] The newest sectoral international is Union Network International (UNI), created from four older and separate organizations, to represent skilled workers' interests in areas such as entertainment, finance, media, and communications. UNI claims it has a network of 920 affiliated unions, representing 15.5 million members in 140 countries.[27]

International solidarity has been advocated both on altruistic grounds as well as by the more self-interested desire to protect domestic labor standards against lower foreign standards. More recently, unions have been concerned with internal corporate decisions involved with the transfer or location of production to low-wage nations. In addition, the increasing merger and expansion of multinational firms makes it rational to build linkages with unions in other nations or to aid in the creation of unions where none may have previously existed. The goals of these federations are to aid struggles in other nations, assist workers in the same corporations, and engage in transnational bargaining. Many difficulties exist, of course, but the rationality of such action may tend to offset the legal, institutional, and nationalistic problems. A few examples of recent solidarity efforts will highlight both the likelihood of further international actions as well as the problems posed by domestic labor law.

Transnational Labor Actions

With the growth of multinational enterprise, management becomes to a large extent an international power—where is the countervailing power? . . . we have management but neither government nor effective union power. The entire basis of our thinking on collective industrial relations and collective labour law is destroyed by this development.[28]

There have been a number of recent transnational solidarity actions, albeit not often reported by the mainstream press. The U.S. Teamsters Union's (IBT) strike against UPS in 1997, to take one example, has often been discussed as a possible harbinger of a renewed militancy of American unions. Little reported, however, were the efforts of foreign unions to support the U.S. Teamsters. The IBT and the International Transport Workers Federation (ITF)[29] created an international strategy, which included a World Council of UPS Trade Unions, aimed at threatening UPS operations abroad.[30] Although UPS dominates the U.S. market, it operates in a much more competitive market in other areas, especially in Europe.

A meeting held in London in February 1997 included American Teamster officials, UPS shop stewards from ITF affiliated unions in Europe and the United States, and union representatives from Brazil and Ireland who planned to organize UPS workers in their own countries. The representatives shared information about UPS and discussed issues that seemed to parallel those of the IBT, such as subcontracting, part-time workers, and health and safety issues. The group was formalized as the World Council of UPS Trade Unions, an organization that would create an information network and support structure, especially in light of the upcoming UPS-IBT negotiations. Since the IBT represents two-thirds of UPS workers globally, the outcome of these negotiations was critical for non-U.S. unions.[31]

A World Action Day was created in the spring of 1997, and a World Council meeting was scheduled in Washington in June to coincide with the final period of the UPS-IBT negotiations. On May 22, 1997, over 150 job actions and demonstrations occurred at UPS facilities around the world, and some short work stoppages occurred in Spain and Italy. The second meeting of the World Council occurred in June, and members of the council were introduced at the bargaining session.[32] After the U.S. Teamsters struck, demonstrations occurred at important distribution centers in Europe, and some sympathy strikes occurred. European unions were requested to make public commitments to support the strike and to create boycott plans for UPS, information that would be delivered to UPS's largest customers. In addition, European public-sector unions were asked to appeal to their "members who were customs officers and labor inspectors to give greater scrutiny to UPS packages and UPS workplace-safety standards during the strike."[33] The function of these actions was to create doubts about the efficacy of UPS's service during the strike.

European workers engaged in sympathetic actions. Since sympathy strikes result in sanctions in the United Kingdom, sickouts occurred. A wildcat strike occurred among UPS distribution center workers in Belgium, although the UPS strike may have been a pretext for local health and safety concerns. Stoppages or interferences with deliveries occurred in nations as widespread as India, the Philippines, and Spain. The settlement in the United States occurred before planned sympathy actions could occur in Germany, France, and the Netherlands. Many of these unions had grievances of their own or used the strike in the United States as an organizing tool. Nevertheless, these actions took place at great risk since many protests that did occur or were planned were probably illegal.[34]

A second example, involving collective action against Renault in Europe, demonstrates how "a transnational realm of European government presents a series of new opportunities and constraints for domestic social actors," leading to claims directed to the European Union (EU) as well as to domestic forms of action.[35] In February 1997, the president of the Renault automobile company announced the closure of its plant in Vilvoorde, Belgium. Having suffered serious financial losses, Europe's sixth largest carmaker announced the closure of the heavily unionized plant. The announcement led to a protest from a number of European nations, concern from the European Union, and the first "Euro-strike."

Belgian, French, and European Union officials expressed outrage, in part because the action violated EU regulations concerning notice of plant closures and resulting negotiations. In addition, Renault had planned to use EU structural funds at the same time as the closing to expand a plant in Spain, leading an embarrassed Spain to withdraw its plan to aid the expansion so as not to appear to replace a viable Belgium operation with production at a cheaper location. Worker demonstrations and strike action occurred across Europe. On March 7, for instance, about half of Renault's workforce in France and Spain struck. The level of support was especially noteworthy given the intensifying competition for jobs across the Union. Imig and Tarrow note that the dispute has come to an "uneasy conclusion." Renault ultimately did close the plant but only after creating "a more extensive social plan for the redundant workers."[36]

An increasingly common story in the United States is illustrated by the protests leveled at Paris-based Imerys involving its Georgia Marble plant in Alabama. Imerys withdrew recognition of the union after it acquired a much larger and nonunion plant, English China Clays, and combined the nearby plant with Georgia Marble. A U.S. delegation met with foreign workers, which led to press conferences and rallies. PACE (Paper, Allied-Industrial, Chemical, and Energy Workers International Union) organized a successful global campaign against Imerys, which included the creation of a web site, a video, and assistance from Imerys workers in the United Kingdom and France. Eventually, the union won an NLRB-sponsored representation election.[37]

Perhaps the most interesting transnational example involves the concerted international boycotts that began when the Merseyside dockers in Liverpool were locked out and replaced for resisting privatization and work force reductions in 1996. The dockers' shop stewards' organization began a campaign for reinstatement, which spread from the United Kingdom to ports around the world. Unlike other workers who have recently faced similar problems, the Liverpool workers became an international cause as the symbol of the "demise of England's unionized longshore industry."

Symbolic as well as direct labor actions occurred in more than one hundred ports, and workers in many locations refused to unload cargo from ships originating in Liverpool.[38] In the United States the ILWU closed down the West Coast for eight hours on January 20, while Oregon ports remained closed for twenty-four hours.[39] As Moody perceptively notes, the "Merseyside dockers had given world labor a lesson in how to counter the power not only of dock, shipping, and the other transportation firms, but of all the TNCs whose vast investments rest on this fragile transportation system."[40]

One result of the troubled situation in the United Kingdom was the international reaction to the voyage of the *Neptune Jade*, a Singapore-owned Orient Lines' freighter. The Jade's cargo had been loaded in Thamesport, England, in 1997, the site of a continuing dispute involving numerous dockers who were sacked by companies in the Liverpool area.[41] The *Neptune Jade* proceeded to Oakland, California, where it was met on September 28, 1997, with a picket line composed of various groups, including the Labor Party's Golden Gate chapter, student members of a labor society at Laney College, and members of various unions, including members of the Industrial Workers of the World who had communicated with each other by e-mail.[42] Over a three-day period, longshore workers refused to cross the picket line and unload the ship.

After three days the ship left the port of Oakland without having been unloaded.[43] The *Jade* then sailed to Vancouver, British Columbia, where a similar scenario unfolded, and, again, the ship was not unloaded.[44] After five hours of picketing by approximately thirty pickets, the *Jade* left for Yokohama, Japan, where the All-Japan Dockworkers' Union refused to unload the ship.[45] Reportedly, the *Jade* was finally unloaded in Taiwan.[46]

Depending on your point of view, the travails of the *Neptune Jade* may be a stimulating example of transnational labor solidarity.[47] Given the international relationship of production and marketing, transportation workers take on a new importance. Nontransportation workers have also been involved in cross-border activity such as providing economic or staff support, for instance, to new independent unions in Mexico, or lending support to strikes or disputes in other countries. The International Trade Secretariats have recently been active, for instance, in bringing together unions representing workers in subsidiaries of TNCs, and unions and international confederations of unions have also waged lobbying and public opinion campaigns.[48]

The future role of such action, however, turns on the legality of such pressure under the domestic law of the state in which a union engages in sympathetic action. When national laws restrict sympathetic or secondary actions by workers, whether wholly within one nation or extending across national borders, they "deconstruct" class, emptying it of social reality and social significance.[49] Indeed, one obvious purpose of secondary boycott restrictions may be precisely to limit the ability of workers to express solidarity *as workers.* The labor laws of many nations treat the very real feeling of solidarity, revealed in the cases discussed below, as unworthy of recognition or protection.

Legal Response to Sympathetic Action

There are a number of national legal responses to sympathetic or secondary labor actions, and thus far little distinction has been made between intra- and international pressure. Most legal systems prohibit sympathetic or secondary action, no matter what form the legal system takes, whether common or civil law, and despite differences in history and culture. Although the same legal rules may be reached, the route by which the result is reached varies.

Some nations, such as the United States and United Kingdom, expressly make most types of secondary or sympathetic action illegal. In the United Kingdom, for instance, the common law of torts and contract regulated strikes throughout most of the twentieth century. There is no positive right to strike, and until the Thatcher period, no concept of legal or illegal strikes. The focus of judicial inquiry was whether the action was a tort or breach of contract, and penalties may affect the individual worker as well as the union.[50]

The absence of positive union rights was offset to some degree by the creation of statutory immunities for acts "in contemplation of a trade dispute." The historical immunities were severely restricted, however, by the Thatcher government in a series of employment acts between 1980 and 1990, now consolidated in the Trade Union and Labour Relations (Consolidation) Act (TULRA) of 1992. In 1980 Parliament banned secondary or solidarity action and picketing away from the worker's own workplace, and in 1982 the definition of "trade dispute" was narrowed to disputes between workers and their own employer. Moreover, action to help workers in another workplace to gain union recognition or consultation from their employer was prohibited. In other words, workers' influence is confined to the workers' own workplace. "[The statutes] prohibit the export of workers' collective influence beyond the boundaries of their own employment unit, itself defined by the employer."[51] The practical effect of such legislation, in Lord Wedderburn's words, "is to fragment and inhibit trade union action while the power of internationalized capital is constitutionally guaranteed the maximum flexibility."[52]

The restriction most relevant to the dockers dispute, for instance, is the "confinement of protected industrial actions to disputes between workers and their own employer and at their own place of work."[53] Thus, secondary actions lost the protection against common law civil liability, and "trade dispute" was narrowed to protect only disputes between workers and their own employer relating to the workers' own conditions.[54] A secondary action, under the recent legislation, will result in an injunction and tort remedies, and a refusal to handle "hot goods" will constitute a breach of contract by the individual employee. Even prior to the Thatcher era statutes, disputes, in order to gain immunity from tort law, had to be in furtherance of a trade dispute, and that term was limited to a dispute between workers and their own employer. Thus, political disputes did not receive immunity.[55]

The message is that employees have no legitimate interest in aiding other workers, thus limiting the scope of disputes to discrete workplaces. As Lord Wedderburn stated in 1985,

> The collective strength of workers is to be limited by the boundaries of their employment units. These boundaries are of course set not by the workers or their unions, but by capital in the private sector, and in the public sector by the state and capital together. Industrial action in solidarity across the boundaries is unlawful; the concept of a trade dispute is not to flow over them; each subsidiary company in a small national or giant multinational group is to retain its own boundaries. . . . In today's labour market in which a work force dreading unemployment . . . face employers increasingly buttressed by transnational connections, that represents a massive legal intervention against the 'collective power' which . . . is the only reality of workers' power.[56]

The ILO's Committee of Experts has found the Thatcher government's proscription of secondary action, based on the U.S. prohibition, provides "excessive limitations" on the right to strike. The U.K. statutes, the committee stated,

> appear to make it virtually impossible for workers and unions lawfully to engage in any form of boycott activity, or "sympathetic" action against parties not directly involved in a given dispute. . . . where a boycott relates directly to the social and economic concerns of the workers involved in either or both of the original dispute and the secondary action, and where the original dispute and the secondary action are not unlawful in themselves, then that boycott should be regarded as a legitimate exercise of the right to strike.[57]

Secondary labor activity in the United States is treated under the vague, but very restrictive, provisions of the National Labor Relations Act. There are two separate aspects of this problem in the secondary context. First, "neutral" employees may not strike to aid workers employed elsewhere nor may striking workers appeal to such workers by, for instance, picketing to induce a labor boycott. Thus, a union clearly may not appeal to neutral workers to cease work either completely or, at a minimum, not to work on hot goods. Nor may the neutral workers cease work on their own, unbidden by the striking union, for this would be a "strike" with an object forbidden by section 8(b)(4)(i).[58] These workers, it will be said, have no dispute with their own employer—there is no primary dispute with their own employer that justifies their work stoppage. Of course, these workers may feel personally or philosophically offended at being forced to handle or work on struck or "hot" goods. Aside from the inherent political nature of this area, it could fairly be argued that these workers indeed have a dispute with their employer since they are required—upon pain of discharge—to work on products which violates their sense of integrity.[59] In addition, such work may well weaken the strike effort.

Moreover, the definition of "neutral" is highly problematic and wholly owned subsidiaries of a firm have been treated as separate, or neutral, employers. If the target of labor action is consumers, the law is more complex. Appealing to consumers to boycott neutral employers via handbilling has been protected despite its secondary nature. The U.S. Supreme Court was moved to state that *picketing* directed to consumers, as opposed to handbilling, would not be protected unless the picketers were following only the struck product.[60]

Various, and wholly unsatisfying rationales have been produced for the legal decisions in the area. For instance, the court has distinguished between political boycotts, protected by the first amendment, and labor boycotts because the latter were merely "economic."[61] Why, however, is labor activity not deemed political? As many have argued, labor standards and communication certainly seem to involve public issues, and the public is the target group in consumer boycott situations.

But even this argument fades away. The U.S. Supreme Court has permitted the application of the secondary boycott statute to a clearly political act—the International Longshoremen's Association's (ILA) withholding of labor to protest the Soviet invasion of Afghanistan.[62] The application of statute would not, said the court, infringe on the first amendment rights of the ILA and its members: "We have consistently rejected the claim that secondary picketing by labor unions in violation of Section 8(b)(4) is protected activity under the first Amendment. . . .

It would seem even clearer that conduct designed not to communicate but to coerce merits still less consideration under the First Amendment." The withholding of labor, therefore, the critical right protected by the statute to make collective bargaining work, was treated as conduct "designed . . . to coerce." The court was willing to assume that the union's aim might be "understandable and even commendable." Even a moral aim, or one aimed at "freeing employees from handling goods from an objectionable source," however, would violate the statute.

In addition, it was irrelevant that the secondary pressure involved no primary employer with whom the union had a dispute. Thus, this was a case of a secondary boycott with no primary dispute. The basic dispute was with the Soviet Union, but the court found no exception for political actions. Indeed, despite the purported use of the political/economic distinction in other decisions, the court stated that "the distinction between labor and political objectives would be difficult to draw in many cases." And this is just the point. With the judicial interring of the "political" distinction, interested observers in the United States are left with no articulated rationale for the lack of protection for secondary labor picketing (as opposed to secondary nonlabor picketing), let alone for the distinction between secondary labor handbilling and picketing.

Nations such as the United States and United Kingdom, which explicitly bar sympathetic actions, place primary emphasis on the protection of neutral employers. It is at this point that courts make a fundamental choice between two views of neutrality. Unions and their members may well believe that firms that continue to work on goods from a struck firm are less than "neutral." As many said in the 1960s, "If you're not part of the solution, you're part of the problem." Moreover, what unions are generally trying to achieve is a fully effective strike, one that ends production at the struck firm. Should that be achieved, there is obviously no production on which workers at other firms can work.[63]

The normal judicial response, however, is that workers taking sympathetic action have no real dispute with their own employer and, thus, they are causing a neutral employer to suffer economic harm unfairly. But a contrary argument exists—if an employer insists that workers handle cargo which the workers find inconsistent with their principles, usually called "hot cargo," either because they wish to aid workers elsewhere or to express political revulsion about the source of the hot goods, why is this not deemed a primary and not a secondary strike? In other words, when workers refuse to work on "hot goods" in order to aid workers elsewhere, can it truly be said that they have no real dispute with their employer? The workers' boycott, after all, may well be based on deeply held beliefs. The answer, no doubt, lies in the limited status courts assign to workers, a status revealed in cases in which workers seek to control some aspect of their work.[64] Why is this type of action more important than a strike to obtain higher wages or, as in the United States, the right to handbill consumers? One could certainly argue that the right to dispose of your labor, especially to defend or assist others, is a more keenly felt and significant interest than the right to persuade consumers how to spend their money.

In the United States, the most noteworthy cases with an international significance have dealt with the legality of secondary action *outside the United States* in order to benefit unions *in the United States*. Two courts of appeals have reached opposite conclusions on the legality of the ILA's request that Japanese longshore workers boycott certain nonunion American shippers. Despite the lack of clarity about efforts by U.S. unions to use the aid of foreign workers, withholding of labor in the United States to aid workers in another country is likely to be treated as an illegal secondary boycott, leading to injunction or an action for damages. It is clear that secondary action within the United States would no doubt fall within the statute.[65]

Second, many nations restrict sympathetic action without explicit statutory prohibitions, although the route taken varies considerably from nation to nation. In Canada, for instance, the legality of strikes at both the federal and provincial level is primarily determined by their timing. In short, strikes are banned during the term of a collective bargaining agreement, and disputes are to be resolved via grievance arbitration. In other words, legislation accomplished in Canada what is normally resolved by contractual no-strike clauses in the United States.[66]

Even if a strike is not related to an underlying collective bargaining purpose, however, as in a sympathetic or political strike situation, the "prevailing view in all Canadian jurisdictions is that disruption of production and concerted employee activity by themselves are all that is required in order for a work stoppage to constitute a strike and be subject to the statutory restrictions on the timing of such activity."[67] Thus, the peace obligation is absolute, even if the dispute is not related to the collective agreement or falls outside the grievance process. In U.S. terms, the obligation not to strike during the contract's term is broader than the obligation to arbitrate contractual issues.[68]

Picketing is regulated primarily through the law of torts, lawful if the underlying strike is lawful, and vice versa. Yet, even picketing in support of a lawful strike may be deemed illegal if its impact is secondary, that is, if it has a "proportionate impact upon a third party unconnected to the labour dispute."[69] Even secondary picketing aimed at consumers is of questionable legality.[70] Thus, whether secondary or not, any strike during the term of an agreement will be deemed illegal even if the matter cannot be resolved through the grievance process. Indirectly, therefore, the peace obligation bars sympathetic strikes, but by a far different route than in the United Kingdom or the United States.

A more common method of restricting, but not necessary prohibiting, sympathetic action is to limit the scope of any collective action to matters affecting the narrow employer-employee relationship. In Japan, for instance, workers can take part in "dispute acts," a concept broader than strikes, as embodied both in postwar legislation and in Japan's constitution. Nevertheless, dispute acts "must be aimed at achieving an objective of collective bargaining."[71] The absence of an explicit statutory prohibition is of doubtful significance given the definition of a lawful strike. Although it is difficult to find reported decisions, it is believed that neither political nor sympathy strikes are proper because they do not involve issues resolvable with the employees' employer. Given the enterprise structure of Japanese unions, however, it is possible that the issue has not frequently arisen.

Interestingly, the ILO's Committee on Freedom of Association, like the Committee of Experts, "considers the right to strike should not be limited solely to industrial disputes that are likely to be resolved through the signing of a collective agreement." That is, "workers and their organizations should be able to express in a broader context, if necessary, their dissatisfaction as regards economic and social matters affecting their members' interests." Moreover, a ban on strike action "not linked to a collective dispute to which the employee or union is a party is contrary to the principles of freedom of association."[72]

Solidarity and sympathy strikes logically direct us to an examination of the workers' interests. It is often stated that European systems, other than the United Kingdom, "reserve some area of legality for solidarity or sympathetic action of some kind."[73] Yet, the absence of precedents makes it difficult to accurately predict judicial responses. The treatment of international boycotts and sympathetic actions is far less clear. Morgenstern, writing in 1984, suggests that some Western nations may permit local boycotts that are intended to aid workers in other countries.[74] As they do with strikes, the law of the place in which the sympathy action occurs usually determines the legality of sympathetic action. This will depend on the domestic law regulating sympathetic action in general, but Morgenstern suggests some protection for such actions as she states that "the most usual requirements in that respect being that the strike being supported must itself be lawful and that the sympathy action must have direct connection with it."[75] There may, however, be special rules dealing with the support of foreign strikes and the manner in which the general restrictions are applied to foreign situations. As Morgenstern notes, however, court decisions on "support of foreign strikes are isolated and relatively old."[76]

Although several countries bar solidarity efforts on the grounds that sympathy or secondary strikes affect those employers not in a position to satisfy the worker's demands, a number of European nations protect solidarity strikes if the workers can demonstrate a sufficient community of interest with the strikers, although the definition of "interest" may vary and may be tested objectively or subjectively. Italian courts, for instance, have held that solidarity actions are protected so long as workers are acting in defense of what they perceive to be their interest in the primary dispute. Worker pressure tactics, therefore, need not be aimed primarily at their own employer. Spain, Ireland, and France take a similar position, and in Belgium sympathy strikes are lawful unless contrary to an absolute peace obligation.[77]

Some nations, like Sweden, have actually recognized the right of unions to engage in boycotts in a transnational context.[78] Such an action is lawful so long as it does not violate any peace obligation in the union's contracts, where the union acts in accordance with its own rules, and where the initial strike is itself lawful. Indeed, even these restrictions have been relaxed if the first strike occurs abroad. In a case involving a strike to support a boycott of goods from Chile, for instance, the Swedish Labor Court noted that Swedish workers have no opportunity to influence the social policies of another nation where the dispute originated.[79] Greece amended its labor laws in 1982 to protect sympathetic action, and unions have a right to take such action against multinational firms where the action abroad can affect domestic working conditions.[80] The most unique example of the recognition of solidarity strikes is Denmark, where such actions are protected, even those contrary to the peace obligation, so long as it is altruistic. "Secondary strikers must not have a material interest of their own in the primary dispute."[81] In such cases, therefore, having no economic interest in the dispute will protect the activity.

Solidarity and Political Strikes

> The attempt to distinguish the economic and political concerns [of unions] rests on the misguided premise that unions can represent the economic interests of workers effectively without engaging in political activity. If this was ever more than a myth, it is certainly not the case in a post laissez-faire society in which government intervention and regulation in most spheres of economic and social life is a daily event.[82]

Transnational efforts may be highly political in nature, for instance, directed at a foreign state's application of labor law or its treatment of its own workers. Generally, the law of many states begins with the assumption that the objectives of the strike must be legitimate, and as already noted, most assume that these must relate to work demands and the process of collective bargaining. German law reflects the approach of many states. Since strikes are legal only if their purpose is to arrive at a collective agreement, it follows that political, secondary, and sympathy strikes are illegal, although narrow exceptions may exist.[83]

Both the secondary and political strike situation create tensions with ILO doctrine. The most central, internationally recognized right of workers is the freedom of association. Although the right to strike is not explicitly set out in any International Labor Organization convention or recommendation, the right is assumed to be basic in various conventions.[84] In addition, the Committee on Freedom of Association considers the right to strike to be "a basic right," even though the right is not explicitly expressed in the body's constitution or important labor conventions such as 87 and 98. Despite the lack of specificity, the ILO's Committee of Experts and the Committee on Freedom of Association

have created a considerable body of law on the right to strike by impli-
cation from a number of articles in the ILO Convention 87, considering the right to be "one of the essential means available to workers and
their organizations for the promotion of their social and economic interests."[85]

The Freedom of Association Committee "has always considered that
strikes that are purely political in character do not fall within the scope
of freedom of association."[86] The committee noted the often difficult
problem of distinguishing between the political aspects of a strike from
those that impact directly on the working conditions of the strikers. The
Committee of Experts has also recognized the workers' right to criticize
government policy, and it has noted that legitimate worker concerns go
beyond securing better working conditions or collective work claims but
also involve the seeking of solutions to social and economic policy issues:

> In the view of the Committee, organizations responsible for defending
> workers' socio-economic and occupational interests should, in princi-
> ple, be able to use strike action to support their position in the search
> for solutions to problems posed by major social and economic policy
> trends which have a direct impact on their members and on workers in
> general, in particular as regards employment, social protection and the
> standard of living."[87]

Similarly, the Committee on Freedom of Association has stated that
a ban or declaration of illegality of a national strike protesting against
the social and labor consequences of a government's economic policy
would constitute a serious violation of freedom of association. Moreover, the committee decided that a twenty-four-hour general strike seeking an increase in the minimum wage, respect of collective agreements
in force, and a change in economic policy is legitimate.[88]

Unsurprisingly, this has proved to be a controversial position, and "in
all countries strikes which are purely *political* in nature are in principle
considered as unlawful."[89] Many countries believe that such strikes
might "affect the system of representative democracy or the competence
of the constitutional bodies, especially where their mode of expression
endangers the sovereignty of public institutions and prevents them from
freely evaluating the requests advanced by other groups."[90] Yet, some

countries have permitted political strikes for short duration, and many have wrestled with the fact that political and occupational aspects may be intertwined in a specific dispute. Japan, Belgium, and the United Kingdom have pronounced such strikes as not legitimate, although Italy, Spain, France, Israel, and the Netherlands have generally recognized political strikes as least so long as they involve the defense of the workers' interests.[91] The right to strike in France includes action for the "defense of the workers' occupational interests and the admixture of political objectives is accepted-but to a different degree in civil and criminal courts."[92] The Italian constitutional right to strike does not extend to "purely" political strikes, but political strikes are not automatically illegal. In 1974, provisions of the penal code were declared unconstitutional "in so far as they penalized 'a political strike not aimed at subverting constitutional order nor at hindering obstructing the free exercise of the legal powers in which popular sovereignty is expressed.'"[93] Thus, such strikes are granted a "liberty" under the labor laws. On the other hand, the full right to strike applies to "strikes in pursuit of 'politico-economic' demands."[94]

One might distinguish domestic and internationally focused "political" disputes on the ground that other channels to affect the labor policies of transnational firms are not available. Since the assertion will often be true, this might be a good argument for allowing international solidarity actions when ordinary channels of political persuasion are nonexistent.[95] The same, of course, may be said for local entities, state or union, over local firms that are under foreign control over which there may be few channels to exert political or social pressure. Trade unions have few avenues to influence international capital, yet it is clear that capital can influence national labor law.[96]

Conclusion

Ironically, the very pressures that are inducing the creation of multinational firms, by merger for instance, may provide openings for unions. Can Chrysler workers in the United States, for example, strike to aid workers at a Daimler-Benz factory in Bavaria? Pressure against one's company in order to aid foreign workers in the same firm may not be deemed secondary, and, thus, the definition of "neutral" takes on a new significance. As subsidiaries of international firms share technology, parts, and production systems, the argument that national borders are irrelevant to the definition of the "primary" grows stronger. In many nations wholly owned affiliates or subsidiaries are considered separate firms for purposes of secondary boycott restrictions, but the internationalization of firms in the same sector weakens the argument for neutrality.[97] Moreover, as Charles Levinson has noted, "If it is legally permissible for a foreign parent company directly to control and decide on management policy from abroad, then it should be equally permissible for workers to act together with other workers of the same company abroad in their common interests without it being held to be an illegal sympathy strike or secondary boycott."[98]

The international merger of companies may create the opening for truly international labor solidarity. If so, it will lead to an ironic, but hardly unprecedented situation. Labor history is filled with thrust and counterthrust and the often-unexpected effects of those efforts. If capital in the nineteenth century, for instance, moved from the putting-out system to factories at least partly to control labor, the unexpected result was the formation of a group of workers with common interests who could form a union. In recent times, the efficiency-generated, just-in-time production process created a windfall for certain unions. In auto, for instance, strikes at particular GM factories in the United States closed down factories in other locales, just as a national strike against GM in Canada quickly affected plants in the United States.[99]

Globalization may create a more "international" worker, aware of common interests with workers in other counties. The possible "internationalization" of unions, however, will confront obstacles of domestic labor law. In some cases, arguments may be made that the firm against whom pressure is being placed is not wholly neutral, that is, it is an integrated part of a larger corporation against whom a foreign union has a dispute. Unions might attempt to argue that a refusal to work on "hot cargo" is not secondary action at all; instead, the pressure is motivated by personal or moral values. Arguments may also be made, especially in the case of political strikes, that traditional assumptions do not apply when the focus of concern extends beyond a nation's borders. The scope of domestic legal restrictions on sympathy strikes will be affected by the actions and resulting litigation. Further, unions may attempt to directly challenge statutory and judicial prohibitions by arguing that the choice of protecting alleged neutral companies denigrates a valuable human right, the right to withhold one's labor in aid of others. The right to withhold one's labor is entitled to great respect, and the traditional labor concern for not working on "hot" goods is as worthy of protection as striking to improve wages.

CHAPTER 9

"All Religions Believe in Justice"

Reflections on Faith Community Support for Worker Organizing

Linda A. Lotz

In religious circles today, Moses is increasingly being remembered as the first labor organizer in "Western" history. Moved deeply by the unjust treatment of Jewish slaves in Egypt, Moses tried to negotiate with their employer, Pharaoh, and, ultimately, the prophet Moses led a dramatic walkout by workers. Sometimes workers involved in organizing campaigns feel like those slaves wandering in the Sinai desert as they alternately gain and lose confidence in their quest. In times of struggle, we must remember that God provided manna to sustain the believers during their journey in the desert and eventually brought them to the land of milk and honey.

Whether one starts with this story, which is significant in Judaism, Christianity and Islam, or tenets of other faiths practiced in the United States today, we find a universal principle: all people should be respected and treated fairly. In different ways, our faiths call on us as believers to undertake a *jihad*—a crusade—for workplace justice.[1]

This paper explores four themes arising from the theological and moral juncture where people of faith and organized labor are increasingly found working together:

• A recent history of faith-labor relations in the United States, setting the stage for why this coalition expanded so rapidly;
• Some stories about faith community activities, drawing primarily from my experiences in Los Angeles;
• The "tool box" used by the faith community to support workers engaged in organizing; and
• Some thoughts about the challenges facing the faith community in the next four years.

A Recent History

From the earliest days of union organizing, there were members of the faith community providing support and assistance. Concern about workers led to the creation of institutions such as labor schools within the Catholic church, YWCA housing for working women, Labor Day prayer breakfasts, and the establishment of an office at the AFL-CIO to engage with the religious community.

During the 1960s and 1970s, mainstream religious community leaders pressed the labor movement to open apprenticeships to members of minority communities and called for the United States to end the Vietnam War.[2] These efforts helped to create friction with the union movement, whose leaders were primarily white and anti-Communist. A joint project of the AFL-CIO and the Central Intelligence Agency, the American Institute for Free Labor Development (AIFLD)—operating in countries such as Brazil, the Dominican Republic, and Nicaragua— taught labor leaders how to suppress independent worker organizing as part of its anti-Communist strategy.[3] Over time, AIFLD efforts to suppress genuine organizing (for fear of Communist or socialist influences) conflicted with the popular education and empowerment activities of missionaries influenced by Paolo Freire.

One significant area of faith-labor cooperation during this period was the campaign for union recognition of farm workers. Cesar Chavez and Delores Huerta understood—from their own deep faith and their political analysis—that the United Farm Workers (UFW) could never win their struggle for unionization without broad public support. Much effort was spent (and continues to be spent) reaching out to religious, student, and other groups. Across the country, people in the faith community embraced the UFW boycott on grapes and lettuce; some joined the UFW staff while others formed the Farmworker Ministry Board to coordinate religious community activities.[4]

Emergency assistance for Central American refugees coming to the United States in the 1980s renewed religious community awareness of U.S. foreign policy objectives. Many of the Salvadoran and Guatemalan refugees—and others fleeing poverty and conflict—lacked the immigration papers needed to obtain decent jobs. Too many undocumented immigrants became the victims of exploitation by employers interested in breaking unions and reducing wages. These situations and the growing desire for "flexible employment" by employers fueled the growth of low-wage jobs offering little or no future for workers of all ethnic and racial backgrounds.

Throughout the 1980s and continuing today, thousands of congregations across the United States sponsored food pantries, shelters, and other projects to address the needs of the poorest in their communities. Some of these people were Vietnam vets, others lost their jobs and homes when manufacturing plants were transplanted to Mexico; hundreds of thousands of people were deeply affected by drastic changes and the elimination of safety net programs. In time, it became clear that no matter how many people were assisted each week, the demand for services continued. By the mid- to late 1990s, food pantry staff found their clients were, increasingly, low-wage workers who, despite holding two, even three, jobs, still could not afford food for their families.

In short, members of the religious community were personally involved with people who were deeply affected by the growing gap between rich and poor in our nation. Most important, faith community leaders could see that something needed to be done.

While these changes were taking place within the religious community, challenges to the old-style leadership of the AFL-CIO culminated with the election of John Sweeney as president in 1995. As head of the Service Employees International Union (SEIU), he preached that the future of the union movement in the United States was dependent on the organizing of thousands of workers in order to compensate for the loss of union jobs due to changes in the global economy. An aggressive new form of union organizing was developed, symbolized by the "Justice for Janitors" model used in Los Angeles and other cities.

To rebuild SEIU, and now the entire U.S. labor movement, John Sweeney has promoted a democratic-based, empowerment model of organizing in which those who are struggling for union representation are respected for their knowledge of their fellow workers, their employer, and their communities. Member unions are urged to shift from the maintenance of current union members to aggressive organizing of new members. Harking back to the UFW organizing model, "the new labor movement" has placed a high priority on building community coalitions. As a result, the new union members are changing the complexion and politics of the union movement.

National changes in leadership and strategies are reflected in Los Angeles. Seasoned labor leaders—such as Miguel Contreras, head of the Los Angeles County Federation of Labor; his wife, Maria Elena Durazo, head of Local 11 of the Hotel Employees and Restaurant Employees Union (HERE); and Eliseo Medina, Western Region vice president of the Service Employees International Union (SEIU)—are applying their skills and experiences from organizing farm workers to the many challenges for labor in Los Angeles, including the need to organize immigrants and other nonunion workers.

In Los Angeles, a campaign for a Living Wage Ordinance provided the spark to bring together people of faith and the labor movement to address low-wage poverty. In the spring of 1996, a small group of clergy and laity came together to start a new organization, Clergy and Laity United For Economic Justice (CLUE), to focus outreach to the religious community for the Living Wage campaign.[5] Clergy and lay religious leaders who had "come of age" in the UFW struggles, the civil rights movements, and the various interfaith coalitions addressing the wars in Central America, the Gulf War, hunger, and homelessness, formed the initial core of CLUE.[6]

During the Living Wage campaign, CLUE members gave sermons about poverty and low-wage workers and made it possible for workers who would benefit from the proposed legislation to speak in their houses of worship. Clergy also encouraged their congregation members to become involved. Several clergy established or rekindled "pastoral" relationships with key city council members in which they discussed theological and moral reasons for a Living Wage policy. By the time the ordinance came before the full city council, a *Los Angeles Times* poll found that a strong majority of Angelenos who would be voting in the April 1999 mayoral race supported a Living Wage.

The Los Angeles City Council adopted the Living Wage Ordinance unanimously in May 1997.[7] All the community organizing, sermons, and visits to members of the city council had paid off. But what ultimately made the campaign successful was the direct involvement of workers who would benefit from the proposed Living Wage ordinance, and their personal expressions of what it meant to live in poverty created by minimum-wage jobs.

While the glow of the victory was still warm, congregation budgets were being prepared. Some clergy had to confront the harsh reality: their congregations had implemented the very same cost-cutting policies that had been the focus of the Living Wage campaign. They, too, depended on people working part-time jobs with no health care benefits and contracted out for janitorial, landscaping, and other services. During the next two years, CLUE members made changes within their own congregations and encouraged others in their denominations to follow suit. The director of one religious institution confided to me that his secretary wept on being told she would begin receiving health care benefits. Although she had worked very closely with the director for several years, she had never been able to tell him how difficult it was to live without this basic benefit.

Over a three-year period (1997–2000), CLUE members worked with regional and national religious bodies—including the Ecumenical Council of Southern California, the Unitarian Universalists, the Episcopal church, the United Methodist church, the Central Conference of American Rabbis, and the Union of American Hebrew Congregations—to adopt strong living wage policies.

Drawing on personal links made during the Living Wage campaign, the Service Employees International Union and the Hotel Employees and Restaurant Employees Union invited clergy and congregation members to support new campaigns to organize low-wage workers and to protect union members whose benefits and union representation were threatened by privatization. As a result of working closely with local union members and leadership on the Living Wage campaign, many CLUE members had come to respect these unions because of their democratic and empowerment models of organizing. Neighborhood committees were established to address each of the campaigns; this outreach helped to build CLUE participation because the clergy could address an economic justice issue in their community and build stronger ties with others in their neighborhoods. By the fall of 1999, CLUE had expanded to a network of more than one hundred key contacts throughout the LA area.

The rapid growth of CLUE in Los Angeles provides only one example of religious community cooperation with unions to address the growing gap between rich and poor—in the United States and around the world.[8]

Today, there are fifty local faith-based groups supporting worker organizing in their communities.[9] The National Interfaith Committee for Worker Justice serves these local groups, provides national leadership, and interfaces with the AFL-CIO; its board is composed of representatives from more than twenty-five different faith bodies. Efforts are being made to involve people of all faiths at the local and national levels.

Other developments are significant as well: Living Wage ordinances have been adopted by thirty-two local government bodies across the country, and the term *living wages* has been adopted by politicians and the media throughout the nation. The National Council of Churches, under the leadership of the Reverend Bob Edgar, has initiated a ten-year project to address poverty. In addition, representatives of various faith groups in Washington, D.C., formed a national coalition to address trade policy issues; and some denominational offices are coordinating activities with the AFL-CIO to address immigration, debt relief, and globalization.

In short, we are witnessing an historic, national movement in which people of faith and labor are joining forces to halt the "race to the bottom." We are working for the benefit of the same people—who are members of our congregations and our unions.

Some Stories

Four projects provide examples of how the faith community can support workers engaged in organizing: (1) The Beverly Hills hotel contract campaign, (2) Catholic Healthcare West union organizing, (3) University of Southern California contract campaign, and (4) the Jewish Commission Against Sweatshops. At the time of these activities, CLUE had a core of about thirty clergy and lay leaders, an active membership of a hundred people, and a staff of two. Following the Quaker practice of speaking about collective action rather than emphasizing individual contributions, these stories reflect the manner in which CLUE planning worked: an idea would blossom through the synergistic input of various members of the faith and labor community.

Not long after the Living Wage campaign, Local 11 of the Hotel Employees and Restaurant Workers Union (HERE) began the process of negotiating a new contract with hotels in downtown Los Angeles and Beverly Hills. The downtown hotels reached a precedent-setting agreement with Local 11 substantially increasing wages and some benefits.[10] The focus next shifted to five prominent hotels in Beverly Hills. In cooperation with Local 11, CLUE organized a series of "Java for Justice" visits to several hotels whose contracts would expire first. After enjoying a cup of coffee or lunch in luxurious surroundings, the religious delegation would pay their bill and then a member of the clergy would stand up and ask for everyone's attention. The minister, priest, or rabbi would explain how the proposed union contract would help to lift the hotel workers from low-wage poverty to middle-class security, and then ask for the diners' support. Because these hotels and restaurants are noted for their discretion and exclusivity, management would politely—but quickly—escort the delegation to the door. These "Java for Justice" visits boosted workers' morale, informed clientele about the contract negotiations, and most important, demonstrated community support for the workers to the hotel management.

During the Beverly Hills campaign, CLUE members participated in Local 11 activities with the workers, but we quickly learned that the rapid pace of union organizing made it hard to turn out more than a few clergy for any one event.

With Easter and Passover fast approaching, CLUE decided to hold an interfaith procession in Beverly Hills. On the Friday before Easter—coinciding with the beginning of Passover—more than seventy clergy in ceremonial robes and prayer shawls walked silently down Rodeo Drive and Wilshire Boulevard to visit three key hotels. In the three weeks between announcing the procession and the actual event, two of the three hotels to be visited agreed to sign the precedent-setting contract with the union! Nevertheless, we decided to hold the procession—but made a slight change in the plans.

Our first stop on the Interfaith Procession was a hotel owned by a prominent member of the Jewish community. A brief Passover Seder was held in front of the hotel using a special Haggadah calling on the owner to stop acting like Pharaoh. We left a plate of bitter herbs and a letter urging the owner to meet with the union to negotiate a new contract.

From there, we went to the "Land of Milk and Honey"—the two hotels where the contract had been signed. The manager of one hotel personally welcomed the delegation and discovered the rector of his church was a part of our procession. After receiving a basket of flowers, honey, and milk, the manager told us that he was deeply moved by this recognition as no one had ever thanked him for signing a union contract. In the next few years, this man initiated several special projects to help HERE members; I believe that our visit encouraged him to look for new ways for management and the union to work together. We also visited the second hotel that signed the contract and presented a similar basket of flowers, honey, and milk but management was a bit shy—and scared. They just didn't know what to do with us!

Not only did we make an impression on the managers of these three hotels, we were seen by hundreds of people in Beverly Hills, and thousands of congregation members heard about our activity that weekend. The message was conveyed far and wide; we appreciate employers who do the right thing—and we will hold accountable those who have not yet learned to treat their workers with respect.

Unfortunately, my second example doesn't yet have an ending. Several years ago, Catholic Healthcare West workers in several parts of California decided to challenge changes occurring at their hospitals: the quality of patient care was plummeting and the warm atmosphere of these traditional Catholic hospitals had been sacrificed to hospital mergers and HMO's. Some workers felt new policies at the hospitals were threatening the lives of their patients. Facing changes in the medical industry affecting day-to-day patient care, the workers hoped a union would give them the power to negotiate with the hospital management about their problems and to partner with the hospital to protect patient care in the public arena.

Although the hospital chain was owned by seven orders of women religious, professional hospital managers were responsible for day-to-day operations. Management brought in one of the thousand-plus firms whose primary function is to help employers fight union drives and before long, workers experienced new pressures from their supervisors, including the spreading of antiunion information. Some worker leaders received anonymous calls at home; other union supporters were followed on the hospital campus. When a delegation of workers described this campaign of harassment to several nuns still affiliated with the hospital chain, it was clear the sisters were moved and disturbed by what they heard. However, the union-busting activities continued.

SEIU Local 399, on behalf of the workers, invited clergy from the Lynnwood area to meet some of the workers and learn about what was happening at St. Francis Hospital. Although these priests and ministers visited the hospital regularly and some of the workers were members of their congregations, the clergy were surprised to learn how bad conditions had become inside the hospital.

In an effort to support workers and learn firsthand about what was happening at St. Francis, small teams of clergy agreed to visit workers in their lunchroom. When the first team of Catholic priests prepared to enter the hospital, security staff told them that they would have to be escorted. The priests were accompanied to the lunchroom and quickly surrounded by hospital supervisors. Not surprisingly, few workers were willing to speak in such a situation. As the team prepared to leave the hospital, a woman came up to one of the priests and asked him to visit her mother, who was very ill. Again, security advised the priest he was not allowed to go into the hospital without an escort. The daughter became extremely distraught when she heard that her priest wasn't welcome in the hospital. Ultimately, the priest was able to visit the mother, accompanied by a security officer. Nevertheless, this incident caused quite a stir around the hospital and the diocese.

Several weeks later, an Episcopal priest agreed to accompany a delegation of workers planning to present a letter to St. Francis's management. The delegation gathered just outside the hospital and the priest led the workers in a brief prayer. When the delegation entered the hospital, workers were allowed to proceed to the meeting but the priest— who had been visiting congregation members in the hospital for many years—was barred from entering the hospital with the delegation. These two small incidents helped the religious community to understand the pressures workers were experiencing as a result of their quest for a union.

Tensions remained at a crisis level for weeks. Efforts to reach out to the women religious who owned the hospital chain were unsuccessful in bringing about any change in management's anti-union tactics. A worker asked the union if it would be possible to have a special period of prayer. CLUE assisted clergy from the neighborhood to plan "twenty-four hours of prayer for peace and reconciliation at Catholic Healthcare West." An invitation was extended to everyone in the hospital chain but unfortunately management and the women religious declined to participate.

The "twenty-four hours of prayer" started with a candlelight vigil at a statue of the Virgin of Guadaloupe, on the St. Francis hospital grounds. From there, workers and members of the religious community walked silently to a local Catholic church and were greeted at the front door by the priest. Over the next twenty-four hours, members of the clergy from around the Los Angeles area dropped by to share a song, a poem, scripture, or a prayer with several workers who remained in the church throughout the entire night. The workers later told us they were profoundly changed by the experience. Messages poured in from around the country from union and religious supporters inspired by the call for reconciliation through prayer. In late afternoon, labor, religious, and political dignitaries attended an interfaith service. The "twenty-four hours of prayer" ended with a silent procession back to the hospital, where candles and a basket of notes with personal messages and prayers, were left at the feet of the Virgin of Guadalupe.[11]

This event gave the workers a lot of hope, and tensions in the hospital were reduced for several weeks. Unfortunately, the spirit of prayer could not overcome the work of the union-busters whose salaries are calculated on their ability to dampen support for a union.

Cardinal Roger Mahoney was kept informed by both sides of developments at CHW. While reminding CHW leadership of the church's century-long support of workers' right to organize, the cardinal exercised strong—but neutral—power by trying to bring the two sides together. Other women religious and priests were involved in efforts to resolve the conflict as well.

This struggle continues. In April 2001, CHW and SEIU signed an historic agreement laying out procedures and conduct that was expected to facilitate union elections once workers sign union cards. In February 2002, the Daughters of Charity split from Catholic Healthcare West to form a separate corporation with seven hospitals including St. Francis, indicating they preferred a simpler corporate structure. Although workers at St. Francis had voted for a union in 2000, a contract was never obtained. It is expected that the new management led by the Daughters will ultimately recognize the union.

My third example highlights efforts to contract out for services previously provided by full-time employees at the University of Southern California (USC). Founded by the Methodist church, USC has been secular for many years, although there are still many in the community who remember its religious origins.

During contract negotiations in 1996, the university asked its janitors, represented by SEIU Local 1877, to include language authorizing the university to contract out some of their work. University of Southern California officials indicated that they didn't expect to do this, but rather wanted the flexibility in case it would be needed. Shortly after the contract was signed, some of the janitors were told to apply with a company holding a new janitorial contract to keep their jobs. Workers with more than a decade of service experienced dramatic cuts in their wages and elimination of health benefits. They also lost access to special mortgage and tuition programs designed by the university. It took more than a year of struggle to bring the janitors back into the union and have their benefits restored. Budget cuts and other pressures were placed on the teaching staff as well, with the effect of stifling freedom of speech with regard to campus employment practices.

Employees working in the restaurants and dormitories were represented by Local 11 of the Hotel Employees and Restaurant Employees Union (HERE). They refused to sign the contract language that allowed the university to contract out janitorial work. Efforts to negotiate a contract between USC and Local 11 dragged on for several years. Fresh from winning the Beverly Hills hotel contracts and the Los Angeles Living Wage Ordinance, Local 11 invited CLUE to join them in seeking resolution to the contracting-out provisions sought by USC.

Because the university had previously obtained an injunction preventing any union gathering of more than a handful of people on campus, University Church extended sanctuary to Local 11 members—as they had earlier extended sanctuary to Japanese Americans, Vietnam veterans, and Central American refugees. A neighborhood committee was established to address the impact of USC on the broader community, addressing this contract as a first project. At one of the first meetings of this community coalition, workers, clergy, and others mapped out USC's complex history with the neighborhood, including respected community service programs, real estate deals, harassment of African-American youth crossing through the campus, and broken promises made to the community.

Next, a series of meetings were held to develop a strategy for community-outreach activities. Teams of workers and clergy attempted to meet with university trustees in order to share their reasons for wanting a just contract. Street theater and rallies were held to pressure several prominent trustees. Recalling the use of civil disobedience during the civil rights movement, scores of workers, clergy, and community supporters blocked several streets in a carefully orchestrated drama and were arrested to highlight Local 11's call for a fair contract.

The workers fasted for several days just before Thanksgiving 1998, for their personal benefit but also to make a point to the USC administration. The following spring, a second fast was held at University Church with a large number of workers and several area clergy participating. At the end of the three-day fast, the charismatic president of HERE Local 11, Maria Elena Durazo, announced she would continue to fast until a new contract was signed. A modest camper was donated for Maria Elena to carry out her fast in a small park across from the USC campus. An altar was filled with candles and flowers, and colorful messages were hung on strings underneath the trees. The widow of Cesar Chavez lent Maria Elena the wooden cross used by the late UFW leader when he fasted.

A powerful drama unfolded as Maria Elena became weaker and weaker until finally her doctor told her to stop the fast. At a special prayer meeting/rally, she announced others would continue the fast on behalf of the workers. Each day a new labor leader, politician, Hollywood star, or member of the clergy would fast and carry the story of the USC workers to their respective communities. CLUE organized daily lunchtime prayers for the workers in the park. The prayers offered spiritual sustenance for the workers—and of course, the person from the religious community was moved as well. On some days, the clergy and the person fasting would lead a procession across the campus to the office of USC president Sample to present a petition or letter calling for a settlement of the contract dispute. When Mrs. Chavez learned about USC's recalcitrance, she asked that a campus monument recognizing her husband be veiled until a contract was signed. Visits to the veiled monument—her rebuke of the USC management—were immediately added to the processions.

Over the summer of 1999, CLUE members worked with the union to prepare an open letter to President Sample. By the time school opened, almost one hundred religious leaders in the USC neighborhood and throughout the Los Angeles area had signed the letter; it was published in the campus newspaper shortly after the fall semester commenced.

Because USC receives direct funding as well as city-funded police support during football games and other activities, a strategy to bring USC under the umbrella of the Living Wage Ordinance and the Worker Retention Ordinance was developed with sympathetic members of the L.A. City Council. City funds would be tied to a requirement that—

should USC try to subcontract any of its restaurant facilities—all employees would have to be retained for a minimum of three months by the subcontractor.[12] Facing the Los Angeles City Council action, the letter signed by one hundred clergy, plus the scheduled appearance of Jesse Jackson and an impending convention of the AFL-CIO in L.A.—the USC administration agreed to sign a contract with Local 11. Although the language is not as strong as the union members would have wished, with the help of the Worker Retention Ordinance it protected workers' jobs.

Out of this "David vs. Goliath" campaign has come a long-term community coalition that is continuing to address a variety of economic and community problems arising from USC's impact on the neighborhood. It is important for unions and the faith community to build this kind of long-term coalition—to give a voice to the needs of a community and to assure that the community will continue to be aware of local labor issues.

The fourth example looks at the garment industry. During the Passover season several years ago, the L.A. chapter of the American Jewish Congress arranged for Latinos working in the LA garment industry to speak at several Jewish congregations. Sparks flew at one congregation where an owner of a major clothing company was a member. Anger was followed by threats to cut contributions to the synagogue and other religious institutions.

Sparked by this controversy, AJC formed a Jewish Commission on Sweatshops composed of rabbis, professors, and other community leaders with the task of studying the garment industry in Los Angeles. The commission was established both because of the historic role played by the Jewish community during the unionization of the garment industry—and because some owners of major apparel companies are prominent members of the Jewish community.

The commission held a series of private "hearings" to learn from people working at all levels of the garment industry. Both the owners of the clothing companies and UNITE, the needlework union, pressured members of the commission on specific issues.[13] Differences arose within the commission particularly when it came time to lay out proposals for further action within the Jewish community. After more than a year and a half of study and debate, a report was published. The final document provides a very helpful explanation of how the contracting-out process itself suppresses wages.[14] A series of actions were recommended to improve working conditions in the apparel industry.

One week after the report was released, the American Jewish Congress closed its Los Angeles office. While the ACJ national board claimed the decision was made because of a budget problem, there were rumors that pressures from the garment industry had played a role in the decision as well. After a series of bicoastal telephone calls and meetings, the Los Angeles AJC board agreed to close the office but the same people would form a new group, the Progressive Jewish Alliance. It turned out that the commission's investigation of the role of Jewish leaders in the garment industry was not the only area of difference between the Los Angeles and the national office, as there had been previous disagreements between the national and Los Angeles offices regarding relationships with local Muslims and public education activities on the topic of terrorism. Nevertheless, this experience provides a stark reminder: religious groups can be subjected to pressure not unlike those experienced by low-wage workers engaged in forming a union.

From these four campaigns in Los Angeles, we can see how the religious community can bring a great deal to the proverbial table of power: religious and moral principles, political clout, "pastoral" relationships, and the ability to inspire people to continue to campaign in spite of whatever pressures may come to bear.

The Tool Box

As CLUE developed experience working on wage and union issues, we began to talk about our "tool box" of activities that could be used to support workers engaged in union organizing. These include prayers, strategic planning, speaking truth to power, model employers, public education, and investigating working conditions.

Prayers

We quickly learned that many—if not most—workers are also people of faith. When workers engage in an organizing campaign, their lives become even more stressful on the job and at home because there is less time to be with their families and paychecks are affected because of harassment and strikes. Many workers confided to us or their union organizers that support from the religious community—such as a brief non-denominational prayer—gave them more inner strength and courage to take action or to speak the truth about their work situations and their needs.

Strategic Planning

As CLUE members became engaged in the Living Wage campaign, they were invited to lead union members in a prayer at meetings and rallies. These "rent-a-collar" invitations came across to us as a late addition to the union's plans rather than one piece of a long-term strategy to involve the religious community in an organizing campaign.

We quickly learned the importance of joining with workers early in preparations for a new organizing campaign or contract negotiations. This gave CLUE members some time to learn about working conditions and specific areas of dispute as well as to become acquainted with the workers who were engaged in the organizing. More important, there was time to identify key pressure points and to build community support for the workers before tensions built to a crisis level.

CLUE operates from the premise that workers should establish the key strategies and the community coalitions should build from these strategies. Our members learned a great deal by participating in the strategic planning process. There were many opportunities for clergy and laity to learn what it means to live in low-wage poverty and to develop personal relationships with some of the workers. Over time, the people sitting around the table built trust and a sense of community. The strength of these relationships became very important when workers experienced pressures from their employers or lost their jobs; our members quickly came to understand the power of union-busting techniques—and the need for strong unions.

Speak Truth to Power

In each organizing campaign, people of faith stood publicly with workers to support their quest for decent wages and working conditions. Clergy and laity brought their considerable moral and political power to these meetings with employers, especially those representing large national and multinational firms.

The presence of the religious community representative put management on notice that it would be held accountable for the treatment of workers. Employers are accustomed to the protection of the complex and drawn-out legal framework established by the National Labor Relations Board, but relatively few owners or managers have been held personally accountable for their treatment of workers in their own congregations or communities.

Engage Public Officials

Whether speaking at a public hearing or meeting; developing a personal, pastoral relationship; or accompanying workers on visits to public officials to discuss low-wage poverty and union-busting techniques, religious participation in both private and public discussions is extremely important. The articulation of religious and moral principles helps to shift the public debate to the ethical and moral reasons for providing better wages and job protections—away from the focus on the bottom line, such as the red-baiting and disinformation tactics used by opponents of the L.A. Living Wage Ordinance. In addition, elected officials understand—and generally respect—the power of clergy to mobilize public opinion in their districts.

Model Employers

As a result of the Living Wage campaign, we were contacted by a number of local religious-based institutions (including congregations, day care centers, schools, nursing homes, and hospitals) to determine if their wages and benefits would match the standards of the Living Wage Ordinance. These employers understood that they bear a special responsibility—due to their religious foundation as well as their nonprofit status—to pay living wages and family health care benefits.

By setting a good example and calling on others to follow their lead, the religious community can influence the policies of other employers in the community—especially those whose managers govern, worship at, or utilize the services of the model institution.

The National Interfaith Committee for Worker Justice is developing special guidelines to assist religious employers facing unionization—based on respect for the other party and trying to find win-win solutions.

Public Education

There are a variety of ways to educate congregation members about the role that low wages play in creating poverty:

- Local workers were invited to make presentations during services and religious education classes; they could also speak at men and women's prayer or discussion groups. The "Labor in the Pulpit" program—in which workers speak in congregations during the Labor Day weekend—provided a special opportunity for CLUE to offer speakers. Nationally, "Labor in the Pulpit" has become a very important vehicle for public education. During the fifth year of Labor in the Pulpit (2001) thousands of congregations in more than one hundred cities held special Labor Day activities.
- Following a CLUE activity such as the Beverly Hills Procession, members of the clergy described their experiences in sermons that same weekend. Clergy can preach about low-wage poverty, respect for workers and immigrants, and globalization as a part of their sermons and lectures throughout the year, whether they are engaged in a specific campaign or elaborating on scripture.
- Ceremonies were used to support workers and could also be used to bring together workers and employers during workplace conflicts. For example, there is a long history of "Labor Seders" in which the traditional Passover dinner commemorating the flight from slavery in Egypt is transformed into a call to address modern-day injustice. Some clergy are creating new ceremonies, such as one Lutheran pastor who holds an annual "Blessing of the Hands of Workers" ceremony each Labor Day. During the ceremony, the congregation honors everyone for the "work" that they contribute, including children who work at their studies, women and the elderly who work in the home to assist their family, and those who work outside the home for money.
- Study groups can relate scriptures and theological principles to poverty, globalization, and modern business practices.
- Congregations can arrange for youth groups to visit union halls to learn about the real, day-to-day issues that workers face in those jobs.

Each of these activities enable congregation members to reflect more deeply about their own lives and the lives of their family members and neighbors.

Investigate Working Conditions

Worker Hearing Boards, special research projects or commissions, and drop-in centers for workers can provide opportunities for the religious community to personally—and independently—research general working conditions in their community and in specific factories or other work places owned by companies based in their communities.

Formal reports, such as the one issued by the Jewish Commission on Sweatshops, can document both positive steps taken by employers as well as problems needing to be addressed. This kind of independent documentation is very helpful for educating and involving the public, especially when employers use heavy-handed, union-busting tactics to frighten workers engaged in union organizing or facts about the situation become cloudy during a lengthy conflict.

There are probably many other "tools" that have been used successfully in the past or will be developed in the future. Creative adaptations can transform these "tools" used in Los Angeles to other settings and circumstances.

Whatever tools are used, we found that it is vital to plan a range of activities focused on a goal (i.e., contacts with city council) so that people with different skills, time-availability, political approaches, and resources can support an organizing campaign. By including fun activities and allowing people to be creative, we found people made special efforts to support our activities and our goal.

The Challenges of the Future

It is critical for the religious community to support the rebuilding of the union movement in the United States and around the world in order to improve the lives of low-wage workers and their families, and to provide some counterbalance to the extraordinary powers of multinational corporations.[15]

Our efforts should focus on the following areas:

1. We need to strengthen existing faith-based organizations addressing worker justice and create new institutions to support this work over the long haul. This means providing a solid financial base for the fifty-plus local groups and the National Interfaith Committee for Worker Justice. It also reflects the need to develop new materials and

resources to educate ourselves and others in the religious community about union-busting and to train our staff and leaders to be more strategic.

2. We need to involve more people in this work. We have to reach out to more clergy and to the people in the pews—with education and opportunities to become involved. How can we help our congregation members to experience and to understand what it means to live in low-wage poverty, or to feel the pressure of a union-busting campaign? Similarly, unions need to find a way to routinely ask: Are workers active in their community—in clubs, political parties, library groups, or faith bodies? When people self-identify themselves this way, they can work together to ask the religious leaders of their church, synagogue, temple, mosque, or other places of worship to support them on a personal basis and to support their fellow workers in an organizing campaign.

One of the most important things that CLUE was able to do was to bring people together from a wide range of religious, ethnic, educational, and economic backgrounds. As they sat together, they were all equal and they learned from each other. This can be a very rich and rewarding experience—by focusing on the empowerment of workers and bridging the gap between peoples of different backgrounds, we will make a substantial contribution to our communities and our country.

3. We need to create new positions in regional and national religious offices to encourage and support faith-labor coalitions, and we need to develop educational programs at business schools, seminaries, and other religious education programs to examine current business practices through the lens of theological and ethical principles.

4. We need to engage with religious-based owners of hospitals, day care centers, and nursing homes. In the current business climate, many religious-based institutions have turned to corporate policies and practices to protect their bottom line and even their very existence. We need to help these institutions maintain their religious foundations and to set positive examples for the treatment of workers in their communities and across the country.

5. We need to enlist business owners and managers who participate in our congregations. Groups of business leaders should be created to address the application of religious principles to the treatment of workers and the practice of union-busting. Such groups could develop

standards and models that could be promoted throughout the business community.

6. We need to consciously, and strategically, build new and stronger relationships with the union movement for the sake of our congregation members and for the sake of our national economy. We must challenge ourselves, within the religious community and our friends in the union movement, to do the best possible organizing and education. We know where our common goals lie—and we know where we differ in styles and objectives. Racism, sexism, and elitism can be found in all of our institutions, past and present. By committing ourselves to this work together—and engaging with each other honestly—we can truly change the lives of millions of workers and their families.

CHAPTER 10

Grasshopper Power

Reverend Jim Lewis

When I am invited to a church supper or a special community dinner, people see my clerical collar as I walk in the door, and it's a sure thing that I'll be asked to say grace over the meal. And more times than enough, the meal I bless will be chicken. I say more grace over chicken than I do over bread and wine, the prime ingredients of my weekly Sunday communion service at the church.

I've been a priest in the Episcopal church for thirty-seven years and have worked on farm and labor issues that center around the production of poultry for the past fifteen years. Some friends who know the wide range of social justice issues I've been involved in over those years are puzzled by the intensity of the work I now do around chickens. It is as if all of the theological training I have had is somehow reduced to a barnyard full of chicken manure. And that is a puzzle to some.

My own understanding of what I do, and the theological justification for it, is pretty simple, not complex at all. All theological education, all piety for that matter, must finally come down out of the sky and come to rest on the earth. All things ethereal must end up on the ground. All things pious must work their way down to the political. In truth, all major religions see a common meal, and the labor that goes into the production and preparation of a meal, as worthy of attention. That is why so many people of faith pause to give thanks over food. That is why I am asked to say grace. That is why I have developed an obsession, a magnificent one, I hope, with chicken.

I have come to understand that most people do not know where the food they eat comes from. They may be eating oranges from Israel, asparagus from Mexico, beef from Nebraska, milk from a neighboring state, and ice cream from Vermont. And chances are good that they will put a knife and fork to a piece of chicken grown and processed on the Delmarva Peninsula, or one of a number of southern states. And chances are also good that they will have no idea how the food on their plate is grown and harvested, nor how much pain and injustice is associated with their meal.

I live on the Delmarva Peninsula. It is the peninsula that extends south of Wilmington, Delaware, and runs through the eastern shore of Maryland and Virginia until the Chesapeake Bay Bridge-Tunnel offers the traveler the opportunity to cross the water into Norfolk and Virginia Beach. The Delmarva Peninsula is tourist country to the east, with summer populations swelling in beach towns like Rehoboth Beach, Ocean City, and Chincoteague Island. On the western shore crabs, oysters, and Chesapeake Bay fish are plentiful. And in the middle of the peninsula the poultry industry booms.

Just over fifty years ago the vertically integrated industrial model of chicken production was invented on the Delmarva Peninsula. ("Vertically integrated" means that the company controls every part of the enterprise with its contracts and policies—like the old "company store" that reigned supreme in Appalachian coal towns.) With this change in the way chicken is produced, what was once mythologized in nursery rhyme as "Old McDonald's Farm" soon became what some now call "new McDonald's farm," the farmyard replication of the McDonald's golden arches. The vertically integrated, factory farm and processing model of poultry production, where every aspect of production and distribution is controlled by the company, is the way business is done these days from the Delmarva on down into North Carolina, Georgia, Mississippi, and Arkansas and right on into Kentucky, West Virginia, and states further west that produce chicken.

A drive through the Delmarva Peninsula, particularly in the springtime or summer months, will cause the motorist to sit up and take notice, even when the car windows are closed. The smell of chicken manure is thick as it rises from the earth where it has been spread to fertilize crops, and from the numerous clusters of chicken houses that hold sixty to one hundred thousand chickens. These chicken farms are called CAFO's, that is, confined animal feeding operations. Birds, once allowed outside to hunt and peck, are now crammed into these chicken houses for a six- to eight-week growing period. When they are ready for the kill the company will come claim their chickens and cart them off to the company-owned processing plant where they are slaughtered, processed, packaged, and shipped to the grocery stores.

Twelve years ago while working in North Carolina, a huge chicken-producing state, I stumbled on to the vertically integrated system of chicken production. At that time I was working with process plant workers, a huge number of whom were black and a rising number of them Latino, from Mexico and Central America. Attempting to address the needs of that population, the church set up one-day clinics in the basement of churches in the area so as to offer medical examinations and counseling for workers who were being injured in the nearby plants. It was then, in those church basements and parish halls, that I discovered the plight of poultry process plant workers.

The daily work of a plant worker is very difficult and often times dangerous. Working on a production line, where chicken carcasses travel by hooks and conveyor belts, workers stand on floors that are wet and endure forty-two degree temperatures while they pull guts, cut, debone, and package as many as fifteen thousand pieces of chicken a day. The pay is poor (a worker on line makes about seven dollars an hour) and injuries abound. Workers lose fingers, have a high rate of carpal tunnel syndrome, lose limbs, suffer from back problems, and put themselves in harm's way daily so that chicken can be marketed from the local grocery stores for barbecues, at fast food carry-outs, church suppers, and family meals at home.

Wendell Berry lives on a farm in Henry County, Kentucky. He has written over thirty books, which include fiction, poetry, and social essays. He loves the land and is a prophetic voice crying out on behalf of humanity in a global economy and stewardship in a world where economic systems slash and burn the very earth, and the creatures of the earth help sustain and nourish human beings.

In a 1997 article in *Christian Century*, Berry addressed the critical issue of an urbanized world unaware of the rural reality that feeds it. Speaking about city folks, Berry says, "Wherever they live, if they eat, people have agricultural responsibilities just as they have cultural responsibilities. Eating without knowledge is the same as eating without gratitude. What's the use in thanking God for food that has come at unbearable expense to the world and other people?" And then Berry drives the nail home. "Every eater has a responsibility to find out where food comes from and what its real costs are, and then to do something to reduce the costs."[1]

In 1965 the Episcopal Diocese of Delaware hired me to live and work on the Delmarva Peninsula. My job was to bring the Episcopal church members in the region into a close working relationship with people who are struggling to make ends met, who are invisible and marginalized to many in the community, and who are caught in economic systems over which they have no control and which take advantage of them. That meant coming to grips with what I have come to call "Big Chicken."

In my mind's eye I see the poultry industry as a big house in which Big Chicken lives. You can enter that house through many doors. There is the consumer door through which folks enter to purchase and eat the chicken. There is the farmer (called "grower") door. Those who enter this door are people who have been to the bank for money to set up a poultry operation and who have contracted with a company to grow chickens. There is the plant worker door through which the process plant workers enter to slaughter, cut, and package chicken. There is the environmental door, one used by people in the community who care about the air, water, and soil, and see the environmental aspect of poultry production. There is the animal-lover door used by people of all ages who believe animals, even the ones eaten by human beings, should be treated carefully and respectfully.

Once inside Big Chicken's house, those who enter from any one of those doors begin to see the harsh reality that Big Chicken owns and controls every room in that house and that all the rooms are connected. It becomes obvious as well that if there is going to be any change inside Big Chicken's house, it will only happen as all parties, no matter what door they entered the house through, find ways to work together.

What's new on the Delmarva Peninsula is a watchdog group, the Delmarva Poultry Justice Alliance (DPJA). The idea behind DPJA is to get all the players associated with the production, distribution, and consumption of chicken around the same table talking with one another. That includes all kinds of people in the community who do not work for the poultry companies but whose lives are affected by the industry.

When we meet the cast of characters seated around the table, it is easy to see that the participants consist of a wide variety of folks.

Seated to my right is a hatchery worker, and across the table is a Guatemalan plant worker, and a third-generation white poultry grower. On my left is a union member from a unionized poultry plant in the area who is seated next to a woman associated with an environmental organization. Regularly present at the table are clergy and lay people from various denominations, along with people who are concerned about the antibiotics and growth additives that the companies put in the feed.

This effort to draw people together across the divisions created in the production and consumption of chicken also brings people together across other barriers that divide us. The membership cuts across race, class, cultural, and language difference, and denominational affiliations. I liken it to a truly "pentecostal" event where people speak different languages with different understandings and orientations and yet find a common ground to unite.

The points of unification are first of all contractual. Everyone works for Big Chicken and has to live under the contract offered by Big Chicken. Poultry growers actually sign a contract with the company, a contract in which they have no say and no negotiating or bargaining power. Once signed, the grower is required to accept company-owned chicks, company-controlled medications, company feed over which they have no say about what is contained in that feed, and a company-designed system of payment that has them compete in a ranking system with other growers on how well they convert feed to the final product. Dan Fesperman and Kate Shatzkin, in a series of articles in the *Baltimore Sun*, say quite powerfully that poultry growers are caught in a system of indentured servitude.[2] The grower takes all the risks and bears all the capital expense, while the companies reap the profits and the growers struggle to make a living and pay the bills.

The poultry workers, be they hatchery workers, chicken catchers, process plant workers, or truck drivers all face serious contractual issues. If a union represents these workers, a definite contract is bargained and negotiations are possible between workers and companies. If they are not represented by a union, these workers will have no way to bargain with the company, which has complete and absolute control over wages, benefits, and safety issues. The poultry industry is notorious for its coercive tactics with workers who try to organize. Workers are threatened, and fired, by the company for participating in a union drive.

Bringing together growers and workers, along with union members, offers an opportunity for each party to see how companies manipulate them around contract issues. They see one another's frustrations and come to recognize that Big Chicken has them in a dependent and vulnerable position. Workers and growers who had previously not known one another are able to appreciate one another and organize together for a fair deal for all parties.

I think of one union official who meets around the table. He was once a meat cutter and a member of the United Food and Commercial Workers union and now holds down a leadership role in the union. He knows the problems that poultry workers face and yet he was unaware, until having come to the DPJA table, of the problems faced by poultry growers, the very people who grow the chicken his members slaughter and process at the plant. Since the DPJA has been in existence, this man has not only become knowledgeable about the growers' situation, he has now become an advocate, along with growers, to address contract issues. At meetings, when he starts talking about how unjust the system is for poultry growers, it is next to impossible to know that he is a representative of process plant workers and not a grower himself.

I've mentioned chicken catchers being around the table. Chicken catchers are a good example of how the poultry industry depends on consumers being kept in the dark about how chicken is produced, processed, and distributed. On close observation, those who enter Big Chicken's house learn that what goes on in the poultry industry goes on in the dark.

Chickens are hatched in buildings without windows, confined in chicken houses that are closed to public view and lighted at night to make the chickens eat more, caught by chicken catchers who enter the chicken houses in the middle of the night or in unobserved daylight to bend and catch and box the live birds, processed in windowless buildings, and shipped in closed up trucks to warehouses and supermarkets where consumers finally get to see a piece of chicken in daylight.

In December 1999, Mike Wallace and *Sixty Minutes* came to the Delmarva Peninsula to tell the story of the DPJA. It was as a result of that program that chicken catchers came out of the dark and into the light. Up until that time a catcher in the minds of most people was someone who was on the other end of a ball thrown by a pitcher. But chicken catching is no game, it is a dirty and dangerous job.

A team of catchers goes into a cluster of chicken houses and gathers up all the chickens and loads them into crates that are then placed on a truck and taken to slaughter at the process plant. Inside the chicken house the men bend over to gather the birds and breath a heavy manure and urine filled dust. Chicken houses can get hot and the continual bending over and gathering of the birds takes its toll on their lungs, their hands, and their backs.

The DPJA assisted chicken catchers as their story was told. In two major lawsuits against Perdue and Tyson, two giants in the poultry industry, catchers have been able to recoup wages denied them by these companies. Working together the men have also conducted a successful union organizing campaign in three Perdue plants. Men once lost in the system—contracted out by the major poultry companies to crew chiefs who often carried no health insurance or pension plans for them—now have a say in the way their work-life will be conducted, and a voice in contract determination.

If growers and plant workers and chicken catchers lack bargaining options and a way to contract, the community is denied a social contract when it comes to the treatment of the environment in which these plants are located.

The Delmarva Peninsula is a small and fragile region, dotted with rural towns and a network of rivers and streams that flow into the Chesapeake Bay to the west and the Atlantic Ocean and the Delaware Bay to the east. Folks who flock here for recreation and retirement have called Delmarva the "land of pleasant living." But environmental problems have reared their ugly heads over the past five years as waterways have been threatened by poultry plant discharge and agricultural runoff.

The agricultural runoff is the manure left over from the poultry industry. Given to the growers to use as fertilizer for crops, the manure is depicted as an asset. The only problem, however, is that what was once an asset is now a liability. Awash in chicken manure, the Delmarva Peninsula has seen its waterways polluted and fish endangered. During the summer of 1998, the waterways saw an outbreak of Pfeisteria, called "the cell from hell" because it infects fish with lesions, kills them, and proves to be harmful to people who are in the vicinity of the streams and rivers where the microbe is working its nasty way.

Excessive amounts of nitrogen and phosphorous, key components of chicken manure, cause this plague and other water-quality problems. Thanks to an aggressive campaign on the part of environmental groups in the area, the DPJA, and community people, the problem has been addressed in the Maryland legislature. In order to get public support and legislative action for a piece of legislation that makes the poultry companies responsible for the manure problem, it was necessary to educate people to the fact that the chicken manure belongs to the company (remember that they own the chickens) and not to the growers. Poultry companies did everything they could to confuse the issue by dividing environmentalists from growers. It was here that the DPJA model of community organizing proved invaluable. Utilizing everyone around the DPJA table, the problem was exposed and the responsibility for a solution fell squarely on the shoulders of the responsible parties—the poultry companies that dot the Delmarva Peninsula.

The fact that the poultry companies thrive off of dividing the community was best illustrated during a trip I took to Moorefield, West Virginia, to support poultry growers in their struggle to get some justice in their contracts with the local poultry company that controls the economy in that small rural town.

The growers asked me to say a few words and when I said to them that they needed a model like the DPJA in order to bring about change, they applauded. When I said that the companies had divided growers from catchers and process plant workers and environmentalists, they applauded. And when the applause quieted down a lone voice in the midst of the crowded school auditorium yelled out, "Preacher, they've divided us growers from one another. Hell, we're competing with one another and we're all losin'. The only winner is the company."

An underlying and most basic aspect of this struggle is the human rights issue connected with people who work in and around the poultry plants.

In Article 23 of the United Nations Universal Declaration of Human Rights, the human rights issue is spelled out clearly: "Everyone has the right to form and to join trade unions for the protection of his interests." This statement, adopted over fifty years ago, combined with statements by all major religious denominations that echo this basic right of workers to organize and bargain collectively, define this issue clearly as a moral issue.

There is a human face to this human rights struggle and it must never be forgotten or lost amidst the philosophical idealism of the term *human rights*. Human rights like the theology mentioned earlier, has to come down to earth and find its focus in the lives of people.

Consuelo, Patrick, Barry and Becky, and George are flesh and blood proof of the human struggle and the moral issues surrounding organizing efforts on the part of people who work in the poultry industry.

Consuelo is a fifteen-year-old girl who has migrated from Guatemala. She is working on the line of a poultry processing plant, outside the law because she does not have legal papers and she is underage. She has gotten her hand caught in a machine and done what may be irreparable damage to herself. But she is afraid to talk with a doctor or a lawyer who could be of help. She is denied legal and medical restitution and relief because she is afraid the company will call the INS in and have her sent back to Guatemala. She needs the work because she needs the money to send back to her family who live in poverty in Guatemala. Organizing through a local union to gain the help and protection she so desperately needs, is far from her mind. She is too frightened.

Patrick is a forty-year-old chicken catcher who has tried to organize other catchers. Because he has engaged in this organizing effort to get medical insurance coverage and pension benefits, Patrick's work has dried up. The crew chief leader no longer hires him on to do the work. He is considered a troublemaker for trying to organize a union drive. He is fearful because he has a family to house, feed, and clothe.

Barry and Becky are poultry growers who live in Georgia. They epitomize the virtues traditionally attributed to hard-working, God-fearing country-folks. They have been organizing growers in Georgia to speak back to the poultry companies around the contractual issues that keep them poor and at the mercy of the poultry companies. They have provided leadership to an alliance movement in Georgia—the Georgia Poultry Justice Alliance—and for engaging in this kind of organizing they have been harassed and threatened by the companies.

George is a fifty-five-year-old waterman who lives and works on the eastern shore of the Delmarva Peninsula. He makes a living off what he brings ashore from catching fish and crabs. Over the years he has seen the depletion of oysters and crabs, as well as the loss of fish due to the overabundance of nitrogen and phosphorus in the water. The large-scale spreading of chicken manure and the wastewater from the many poultry processing plants is largely responsible for these problems. He is concerned that the precious water and land he loves so much will be poisoned if something isn't done to make the companies responsible for the manure and the point-source dumping at the poultry processing plants.

These are the faces that the DPJA is gathering throughout the community in order to meet and converge around problems that affect each one of them and which affect the communities in which they live.

The poultry industry operates out of a hired-hands mentality. Despite all the problems associated with the growing of chickens, the farms must keep moving the birds to the processing plants, and the plants to the consumer, in order to satisfy the public's demand for cheap chicken on the dinner plate. If someone is hurt along this poultry production line, new hands are needed to step in and pick up the slack. Workers are expendable in this process. When injured workers are no longer capable of working, they are disposed of and replaced by new workers and a new work force, largely made up of immigrants.

The role of the religious community (the church in this case) is to bring together all of the parts of the community which are engaged and affected by the production of chicken. It is the work of the church to address the fundamental justice issues relevant to the production of chicken.

What the poultry industry is comfortable with is the religious community being available to do the personal and charitable tasks so long associated with the church and religious work. What that means is that companies are not troubled by clergy and churches calling on the injured and sick, assisting the unemployed with meals and canned goods, and burying members of the community. What they object to is seeing clergy and churches move from a charitable and traditionally pastoral role to a more activist role of addressing the justice issues involved with the injured, unemployed, and deceased. When a local preacher or congregation start asking questions and directing attention to what causes people to be injured in the workplace, what economic forces have caused people to be unemployed, and what the workplace situation was that caused a person to die, that's when the preacher, according to company standards, has gone to meddling.

The DPJA has drawn the religious denominations around the table to address those underlying economic justice issues. Once around the table, clergy and church members focus on economic issues, contractual issues between the employer and those who work for the poultry companies, environmental issues, workplace safety issues, and issues that speak of community sustainability.

The great challenge facing the DPJA is the organizing task necessary for all the parties around the table to be strong enough to engage in major campaigns against the numerous illegal and unjust practices that exist in the industry. Identifying individuals within each of the constituencies (growers, workers, religious community, environmentalists, animal rights advocates, etc.), and providing them with the leadership and organizational training they need, is the day-to-day work of the DPJA. On top of this, each one of the constituencies is called to work alongside one another in an interdependent way, and this is a challenge to folks who come from a variety of racial and cultural backgrounds.

Key to all of this work has been the participation of the unions. Without a union, workers are unable to stand up to the injustices they experience daily while working in the hatcheries, catching chickens, or working on the line in a poultry processing plant. In order to make a difference, however, unions are being challenged to address critical issues that, heretofore, they may have avoided. Any union attempting to organize low-wage poultry workers will have to face the fact that, by and large, the work force in poultry has changed dramatically. Immigrants, many from Mexico and Central America, have replaced poor white and African American workers in poultry-production jobs. Unions cannot assume any longer that they are in touch with this new work force, as long as contracts are not in Spanish and leadership in the local unions does not have a Latino face.

Even more important in any union organizing work is for the union to identify with the basic problems faced by this new and growing Latino work force. Unions will have to get down and dirty with these workers around the most basic issues faced by the population. When the AFL-CIO made the decision to change its posture toward this work force and declared that it would work on a political agenda that would result in national legislation to give legal status to immigrant workers without proper documentation, the union movement took a bold step in the right direction. It said, in that change of policy, that it cared about the most important issue in the lives of immigrant workers. It said also that it recognized that the future of unions in this country rests in developing new members and new leaders from this immigrant population.

I speak about chicken, and the injustices surrounding that industry, in churches all over the country. When I have concluded my remarks, often made after we have eaten a chicken dinner, people are angry and want to know what they can do. I tell them we need to organize around a major campaign to change the poultry industry in this country and that it can start right here at the local level. But I do not kid myself, or them. It will take a lot of work and it will require forming alliances that cut across the entire industry.

An alliance approach to the problems created by the poultry industry recognizes that there will be no sustainable community unless all the parts of the community see themselves related in a holistic way, not only in regard to the problems, but also to the solution of those problems.

Local communities are the final dumping ground, not only for the enormous environmentally destructive manure and waste deposited on the land and in the water in the production of chicken. Poultry-producing communities are the dumping ground for diseased dead birds and chemical residue. These communities are also the dumping ground for bankrupt chicken farmers suffering from the one-sided contracts controlled by the poultry industry. These rural communities are the dumping ground for injured workers who often have poor housing and no adequate medical care. These communities, along with every city and town across the nation, are the dumping ground for a marketed piece of chicken full of antibiotics and growth-producing substances harmful to the consumer.

The Episcopal church put me to work on the Delmarva Peninsula in recognition that there are deep moral issues at stake around the chicken we bless and eat. And I can say quite assuredly that people are getting that message as alliances are being formed in poultry producing states and as the problems associated with the production of poultry are being aired.

When chicken catchers were demonstrating in front of a Food Lion store in Salisbury, Maryland, for a just contract and the payment of wages they had been denied, a woman on her way into the store to buy her groceries rose to the occasion and exemplified this growing awareness on the part of the public to the plight of poultry workers. And not only that, she displayed her knowledge and her indignation publicly by speaking into the microphone of a local television camera, and by saying that it was just plain "not right" the way the company was treating these chicken catchers.

When a man, working on a local poultry farm tending to company chickens, came into the DPJA office and let it be known that the company was telling him to dump dead birds illegally on land adjacent to one of the local waterways, he declared that what the company was ordering him to do was "just not right." His willingness to act on that moral conviction resulted in an EPA fine for the company involved.

"It's just not right." Those words say it all. What the poultry industry, this vertically integrated, factory-farm business enterprise, is doing to the environment, the workers, the growers, the consumers, and the people who care about the health and welfare of the community, is wrong. And change will take place only as communities organize in new and creative ways across lines in the community, lines created and exploited by the poultry companies, and present a united face in support of truly sustainable and healthy communities.

Linda Lord, a woman who for years had worked in a poultry plant in Belfast, Maine, tells her story in a marvelous book that shines light on the ills of working for a poultry company. When asked by the interviewer how she liked her work over the years inside that plant, she replied, "I was content and not content."[3]

That's it in a nutshell for poultry workers and people in communities who rely on the poultry industry for their economic survival. They are content and not content. Content with being able to have a job and bring some money home to support a family, even if it is too little to support a family adequately, and it comes at the expense of the worker's own health and safety. Not content in the way the entire community has to live in a dependent relationship with the poultry companies, one that is full of injustices.

The religious community that sits at the table of an alliance like the DPJA brings a learned awareness that all is not right in the community when it comes to the production of chicken. A covenant has been broken with God and with one another when injustice exists. The religious community, expert in speaking of "sin," comes prepared to connect that theological understanding with the evil of an industry so caught up in profit-making that it is not capable of seeing what trouble it is creating in the production and consumption of chicken. Creation itself has been disrupted by the practices of the poultry industry, all parts of creation, which includes animals, the fish of the surrounding waterways, the earth, and an assortment of people from all races and creeds, and the only remedy is to right what is wrong.

Faith-based communities in poultry-producing communities are coming into an active awareness that love and justice are down-to-earth realities when it comes to addressing the many fears associated with challenging the poultry industry. (To raise serious justice issues in poultry-producing-communities is to live with the fear of losing a contract, or a job, or the economic security of poultry plants that threaten to pick up and move to a more "friendly" community if people raise their voices in protest at the way things are and how wrong things are.)

A chicken catcher, who also happens to be a lay-preacher, once told me that "there is a serious lack of love in the poultry industry." What he means is that things are not right because there is injustice in the poultry industry. The old saying that justice is love with its working clothes on is the lesson this catcher-preacher knows personally, and which people of faith finally are waking up to.

The town of Georgetown, Delaware, with a population of about six hundred people, could once count the Latino members in the community on one hand. That county seat now has a Guatemalan population estimated to be 40 percent of the town's population. These folks have come to the region to work in local poultry plants.

The Episcopal church, along with Roman Catholics in the area, has opened a Latino welcoming center. La Esperanza (Place of Hope) is there to assist this immigrant population as people from all over Mexico and Central America attempt to find their way in a new and strange land.

La Esperanza has adopted as its appropriate logo the grasshopper.

The grasshopper brings to mind the small creature that, in large numbers, brought to Pharaoh one of the many plagues sent by God as a warning to let people held in slave labor go free. The grasshopper also calls to mind the story of the Hebrew people on their way to a promised land where people would be able to own land and be able to find a justice that would enable them each to sit under their own vine and fig tree and live in economic peace. When Moses sent a party of tribal scouts over into the land they were seeking to enter, the scouts came back with the story that the people who inhabited the land were like giants. Surely there would be no way to come into that new land because what were they, the Hebrew people, but nothing more than grasshoppers as opposed to these giants. As they say, the rest is history.

The rest is history, but the future has yet to be realized when it comes to economic and community justice in terms of the poultry industry.

What may well be called for here is what we might call "grasshopper power," the kind of unity between all parts of the community capable of coming together across all divisions to bring about real structural change in the way poultry is produced in this nation.

The cry well might be, "Grasshoppers Unite!"

Notes

1. A Long Overdue Beginning

1. Pub. L. No. 74–198, 49 Stat. 449–50 (1935) (Codified as Amended at 29 U.S.C. § 141–44, 167, 171–87 (1944).

2. For example, Human Rights Watch pointed out in its report, *Unfair Advantage: Workers' Freedom of Association in the United States Under International Human Rights Standards* (2000), that some provisions of the Wagner Act, such as the exclusion from coverage of agricultural and domestic workers, openly conflict with international human rights norms that affirm the right of "every person" to form and join trade unions and to bargain collectively. Citing these exclusions, the denial by many states of the right to bargain collectively to public-sector employees, as well as additional exclusions in the Taft-Hartley amendments to the Wagner Act, Human Rights Watch concludes that "millions of workers in the United States are excluded from coverage of laws that are supposed to protect the right to organize and bargain collectively." As a consequence, "workers who fall under these exclusions can be summarily fired with impunity for seeking to form and join a union."

3. James A. Gross, "Conflicting Statutory Purposes: Another Look at Fifty Years of NLRB Law Making," *Industrial and Labor Relations Review* 39 (7) (1985): 10.

4. Ibid.

5. James A. Gross, *Broken Promise: The Subversion of U.S. Labor Relations Policy: 1937–1994* (Temple University Press: Philadelphia, 1995).

6. 29 U.S.C. § 157 (1947). Under the Wagner Act workers were free, of course, to vote against unionization in secret ballot representation elections.

7. Gross, *Broken Promise*, 13.

8. 28 U.S.C. § 158(c) (1947).

9. Robert Wagner, "The Wagner Act-A Reappraisal," *Congressional Record* 93 (1947): A895–A896. Reprinted in Vol. 2, *Labor Management Relations Act History* (U.S. Government Printing Office: Washington D.C., 1948), 935, 938.

10. Subcommittee on Labor-Management Relations of the House Committee on Education and Labor, 98th Cong., Vol. 1, "The Failure of Labor Law—A Betrayal of American Workers" (Committee Print 1984).

11. Ibid., 24.

12. Ibid.

13. "Examination of the Relationship Between the United States and the International Labor Organization," Hearing Before the Senate Committee On Labor And Human Resources, 99th Cong., 1st Sess., Vol. 1 (1985), 35–36.

14. Ibid., 36.

15. Ibid., 111.

16. Ibid., 11.

17. Virginia Leary, "The Paradox of Workers' Rights as Human Rights," in *Human Rights, Labor Rights and International Trade*, eds. Lance A. Compa and Stephen F. Diamond (Philadelphia: University of Pennsylvania Press, 1996), 22, 25.

18. Statement to the World Conference on Human Rights on Behalf of the Committee on Economic, Social, and Cultural Rights, UN Doc. E/1993/22, Annex III reprinted in *International Human Rights In Context: Law, Politics, Morals*, eds. Henry Jr. Steiner and Philip Alston (Clarendon: Oxford, 1996), 266.

19. Darryl M. Trimiew, *God Bless the Child That's Got Its Own: The Economic Rights Debate* (Atlanta, Ga: Scholars Press, 1997), 123.

20. See James A. Gross, "The Broken Promises of the National Labor Relations Act and the Occupational Safety and Health Act: Conflicting Values and Conceptions of Rights and Justice," *Chicago-Kent Law Review* 73 (351): 384–85.

21. Ibid., 378–79.

22. The Universal Declaration of Human Rights is reproduced in *International Human Rights in Context*, 1156–1160.

23. The International Covenant on Civil and Political Rights is reproduced in Ibid., 1161–171.

24. Ibid., 1159.

25. Ibid., 1167.

26. The International Covenant on Economic, Social, and Cultural Right is reproduced in Ibid., 1175–181.

27. Hurst Hannum and Dana D. Fischer, *U.S. Ratification of the International Covenants on Human Rights* (Irvington-on-Hudson, N.Y.: Transnational Publications, 1997), 121.

28. James A. Gross, "A Human Rights Perspective on United States Labor Relations Law: A Violation of the Right of Freedom of Association," *Employee Rights and Employment Law Journal* 3 (1999): 65, 74. For a more thorough discussion see James A. Gross, "The Common Law Employment Contract and Collective Bargaining: Values and Views of Rights and Justice," *New Zealand Journal of Industrial Relations* 23 (1) (1998): 63–76.

29. "Review of Annual Reports Under the Follow-up to the ILO Declaration on Fundamental Principles and Rights at Work, Part II: International Labor Office," (Geneva, 2000), 144–58.

30. Ibid., 153.

31. Ibid.

32. Ibid., Part I, par. 44, 10–11.

33. Human Rights Watch, *Unfair Advantage*.

34. Ibid., 50.

35. Conference Minutes, "Human Rights in the American Workplace: Assessing U.S. Labor Law and Policy," October 20–21, 2000, Panel on U.S. Labor Law and Policy, 95.

36. Ibid., Panel on Workers' Rights, 30.

37. Conference Minutes, "Human Rights in the American Workplace: Assessing U.S. Labor Law and Policy," Panel on "Human Rights Implications," 49–50.

38. ILO, Convention Concerning Freedom of Association and Protection of the Right to Organize (No. 87), 31st Sess. (1948), Vol. 1, International Labour Conventions and Recommendations 435 (1992).

39. ILO, Convention Concerning Right to Organize and Collective Bargaining (No. 98), 32d Sess. (1949), Vol. 1 International Labor Conventions and Recommendations 524 (1992).

40. Michael J. Perry, *The Idea of Human Rights: Four Inquiries* (Oxford: Oxford University Press, 1998), 4–5.

41. For a discussion of some of these cases, see Gross, "A Human Rights Perspective," 81–88, 96.

42. Ibid., 85.

43. Edward E. Potter, *Freedom of Association, the Right to Organize and Collective Bargaining: The Impact on U.S. Law and Practice of Ratification of ILO Conventions No. 87 and No. 98* (Washington, D.C.: Labor Policy Association, 1984).

44. Ibid., 45.

45. Ibid., 88.

46. Philip Allott, *Eunomia: New Order for a New World* (Oxford: Oxford University Press, 1990), 287, reprinted in *International Human Rights in Context,* 454.

47. Conference minutes, "Human Rights in the American Workplace: Assessing U.S. Labor Law and Policy," Panel on "Workers' Rights," 35.

48. Jack Donnelly, "International Human Rights: A Regime Analysis," *International Organization* 40 (1986): 599, 613, reprinted in *International Human Rights in Context,* 452.

49. Conference Minutes, "Human Rights in the American Workplace: Assessing U.S. Labor Law and Policy," Panel on "U.S. Labor Law and Policy," 95.

50. Conference Minutes, "Human Rights in the American Workplace: Assessing U.S. Labor Law and Policy," comment by Pharis Harvey, executive director, International Labor Rights Fund, Panel on "Agents of Change," 157.

51. Ibid., 150.

52. Ibid., 151.

2. Workers' Freedom of Association in the United States

1. For additional treatment of human rights principles regarding freedom of association for workers, see James A. Gross, "A Human Rights Perspective on United States Labor Relations Law: A Violation of the Right of Freedom of Association," *Employee Rights and Employment Policy Journal* 3 (1999): 65; see also papers and other information available at the web site of the Society for the Promotion of Human Rights in Employment (SPHRE) at http://www.mericleinc.com/Sphre/.

2. Universal Declaration of Human Rights, G.A. Res.217A (III), U.N. GAOR, 3d Sess., pt. 1, at 71, U.N. Doc. A/810 (1948) (art. 20(1); art. 23(4)).

3. International Covenant on Civil and Political Rights, Dec. 16, 1966, 999 U.N.T.S. 171 (art.22).

4. International Covenant on Economic, Social, and Cultural Rights, Dec. 16, 1966, 993 U.N.T.S. 3 (art. 8).

5. International Covenant on Civil and Political Rights, Article 2.

6. See U.S. Senate, Ratification of ICCPR, April 2, 1992. Reservations, understandings, and declarations are accepted under international law as a means of ratifying complex international instruments while taking exception to certain details, so that wider ratification of the instruments can be achieved.

7. In a written exchange between the Senate and the White House on questions posed by Senator Daniel Moynihan, first as to whether ICCPR Article 22 alters or amends U.S. labor law, the administration responded, "No," asserting that Article 22's "general right of freedom of association, including the right to form and join trade unions . . . are fully contemplated by the First Amendment to the U.S. Constitution." On the question of whether ratification of Article 22 commits the U.S. to ratify ILO Convention 87, the administration again responded in the negative, saying "the two agreements are different in the scope of the rights and obligations they provide." This exchange, not reflected in the instrument of ratification, does not lessen the United States' obligation to fully comply with Article 22 of the ICCPR.

8. See Office of the Legal Advisor, U.S. Department of State, "Civil and Political Rights in the United States: Initial Report of the United States of America to the U.N. Human Rights

Committee under the International Covenant on Civil and Political Rights," Department of State publication 10200 (July 1994; released September 1994).

9. Ibid., 166.

10. American Declaration of the Rights and Duties of Man,´ 1948, in Final Act, Ninth International Conference of American States, Bogota, Colombia, Articles 21, 22. "American" here refers to the Americas, including North, Central, and South America and the Caribbean region.

11. American Convention on Human Rights, OAS Official Records, OEA/Ser.A/16 (English), T.S. No. 36 (Nov. 7–22, 1969), Article 16.

12. European Convention for the Protection of Human Rights and Fundamental Freedoms, Nov. 4, 1950, E.T.S. No. 5 (entered into force, Sept. 3, 1953), Article 11.

13. "European Union, Community Charter of Fundamental Social Rights of Workers," in *European Labour Law*, eds. Roger Blanpain and Chris Engels (The Hague: Kluwer Law International, 1998), Articles 11–13.

14. ILO Convention No. 87, Articles 2, 11.

15. ILO Convention No. 98, Articles 1, 3, 4.

16. Cited in OECD, *Trade, Employment, and Labour Standards: A Study of Core Workers' Rights and International Trade* (Paris: Organization for Economic Cooperation and Development, 1996) (hereafter *Trade, Employment and Labour Standards*); see also Hilary Barnes and Andrew Jack, "Nations Agree on Fighting Poverty," *Financial Times*, March 13, 1995: 6.

17. See *ILO Focus* (winter/spring 1997); the conventions cited are nos. 87 and 98 on freedom of association and the right to organize and bargain collectively, 29 and 105 on forced labor, 100 and 111 on nondiscrimination, and 138 on child labor.

18. Organization for Economic Cooperation and Development, "Guidelines for Multinational Enterprises" (1976).

19. See OECD, *Trade, Employment and Labour Standards* (1996).

20. See U.S. Labor Department News Release, June 18, 1998, available at www.dol.gov.

21. See Fact Finding and Conciliation Commission on Chile, International Labour Organization, Geneva, Switzerland (1975), para. 466.

22. See ILO, CFA Cases nos. 1130 (1987), 1401 (1987), 1416 (1988), 1420 (1988), 1437 (1988), 1467 (1988), 1543 (1991), 1523 (1992), 1557 (1993), available at www.ilolex.ilo.ch.

23. To take one example, the exclusion of agricultural workers from protection of the right to organize clashes with ILO norms. The argument against ratification is developed in detail in Edward E. Potter, *Freedom of Association, the Right to Organize and Collective Bargaining: The Impact on U.S. Law and Practice of Ratification of ILO Conventions No. 87 and No. 98* (Washington, DC: Labor Policy Association, 1984). Ratification of ILO conventions is further complicated by the fact that, in the U.S. system, later-in-time statutes passed by Congress and signed by the president supersede earlier-ratified international treaties.

24. See statement of Abraham Katz, president, U.S. Council for International Business, "Examination of the Relationship Between the United States and the International Labor Organization," U.S. Senate, Hearing before the Senate Committee on Labor and Human Resources, 99th Cong., 1st Sess., Vol. 1 (1985), 74–101.

25. See, e.g., *U.S. Report* for the period ending 31 December 1997 under Article 19 of the ILO constitution on the position of national law and practice in regard to matters dealt with in conventions 87 and 98, available from the U.S. Department of Labor and on file with author.

26. See *Annual Report for 1999* to the ILO regarding aspects of conventions 87 and 98, available from the U.S. Department of Labor and on file with author.

27. See "Review of Annual Reports under the Follow-up to the ILO Declaration on Fundamental Principles and Rights at Work," ILO Governing Body, March 2000, para. 44.

28. See, for example, Generalized System of Preferences Act, 91 U.S.C. sec. 2462(b)(7).

29. 19 U.S.C.A. § 2461 et.seq. The GSP program permits a developing country to export goods to the United States on a preferential, duty-free basis as long as they meet the conditions for eligibility in the program.

30. 22 U.S.C.A. § 2191 et.seq. OPIC insures the overseas investments of U.S. corporations against losses due to war, revolution, expropriation, or other factors related to political turmoil, as long as the country receiving the investment meets conditions for eligibility under OPIC insurance.

31. 19 U.S.C.A. § 2702 et seq. A 1990 labor rights amendment to what is now called the Caribbean Basin Economic Recovery Act (CBERA) expanded the worker rights clause to comport with GSP and OPIC formulations. CBERA grants duty-free status to exports into the United States from Caribbean basin countries on a more extensive basis than under GSP provisions.

32. 19 U.S.C.A. § 2411 et.seq. Section 301 defines various unfair trade practices, now including worker rights violations, making a country that trades with the United States liable to retaliatory action.

33. Amendment to the Foreign Assistance Act, 22 U.S.C.A. §§ 2151 et seq.

34. 22 U.S.C. § 1621 (1994).

35. See H.R. Conf. Rep. No. 4426, 103rd Cong., 2d Sess., §1621 (a) (1994), codified at 22 U.S.C. §1621 (a).

36. See General Accounting Office, "Assessment of the Generalized System of Preferences Program," GAO/GGD-95–9 (November 1994), 99–100.

37. See U.S. Department of State, *Country Reports on Human Rights Practices for 1999* (February 2000), Appendix B, "Reporting on Worker Rights."

38. Ibid.; see also Hodges-Aeberhard and Odero de Diós, "Principles of the Committee of Association Concerning Strikes," *International Labour Review* 126 (1987): 544.

39. See Gov. Bill Clinton, "Expanding Trade and Creating American Jobs," Address at North Carolina State University, Raleigh, North Carolina (1992).

40. North American Agreement on Labor Cooperation, Annex 1, Labor Principles 1–3.

41. Ibid., Article 2.

42. 29 U.S.C. §§ 151–169, Section 7.

43. See, for example, Subcommittee on Labor-Management Relations of the House Committee on Education and Labor, 96th Cong., 2d Sess., "Report on Pressures in Today's Workplace" (1980); 98th Cong., "The Failure of Labor Law: A Betrayal of American Workers" (1984); U.S. Department of Labor, Bureau of Labor-Management Relations, Report No. 134: "U.S. Labor Law and the Future of Labor-Management Cooperation" (1989); U.S. Department of Labor, U.S. Department of Commerce, Commission on the Future of Worker-Management Relations (Dunlop Committee), *Fact Finding Report* (1994).

44. See NLRB Annual Reports 1950–1998; 1998 Table 4, 137.

45. Author interview, Palm Beach, Florida, July 24, 1999.

46. See NLRB Decision and Order, *PVMI Associates, Inc. D/b/a King David Center et al. and 1115 Nursing Home Hospital & Service Employees Union-Florida*, 328 NLRB No. 159 (August 6, 1999).

47. Ibid., 13.

48. Ibid., 18.

49. Author interview, Palm Beach, Florida, July 24, 1999.

50. These unfair labor practices are described in more detail in NLRB Region 11, Order Consolidating Cases, Complaint, and Notice of Hearing, *Smithfield Foods, Inc. and United Food & Commercial Workers*, Case No. 11–CA-18316 (January 21, 2000).

51. Author interview, Wilson, North Carolina, July 13, 1999.

52. See *NLRB v. Village IX, Inc.*, 723 F.2d 1360 (7th Cir. 1983).

53. Author interview, Baltimore, Maryland, March 19, 1999.

54. Author interview, New Orleans, Louisiana, May 11, 1999.

55. Quoted in NLRB, Decision of administrative law judge David L. Evans in *Avondale Industries, Inc. and New Orleans Metal Trades Council,* Cases 15–CA-12171–1 et al., February 27, 1998.

56. See *Avondale Industries, Inc. v. NLRB,* No. 97–60708, 1999 U.S. App. LEXIS 15036, July 7, 1999.

57. This is the standard NLRB remedy for unfair labor practices. Reinstated workers are entitled to back pay for time off the job, "mitigated" by subtracting all interim earnings the worker was able to obtain.

58. Author interview, May 11, 1999.

59. Author interview, May 11, 1999. Litton Industries purchased Avondale in late 1999. Litton agreed to recognize the union after a majority of workers signed cards authorizing representation and collective bargaining. However, Litton did not agree to reinstate fired workers. Their cases remained on appeal.

60. Author Interview, Chicago, Illinois, July 8, 1999.

61. See *NLRB v. Lovejoy Industries, Inc.,* 904 F.2d 397 (7th Cir. 1990).

62. Author interview, Chicago, Illinois, July 5, 1999.

63. Ibid.

64. Author interview, July 8, 1999.

65. U.S. Bureau of Labor Statistics, unpublished tabulations from 1998–1999 population survey, on file with author.

66. See Ruben Castañeda, "Man Found Guilty in Slave Case; Md. Couple Brought Woman From Brazil," *Washington Post,* February 11, 2000: B1.

67. Author interview, Seattle, Washington, November 4, 1999.

68. See Leslie Helm, "Technology: 16 Microsoft Temps Organize into Bargaining Unit; Labor: Group Hoping for Improved Benefits Signs a Petition Seeking Representation by Local Union," *Los Angeles Times,* June 4, 1999: C3.

69. Author interview, November 4, 1999.

70. See Paul Andrews, "Microsoft Drops TaxSaver Software; Workers on Project Call Decision a Shock," *Seattle Times,* March 24, 2000: D3.

71. Author interview, April 25, 2000.

72. See Steven Greenhouse, "Two-Thirds of Garment Shops Break Wage Laws, U.S. Says," *New York Times,* October 17, 1997: A37.

73. See Report, Los Angeles Jewish Commission on Sweatshops (Los Angeles, January 1999); Patrick J. McDonnell, "Jewish Group Urges Reform of Sweatshops," *Los Angeles Times,* February 1, 1999: B1.

74. Author interview, New York City, June 15, 1999, and following Ramírez and Rodríguez statements.

75. See International Labour Organization, Committee on Freedom of Association, *Complaint against the Government of the United States Presented by the American Federation of Labor and Congress of Industrial Organizations (AFL-CIO),* para. 92, Report No. 278, Case No. 1543 (1991).

76. See, e.g., *Denver Post* classified advertising section, October 1, 1997; "Notice to Permanent Replacement Employees," Oregon Steel (notice distributed to replacement workers, 1997).

77. See Decision of ALJ Albert A. Metz, *New CF&I, Inc. and Oregon Steel Mills, Inc. and United Steelworkers of America,* Cases 27–CA-15562 et al., May 17, 2000.

78. See NLRB Region 19, Order Consolidating Cases, Consolidated Complaints and No-

tice of Hearing, *Stemilt Growers, Inc., Ag-Relate, Inc. and International Brotherhood of Teamsters,* Case Nos.19–CA-25403 et al.; *Washington Fruit and International Brotherhood of Teamsters,* Case Nos. 25702 et. al. (1998).

79. Stemilt worker affidavit to NLRB.

80. See Leah Beth Ward, "N.C. Growers' Trade in Foreign Farm Workers Draws Scrutiny," *Charlotte Observer,* October 30, 1999: 1.

81. Author interview, Lori Elmer and Alice Tejada, staff attorneys of Legal Services of North Carolina, Farmworker Unit, Raleigh, North Carolina, July 13, 1999.

82. Author interview with migrant H-2A workers, near Mt. Olive, N.C., July 14, 1999.

83. See affidavit of Juan Carlos Vieyra Ornelas, intern with Farm Worker Project of Benson, North Carolina, August 10, 1999, on file with author.

84. Author interview, near Mt. Olive, N.C., July 15, 1999.

85. Ward, "Growers' Trade," 30.

86. See Demetrios G. Papademetriou and Monica S. Heppel, *Balancing Acts: Toward a Fair Bargain on Seasonal Agricultural Workers* (Washington, D.C.: International Migration Policy Program, Carnegie Endowment for International Peace, 1999), 13.

3. Closing the Gap between International Law and U.S. Labor Law

1. The constitution of the ILO proclaimed, at the end of World War I, that "there can be no lasting peace without social justice."

2. The Employment Policy Convention, 1964 (Convention 122).

3. The Labor Statistics Convention, 1985 (Convention 160).

4. The Labor Administration Convention, 1978 (Convention 150).

5. The Labor Inspection Convention, 1947 (Convention 81) and the Labor Inspection (Agriculture) Convention, 1969 (Convention 129).

6. ILO Convention 29 was adopted at the suggestion of the league in order to lend a labor aspect to this question. The United Nations has not created a supervisory machinery for the Slavery Convention, nor for the Supplementary Convention on the same subject adopted in 1953.

7. Ratified by the United States in 1991.

8. Submitted to the U.S. Senate for advice and consent for ratification, in 1998. Not yet approved.

9. All ratification figures here as of 25 March 2002. Convention 87 has 139 ratifications, Convention 98 has 151, Convention 100 has 156, Convention 111 has 154, and Convention 105 has 157.

10. The social clause usually means a measure that would link trading privileges with demonstrated respect for fundamental labor standards.

11. In addition to the procedure of the Committee on Freedom of Association, created in 1951 for precisely this purpose.

12. ILO, *Review of Annual Reports under the Follow-up to the ILO Declaration on Fundamental Principles and Rights at Work, Part II: Compilation of Annual Reports* (ILO, Geneva, each year as of 2000).

13. One of only thirteen conventions the United States has ratified. Five concern seafarers' working conditions (Conventions 53, 55, 58, 74 and 147), one is a procedural instrument on revision of the final articles of older ILO standards (Convention 80), and two are fundamental human rights conventions (Conventions 105 and 182). In addition the United States has ratified conventions 144 on tripartite consultations, 150 on Labor Administration, and 160

on Labor Statistics. Two older seafarers' conventions (Conventions 54 and 57) were ratified, but were "automatically" denounced on the ratification of a revising convention.

14. The general survey carried out by the ILO Committee of Experts in 2000, published in 2001, and discussed in the conference that year contains a review of the standards on night work. It concluded that while prohibitions on women working at night are discriminatory, there may be some very special circumstances that justify their retention, on condition of consultations with the women concerned and other factors.

15. But as of this writing it is generally felt that it will receive its twentieth ratification in the course of 2002 and enter into force shortly thereafter.

16. As indicated above, most of the conventions the United States has ratified in fact relate to the conditions of work of seafarers, one of the few labor law subjects covered entirely by federal law.

17. This may appear to be an unusual convention for the ILO to have adopted, but in fact these are the only international standards applying specifically to these peoples and was adopted on behalf of the entire United Nations system. These peoples are, in the end, workers in the informal sector when they follow their traditional economic activities.

18. General surveys are carried out to set out the current way in which all member states are applying a certain set of conventions and recommendations, to explain their provisions, and to examine difficulties in their application and in ratifying them. Examples of subjects covered in recent years are night work for women (for the November 2000 session), tripartite consultations (1999), and migrant workers (1998).

19. Report III (Part 4A), International Labor Conference, 63rd Session, 1977, General Report, para. 31.

20. They may however be found in the ILOLEX database, distributed annually on CD-ROM. The online version published by the ILO on its web site, http://www.ilo.org, does not contain the direct requests.

21. Now Report III (Part IA).

22. Only fourteen representations were submitted between the end of World War II and 1978, but since then they have been arriving with far greater frequency.

23. See a recent article on just this subject: Edward Weisband, "Discursive Multilateralism: Global Benchmarks, Shame, and Learning in the ILO Labor Standards Monitoring Regime," *International Studies Quarterly* 44 (2000): 643–66.

24. Human Rights Watch, *Unfair Advantage: Workers' Freedom of Association* (New York: Human Rights Watch, 1999).

4. Risks and Rights

1. It is *not* my purpose to explore the philosophical and religious bases for rights concepts, to respond to the difficult questions regarding trade agreements, to set out the specific rules that should govern workplace risks, or to provide a detailed analysis of the U.S. health and safety regime.

2. Robin Herbert and Philip J. Landrigan, "Work-Related Death: A Continuing Epidemic," *American Journal of Public Health* 90 (2000): 541–45. Note that there are enormous difficulties (even in the United States where reporting is required) with determining the real numbers of occupational injuries, fatalities, and illnesses. For ongoing discussions of these problems, see, e.g., Daniel M. Berman, *Death on the Job: Occupational Health and Safety Struggles in the United States* (New York: Monthly Review Press, 1978), 38–53; Marc Linder, "Fatal Subtraction: Statistical MIAs on the Industrial Battlefield," *Notre Dame Law Review* 20 (1994): 99–145 ("implausible as it may seem, despite the fact that the last state [Mississippi]

enacted a workers' compensation statute almost a half-century ago, the United States still lacks comprehensive and accurate data on work-related fatalities." Ibid., 100); Emily A. Spieler, "Perpetuating Risk? Workers' Compensation and the Persistence of Occupational Injuries," *Houston Law Review* 31 (1994): 119–240; Sidney Shapiro and Thomas McGarity, *Workers at Risk: The Failed Promise of the Occupational Safety and Health Administration* (Westport, Conn.: Praeger, 1993). It is reasonable to assume that the counting of these events in less well-developed countries is even more problematic.

3. 6,023 workers died from traumatic injuries in 1999. Bureau of Labor Statistics, U.S. Dept. of Labor, *National Census of Fatal Occupational Injuries 1999*, USDL 00–236 (2000). According to this report, in the last decade people have died at work at a rate of 4 to 5 workers per 100,000 workers per year.

4. U.S. Dept of Labor News, *Lost-Worktime Injuries and Illnesses: Characteristics and Resulting Time Away from Work, 1999*, USDL 01–71, March 28, 2001.

5. Hugh Conway and Jens Svenson, "Occupational Injury and Illness Rates, 1992–96: Why They Fell," *Monthly Labor Review* 121 (Nov. 1998): 36–58.

6. For attempts to estimate the total costs, see, e.g. J. P. Leigh, Steven B. Markowitz, M. Fahs, C. Shin, and Philip J. Landrigan, "Occupational Illness and Injury in the United States: Estimates of Costs, Morbidity, and Mortality," *Archives of Internal Medicine* 157 (1997): 1557–568; Ted R. Miller, "Estimating the Costs of Injury to U.S. Employers," *Journal of Safety Research* 28 (1997): 1–13; Ted R. Miller and M. Galbraith, "The Costs of Occupational Injury in the United States," *Accident Analysis and Prevention* 17 (6) (1995): 741–47; Tim Morse, Charles Dillon, Nicholas Warren, Charles Levenstein, and A. Warren, "The Economic and Social Consequences of Work-related Musculoskeletal Disorders: The Connecticut Upper-Extremity Surveillance Project (CUSP)," *International Journal of Occupational and Environmental Health* 4 (1998): 209–16.

7. For data regarding injury and fatality rates, see the website of the ILO (www.ilo.org). For a discussion of occupational safety and health in the global economy see Howard Frumkin, "Across the Water and Down the Ladder: Occupational Health in the Global Economy," *State of the Art Reviews: Occupational Medicine (Special Populations)* 14 (3) (1999): 637–63.

8. See Jukka Takala, "Global Estimates of Fatal Occupational Accidents," ICLS/16/RD 8, *Sixteenth International Conference of Labour Statisticians*, Geneva, October 6–15, 1998; Asian-Pacific Newsletter, "Indicators of Death, Disability and Disease at Work," http://www.occuphealth.fi/e/info/asian/ap100/indicators02.htm, showing the following:

Table 4.1

Region	Fatality Rate (estimates)
Established market economies	5.3
Formerly Socialist economies of Europe	11.1
India	11.0
China	11.1
Other Asian countries	23.1
Sub-Saharan Africa	21.0
Latin America/Caribbean	13.5
Middle Eastern crescent	22.5

9. Herbert and Landrigan, "Work Related Death," 541.

10. See, e.g. "Toy Factory Fire Shows Laxness of Safety Rules," *Asian Wall Street Journal,*

May 13, 1993: 1 (number of accidents doubled in Malaysia from 1985 to 1990 from 61,724 to 121,104).

11. ILO Declaration on Fundamental Principles and Rights at Work and Its Follow-up, adopted by the ILO at its 86th Session, Geneva, June 18, 1998.

12. I have chosen to characterize these as four rights, although these rights are sometimes listed as five or more rights because of the multiple ILO conventions that address some of the issues. In fact, these four rights do not track preexisting ILO conventions. See Lance Compa, "The Promise and Perils of 'Core' Labor Rights in Global Trade and Investment," unpublished manuscript presented at conference Human Rights for the Twenty-First Century at The Graduate Center, City University of New York, November 17–18, 2000, publication of conference papers pending, 5 n.1 ("References to core labor standards sometimes speak of four standards, or six, or seven, or eight such standards; the confusion arises because the ILO has more than a single relevant convention on the four core issues contained in the declaration—two on forced labor, two on child labor, two or more on freedom of association and collective bargaining [which are taken to include the right to organize], two or more on discrimination. Readers who come across references to differing numbers of "core" standards should keep this in mind. The consensual "core" is contained in items [a]–[d] of the ILO declaration.")

13. Compa, "Promise and Perils," 5.

14. See Clyde Summers, "The Battle in Seattle: Free Trade, Labor Rights, and Societal Values," *University of Pennsylvania Journal of International Economic Law* 22 (spring 2001): 61–90. Summers reviews the arguments regarding the imposition of labor standards in international trade and argues persuasively that the resistance to inclusion of even these four core rights in trade agreements represents "laissez-faire absolutism." Ibid., 81.

15. For discussion of this point, in addition to Summers, "The Battle in Seattle," and Compa, "Promise and Perils," also see Raj Bhala, "Clarifying the Trade-Labor Link," *Columbia Journal of Transnational Law* 37 (1998): 11–56 (providing a more extensive summary of the arguments on both sides of the debate), and Janice R. Bellace, "ILO Fundamental Rights at Work and Freedom of Association," *Labor Law Journal* 50 (3) (1999): 191–203 (history of the ILO discussions). According to Summers, "The argument that free trade requires recognition of a country's comparative advantage regardless of the source of that advantage legitimates labor conditions that violate fundamental rights." Summers, "The Battle in Seattle," 87.

16. These rights were analogized to nineteenth-century American law by Elaine Bernard, director, Harvard Trade Union Program, at the conference Human Rights in the American Workplace, sponsored by Cornell's ILR school, October 2001. She is clearly right, with the important exception that the explicit protection of rights of association goes beyond the protections under U.S. law at that time.

17. See Organization for Economic Co-Operation and Development (OECD), *Trade, Employment & Labour Standards: A Study of Core Workers Rights and International Trade* (Paris: OECD, 1996).

18. See Drusilla K. Brown, Alan V. Deardorff, and Robert M. Stern, "International Labor Standards and Trade: A Theoretical Analysis," in *Fair Trade and Harmonization*, ed. Jagdish Bhagwati and Robert E. Hudec (Cambridge: MIT Press, 1996), 227–80.

19. See Compa, "Promise and Perils," 5 (citing U.S. Council for International Business, the U.S. employer delegation to the ILO), International Labor Affairs Update, April 1998 and August 1998, at its web site, www.uscib.org. ("The Declaration is necessary for staving off pressure for the social clause. . . . The goal of this initiative has been to place the ILO at the center of the debate on linking worker rights with trade, thereby decreasing the pressure to use trade sanctions to enforce labor standards.")

20. "Easy consensus against the 'worst' masks failure to act against much more widespread commonplace forms of child labor." Compa, "Promise and Perils," 12.

21. Steve Charnovitz, "Green Roots, Bad Pruning: GATT Rules and Their Application to Environmental Trade Measures," *Tulane Environmental Law Journal* 7 (summer 1994): 299–352. See also Steve Charnovitz, "Environmental Trade Sanctions and the GATT: An Analysis of the Pelly Amendment on Foreign Environmental Practices," *American University Journal of International Law and Policy* 9 (spring 1994): 751 (citing Convention Respecting the Prohibition of the Use of White [Yellow] Phosphorus in the Manufacture of Matches, Sept. 26, 1906, 203 Consol. T.S. 12). Charnovitz notes that several countries banned import shortly thereafter: Australia in 1908 (citing Proclamation of 19 Dec. 1908, *Gazette*, 1707); the United States in 1912, White Phosphorus Matches Act, ch. 75, 37 Stat. 81–84 (1912) (repealed in 1976).

22. Steve Charnovitz, "Environmental Trade Sanctions," 751–807, 755.

23. Treaty of Versailles, Covenant of the League of Nations, Part I of the Treaty of Peace signed at Versailles, June 28, 1919. *I Int'l Legis.* 1919–921 1 (1931).

24. Constitution of the International Labour Organization Preamble, 15 U.N.T.S. 40 (1948) <http://www.ilo.org/public/English/about/iloconst.htm#pre>

25. Declaration Concerning the Aims and Purpose of the International Labour Organization, 10 May 1944 <http://www.ilo.org/public/English/about/iloconst.htm#annex>.

26. Article 23 (1), Universal Declaration on Human Rights, U.N.T.S. Res. 217A (III), U.N. Doc. A/810 (1948).

27. International Covenant on Economic, Social, and Cultural Rights, Article 7. Adopted 16 Dec. 1966, G.A. Res. 2200 (XXI), U.N. GAOR, 21st Sess., Supp. No. 16 (1966) 993 U.N.T.S. 3 (entered into force 3 Jan. 1976).

28. ILO Convention, Occupational Safety and Health, No. 155, 1331 U.N.T.S. 280 (adopted 22 June 1981). ILO Conventions are also available on the ILO website: http://www.ilo.org/.

29. Trade Act of 1974, 19 U.S.C. § 2101 et seq. (1994). See also United States-Caribbean Basin Trade Partnership of 1983, 19 U.S.C. §§ 2701- 2707 (1994); Foreign Assistance Act of 1969, 22 U.S.C. §§ 2192–200 (1994) (also providing for the extension of trade benefits based upon recognition of labor standards).

30. North American Agreement on Labor Cooperation ("NAACL"), Sept. 13, 1993, U.S.-Can.-Mex., 32 I.L.M. 1499, annex I.

31. See, e.g. Charter of Fundamental Social Rights (European Union, Dec. 1989); Maestricht Protocol and Agreement on Social Policy, Treaty on European Union, 31 I.L.M. 247 (1992) (done at Maestricht, Feb. 7, 1992); European Social Charter, Oct. 18, 1961, 529 U.N.T.S. Article 3.

32. Most labor issues require a unanimous vote, giving each country a veto, while freedom of association and collective bargaining are excluded from EU consideration. This means that EU members view health and safety as a vital issue in their relations with one another, not something to be left entirely to national sovereignty—in other words, it is viewed as a "core" issue for them as partners, precluding the existence of outlier economies in this area. See 1992 Maestricht Protocol on Social Policy, art. 2.

33. U.N. Charter, art. 55 ("the United Nations shall promote . . . solutions of international . . . health . . . problems"); UDHR, art. 25 (right to a standard of living "adequate for . . . health and well-being"); Universal Declaration of Human Rights, G.A. Res. 217 (III), U.N. GAOR, 3d Sess., at 71, U.N. Doc. A/810 (1948); International Covenant on Economic, Social and Cultural Rights, G.A. Res. 2200, U.N. GAOR, 21st Sess., Supp. No. 16, at 51, U.N. Doc. A/6316 (1966); International Convention on the Elimination of All Forms of Racial Discrimi-

nation, G.A. Res. 2106 A (XX), U.N. GAOR, 23d Sess., 660 U.N.T.S. 195 (1969); Convention on the Elimination of All Forms of Discrimination Against Women, G.A. Res. 34/180, U.N. GAOR, 34th Sess., Supp. No. 46, at 80, U.N. Doc. A/34/46 (1980); Convention on the Rights of the Child, G.A. Res. 25, U.N. GAOR, 44th Sess., Annex, Agenda Item 108, at 12–13, U.N. Doc. A/Res/44/25 (1989).

34. Constitution of the World Health Organization, opened for signature July 22, 1946, 14 U.N.T.S. 185, 186.

35. International Covenant on Economic, Social and Cultural Rights, Article 12.

36. Jonathan M. Mann, "Public Health and Human Rights," *Human Rights* 25 (Fall 1998): 2. For other recent discussions of the right to health, see also Virginia Leary, "The Right to Health in International Human Rights Law," *Health and Human Rights* 1 (1) (1994): 24–56; Steven D. Jamar, "The International Human Right to Health," *Southern University Law Review* 22 (1) (1994): 2–68; Paul Hunt, "The Right to Health: A Way Forward at the International Level," in *Reclaiming Social Rights: International and Comparative Perspectives*, ed. Paul Hunt (Brookfield, Vt.: Dartmouth, 1996), 107–51; Audrey R. Chapman, "Conceptualizing the Right to Health: A Violations Approach," *Tennessee Law Review* 65 (1998): 389–418; Sheetal B. Shah, "Illuminating the Possible in the Developing World: Guaranteeing the Human Right to Health in India," *Vanderbilt Journal of Transnational Law* 32 (1999): 435–93.

37. See, e.g. David L. Parker and Sarah Bachman, "Economic Exploitation and the Health of Children: Towards A Rights-Oriented Public Health Approach," (2001) Unpublished paper (on file with author) (tying together social policy questions concerning child labor and health and safety and noting that a "rights based public health orientation could add four dimensions to an understanding of the issue. First, it ensures that exploitative and abusive work is not only considered a labor market or health problem, but also an issue of human rights. Second, it focuses attention on the legislative and policy framework that exists to promote and ensure the rights of children to protection, and to the exercise of their individual rights. Third, it draws attention to the relationship among individuals, their community and the state. Fourth, it helps to identify potential burdens on the lives of individuals that are created by the presence (or absence) of government programs and policies that address child health and child labor" and noting further "it is the hypothesis of this paper that children's work that is harmful, hazardous and carried out in subhuman working conditions can create, exacerbate, or perpetuate an intergenerational cycle of poverty, malnutrition and social disadvantage.").

38. See Peter Dorman, *Markets and Mortality: Economics, Dangerous Work, and the Value of Human Life* (Cambridge: Cambridge University Press, 1996); Paul J. Leigh, "Compensating Wages, Value of a Statistical Life, and Inter-industry Differentials," *Journal of Environmental Economics and Management* 28 (1) (January 1995): 83–97; Paul J. Leigh, "No Evidence of Compensating Wages for Occupational Fatalities," *Industrial Relations* 30 (3) (fall 1991): 382–95. For a summary of the arguments on both sides of this debate, see John F. Burton, Jr., and James R. Chelius, "Workplace Safety and Health Regulations: Rationale and Results," in *Government Regulation of the Employment Relationship*, ed. Bruce E. Kaufman (Madison, Wis.: Industrial Relations Research Association, 1997), 253–93. See, also Susan Rose-Ackerman, "Progressive Law and Economics—and the New Administrative Law," *Yale Law Journal* 98 (1988): 341–68.

39. This is the classic explanation for any failure of hazard pay to compensate fully for risks. See W. Kip Viscusi, *Risk by Choice: Regulating Health and Safety in the Workplace* (Cambridge: Harvard University Press, 1983) (noting that in some cases information should be supplied to overcome market failure to produce optimal health and safety).

40. See James A. Gross, "The Broken Promises of the National Labor Relations Act and the Occupational Safety and Health Act: Conflicting Values and Conceptions of Rights and Jus-

tice," *Chicago-Kent Law Review* 73 (1998): 374–76. Note that "bargain" is used here in the sense of competitive markets and the behavior at the margin, not in the sense of the striking of an individual bargain.

41. For a discussion of this and related issues, see Rose-Ackerman, "Progressive Law and Economics," 355–56 (where she notes a variety of problems with a purely informational approach).

42. Mark Geistfeld, "Reconciling Cost-Benefit Analysis with the Principle that Safety Matters More than Money," *New York University Law Review* 76 (1) (2001): 114–87, 123 n. 27.

43. See, e.g. Rose-Ackerman, "Progressive Law and Economics," 355–56 ("Even in this simple competitive world, one complication must be introduced immediately. Knowing that they must compensate workers to take risks, employers would like to keep job hazards secret. Therefore, the market will then only work efficiently if potential new employees can observe the riskiness of jobs. One way such information might be provided is through a learning process. The first round of employees are uninformed, but after they are injured, other members of the labor force observe their injuries and illnesses and demand that the company pay a wage premium or reduce workplace hazards. There are many reasons why this learning process will work poorly in the real world. First, many hazards take a long time to produce injuries. Second, even if they happen quickly, participants in a large labor market will not observe many of the injured. Third, the level of hazard depends on workers as well as workplaces. Some workers are more susceptible to hazards because of their genetic characteristics or their life style— for example, whether they smoke. Therefore, it may be difficult for job applicants correctly to infer their own risk by observing the harm suffered by others. Fourth, workplace conditions change with technology—so the past may be a poor guide to the future. For all these reasons, regulations that require employers to inform employees of hazards are easy to justify. The information must, however, be provided in a form that employees can understand and use to compare job market options.")

44. Arthur M. Okun, *Equality and Efficiency: The Big Tradeoff* (Washington D.C.: Brookings Institution, 1975), 20 (comparing the regulation of risk with extending the "logic of the ban on indentured service"). See, also Gross, "The Broken Promises of the National Labor Relations Act," 20–21 ("Minimum-wage laws and work-safety legislation can be viewed most fruitfully as further examples of prohibitions on exchanges born of desperation, extending the logic of the ban on indentured service . . . some economists wonder whether work-safety legislation is warranted by lack of information about on-the-job dangers. As I read the laws, they declare that anyone who takes an absurdly underpaid or extremely risky job must be acting out of desperation. That desperation may result from ignorance, immobility, or genuine lack of alternatives, but it should be kept out of the marketplace. Recognizing that objective still leaves plenty of room for debate about the proper scope of these laws. With these bans, society assumes a commitment to provide jobs that are not excessively risky or woefully underpaid.")

45. For discussions of this principle, see David Weil, "Are Mandated Health and Safety Committees Substitutes or Supplements for Labor Unions?" (1998) working paper, http://papers.ssrn.com/sol3/delivery.cfm/98101512.pdf?abstractid=137397, 8 ("The exercise of right taken at the individual level leads to a 'higher threshold' . . . than the threshold that would prevail if the preferences of all workers were considered. . . . Workplace rights . . . will be underutilized because the collective benefits arising from their action are not factored into the individual decision."); Rose-Ackerman, "Progressive Law and Economics," 356 ("Many actions employers take are 'local public goods.' If dust collectors are installed, they will benefit all employees on a shop floor, and if a harmless chemical is substituted for a toxic, everyone who comes in contact with the material will benefit. However, if the employees are not organized into a union, individual workers may be unwilling to modify their wage demands enough to

make the health and safety investment worthwhile. If employers do not know the value work-ers place on safety, they may be unwilling to experiment with costly changes that may not pay off in lower wage increases or improved productivity. Established employers are especially un-likely to act if money wages are sticky downward and thus cannot be reduced in the face of an acknowledged improvement in working conditions."); Cass R. Sunstein, "Human Behavior and the Law of Work," *Virginia Law Review* 87 (2) (2001): 205–76, 255. ("If safety is a local private good—something that, when provided to some, will also be provided to all—rational individual choices, by workers, are likely to lead to a large number of waivers, and hence a fail-ure to create incentives to increase safety.")

46. Studies showing the extent of wage loss as well as the failure of workers' compensation systems to replace these losses include: Robert T. Reville, "The Impact of a Disabling Work-place Injury on Earnings and Labor Force Participation," in *The Creation and Analysis of Linked Employer-Employee Data, Contributions to Economic Analysis*, ed. J. Lane (New York: Elsevier Science, 1999), 147–73; Robert T. Reville, J. Bhattacharya and L. Sager, "New Methods and Data Sources for Measuring Economic Consequences of Workplace Injuries," *American Jour-nal of Industrial Medicine* 40 (2001): 452–63; Jeff Biddle, Leslie I. Boden, and Robert T. Re-ville, "Permanent Partial Disability from Occupational Injuries: Earnings Losses and Replacement in Three States," in *Ensuring Health and Income Security for An Aging Workforce*, ed. Peter P. Budetti, Richard V. Burkhauser, Janice M. Gregory, and H. Allan Hunt (Kalama-zoo, Mich.: W. E. Upjohn Institute for Employment Research, 2001), 263–90; Leslie I. Bo-den and Monica Galizzi, "Economic Consequences of Workplace Injuries and Illnesses: Lost Earnings and Benefit Adequacy," *American Journal of Industrial Medicine* 36 (5) (1999): 87–503.

Further, recent analyses suggest that the labor market has remarkable rigidity in the exclu-sion of disabled people. During the 1990s, people with disabilities fared poorly in the work force, despite the passage of the Americans with Disabilities Act, a boom economy, rising wages (for all other groups), and low unemployment. Richard V. Burkhauser, Mary Daly, and An-drew J. Houtenville, "How Working-Age People with Disabilities Fared over the 1990s Busi-ness Cycle," in *Ensuring Health and Income Security for An Aging Workforce*, ed. Peter P. Budetti, Richard V. Burkhauser, Janice M. Gregory, H. Allan Hunt (Kalamazoo, Mich.: W. E. Upjohn Institute for Employment Research, 2001), 291–346.

47. The question of whether workers' compensation provides a successful safety incentive is heavily debated in the literature. See John F. Burton, Jr. and James R. Chelius, "Workplace Safety and Health Regulations: Rationale and Results"; Viscusi, *Risk by Choice*; Spieler, "Per-petuating Risk." For a description of the position of the old institutionalists, see Bruce E. Kauf-man, "Labor Markets and Employment Regulation: The View of the 'Old' Institutionalists," in *Government Regulation of Employment*, ed. Bruce E. Kaufman (Madison: Industrial Rela-tions Research Association, 1997), 11–56. Kaufman suggests the following: "When firms can rent labor by the hour or week and the costs of maintenance and training fall upon the worker or community, management's time horizon shortens and the incentives change, particularly when an excess supply of labor is available, whether from cyclical unemployment, immigra-tion, or some other source, the optimal labor policy is to get the maximum work effort from the employee each and every hour and when the employee's health or physical stamina cracks, replace him or her with a new worker." Ibid., 24–25.

48. There has been an explosion of this literature, including a number of symposia in law reviews on this issue. See, e.g., Symposium, Research Conference on Behavioral Law and Eco-nomics in the Workplace, *New York University Law Review* 77(2002): 1–134; Christine Jolls, Cass R. Sunstein, and Richard Thaler, "A Behavioral Approach to Law and Economics," *Stan-ford Law Review* 50 (1998): 1471–550; Russell B. Korobkin and Thomas S. Ulen, "Law and

Behavioral Science: Removing the Rationality Assumption from Law and Economics," *California Law Review* 88 (2000): 1051–120; Symposium, Law Economics and Norms, *University of Pennsylvania Law Review* 144 (1996): 1643–2339; Symposium, The Legal Construction of Norms, *Virginia Law Review* (2000): 1577–2021; Symposium, Social Norms, Social Meaning, and the Economic Analysis of Law, *Journal of Legal Studies* (1998): 537–823; Lynn A. Stout, "Other-Regarding Preferences and Social Norms" 2001 (unpublished paper http://papers. ssrn.com/sol3/delivery.cfm/SSRN_ID265902_code010405520.pdf?abstractid=265902) (noting that the classical theory rests on both an assumption of rationality and an assumption of selfishness; the cab driver who returns a large denomination bill that was proffered in error says, "I have to live with myself"). And finally see Amir N. Licht, "The Pyramid of Social Norms: A New Perspective," 2001 (unpublished paper http://papers.ssrn.com/sol3/delivery. cfm/SSRN_ID264970_code010411510.pdf?abstractid=264970) (bringing us full circle to the conclusion that "values are the core terms of social norms.")

It is interesting to note that these arguments were raised against classical economic theory by the institutionalists. For a very good description of this, see Kaufman, "Labor Markets and Employment Regulation." One is again left feeling that indeed there is nothing new under the sun! For a comparison of the neoclassical "Chicago school" economics approach and the institutionalist approach, see James B. Zimarowski, Michael J. Radzicki, and William A. Wines, "An Institutionalist Perspective on Law and Economics (Chicago Style) in the Context of United States Labor Law," *Arizona Law Review* 35 (1993): 397–442.

49. See Leary, "The Right to Health," 37; Summers, "The Battle in Seattle," 84–85; Cass R. Sunstein, "Switching the Default Rule," University of Chicago Law & Economics, Olin Working Paper No. 114 (2001) http://papers.ssrn.com/sol3/delivery.cfm/SSRN_ ID255993_code010112520.pdf?abstractid=255993 ("There are always winners and losers when market principles are applied.") now published as "Switching the Default Rule," *New York University Law Review* 77 (2002):106–34.

50. For a brief summary of the economics of segmented labor markets, see Glen G. Cain, "Segmented Labor Markets," in *New Palgrave Social Economics*, ed. John Eatwell, Murray Milgate, Peter Newman (New York: W. W. Norton, 1989), 225–30 (noting also the differences in ideological perspectives on the observation that barriers to successful participation in the labor market are not equal across race, ethnic, class, gender, and immigration status lines).

This notion of a floor is not, of course, new. See Okun, *Equality and Efficiency*, 18 ("Basic rights are the morality of the depths. They specify the line beneath which no one is allowed to sink.").

51. A copy of O'Neill's speech is on file with author. This speech caused significant consternation in political circles in Washington, as O'Neill was quite obviously "off message" for the new Bush administration; at almost the same time that this speech was delivered, President Bush signed legislation revoking the just-promulgated OSHA standard governing ergonomics hazards. For an unsympathetic portrait of O'Neill, see William Grieder, "The Man from Alcoa," *The Nation* 273 (3) (2001): 11–14.

52. The issue of commensurability is one that arises in the dispute over whether there is a common metric for measuring success of an option or a decision or a system that can be normatively justified. Purist economists might argue, for example, that monetary exchange units are a universal metric. Thus, measurement of the value of a life in cost-benefit analyses involving regulations are straightforward. On the other hand, others may argue that there are options, choices, values, or things that cannot be appropriately or accurately valued through use of this or any other universal metric. Entire law review symposia have been devoted to this issue. See, e.g., Symposium: Law and Incommensurability, *University of Pennsylvania Law Review* 146 (1998): 1169–731. The problem of incommensurability is often presented as an

objection to economic arguments regarding the normative value of wealth maximization. For the argument that the assertion of incommensurability is made only to assert strategic advantage, see Eric Posner, *Law and Social Norms* (Cambridge: Harvard University Press, 2002), 187 ("Incommensurability claims do not reflect people's interests and values; they conceal them.").

53. This Clinton administration program could be found at U.S. State Department, Promoting the Model Business Principles (visited Jan. 12, 2000) <http://www.state.gov/www/about_ state/business/business_principles.html> [hereinafter Model Business Principles Web Page]. The Clinton administration Model Principles contained the following provisions: "1) Provision of a safe and healthful workplace; 2) Fair employment practices; including avoidance of child and forced labor and avoidance of discrimination based on race, gender, national origin or religious beliefs; and respect for the right of association and the right to organize and bargain collectively; 3) Responsible environmental protection and environmental practices; 4) Compliance with U.S. and local laws promoting good business practices, including laws prohibiting illicit payments and ensuring fair competition; 5) Maintenance, through leadership at all levels, of a corporate culture that respects free expression consistent with legitimate business concerns, and does not condone political coercion in the workplace; that encourages good corporate citizenship and makes a positive contribution to the communities in which the company operates and where ethical conduct is recognized, valued and exemplified by all employees." Perhaps the Bush administration has moved on from these principles. Implementation of the Clinton administration Model Business principles was limited to the Commerce Department's Best Global Practices program. This program included "1) an award to be presented to a U.S. company in recognition of exemplary achievement in meeting the goals of one or more of the Model Business Principles; 2) an electronic clearinghouse of corporate codes of conduct to serve as models for others; and 3) a resource directory of NGOs that may be consulted for additional information on social responsibility and best business practices." Perhaps not surprisingly, critics of these corporate best practices have always argued that the approach was always more rhetorical than real. As of July 25, 2001, this web site reads: "Sorry, you have tried to access a page that is not available."

54. Okun, *Equality and Efficiency*, 17.

55. The safety principle, that "in the context of nonconsensual risk impositions, the safety interests of potential victims deserve greater weight than the ordinary economic interests of potential injurers" is described at length in Geistfeld, "Reconciling Cost-Benefit Analysis." Professor Geistfeld assumes however that the risks of workers are consensual, a conclusion that I would dispute. The purpose of Geistfeld's article is, somewhat paradoxically, to propose a mechanism to quantify the safety principle within cost benefit analysis. Geistfeld provides a lengthy list of other sources that discuss this safety principle at 117, note 6. Those who accept the idea of a basic safety principle vary considerably in their basic ideological views. See, for example Henry Shue, *Basic Rights: Subsistence, Affluence, and U.S. Foreign Policy* (Princeton: Princeton University Press, 1980), 20–22 (basic right to physical security); Robert Nozick, *Anarchy, State, and Utopia* (New York, Basic Books, 1974), 66 (suggesting that some risks cannot successfully be compensated on either an ex ante or ex post basis: "A system that allowed assaults to take place provided the victims were compensated afterwards would lead to apprehensive people, afraid of assault, sudden attack, and harm. . . . under a general system which permits assault provided compensation is paid, a victim's fear is not caused by the particular person who assaulted him. . . . Some things we would fear, even knowing we shall be compensated fully for their happening or being done to us . . . these acts are prohibited and made punishable.").

56. Sunstein, "Human Behavior and the Law of Work," 248; Rose-Ackerman, "Progressive Law and Economics," 359.

57. Gross, "The Broken Promises of the National Labor Relations Act," 377. It is important to note here that I am not arguing for the absolutist position that cost-benefit analyses are never appropriate to determine the appropriateness of regulation or (conversely) that any regulation is appropriate if it will save a single life.

58. For an interesting discussion of default principles in employment, see Sunstein, "Switching the Default Rule." It must be acknowledged that even in those countries that have ratified ILO conventions or have enacted national legislation that might restrict employer discretion, these restrictions are often not enforced. The idea behind assertion of rights within employment is to change expectations regarding treatment, a necessary precursor to effective enforcement of laws. The question of where the default lies, and whether this matters (in terms of the ultimate bargain that is struck) is, of course, a major focus of the interpretation of Coase's theorem. As Richard Posner acknowledges, "If market transactions were costless, the economist would not care where a right was initially vested. The process of voluntary exchange would costlessly reallocate it to whoever valued it the most. But once the unrealistic assumption of zero transaction costs is abandoned, the assignment of rights becomes determinate." Richard Posner, *The Economics of Justice* (Cambridge: Harvard University Press, 1981), 71.

59. Lance Compa, *Unfair Advantage: Workers' Freedom of Association in the United States under International Human Rights* (New York: Human Rights Watch, 2000).

60. Gary Fields, *Trade and Labour Standards: A Review of the Issues* (Paris: Organization for Economic Cooperation and Development, 1995), 13.

61. For example, in responding to the hundreds of deaths from acute silicosis during Union Carbide's construction of the tunnel at Gauley Bridge, West Virginia, the *Fayette Tribune* characterized conditions as "atrocious conditions against humanity." *Fayette Tribune*, May 20, 1931, as quoted in Martin Cherniak, *The Hawks Nest Incident: America's Worst Industrial Disaster* (New Haven: Yale University Press, 1986), 51. Similarly, the *Bangkok Post* responded to a fire in a Bangkok toy factory in which almost two hundred workers died: "No aspect of our economy should be based on a disregard for human life." As quoted in Sutin Wannbovorn (Reuters), "Guards: Thai Fire Victims Were Locked In," *Chicago Tribune*, May 12, 1993, 6.

62. Sunstein, "Human Behavior and the Law of Work," 248; Rose-Ackerman, "Progressive Law and Economics," 359 ("risks that most people would not plausibly pay to accept"). According to Sunstein, the "nonwaivable minima" would be supplemented by more protective "benchmark standards" to which workers would have a "presumptive right," a right they could waive for additional compensation. The nonwaivable minima must therefore be adequate, since there is a danger that workers might "waive their rights for too little."

63. Sunstein, "Human Behavior and the Law of Work," 248.

64. "Safety is obviously a highly relative attribute that can change from time to time and be judged differently in different contexts. Knowledge of risks evolves, and so do our personal social standards of acceptability." William W. Lowrance, *Of Acceptable Risk: Science and the a-Determination of Safety* (Los Altos, Calif.: W. Kaufmann, 1976), 8–9.

65. A similar standard is proposed by David Rosner for criminal prosecutions of workplace deaths. See David Rosner, "When Does A Worker's Death Become Murder?" *American Journal of Public Health* 90 (2000): 535–40, 536.

66. See, e.g., W.Va. Code §23-4-2(b) (employee may both sue in tort and collect workers' compensation benefits if the injury or death results "from the deliberate intention of his or her employer to produce such injury or death").

67. Examples of this kind of behavior are described in Anita Chan, "Labor Standards and Human Rights: The Case of Chinese Workers Under Market Socialism," *Human Rights Quarterly* 20 (1998): 886–904; Anita Chan, *China's Workers Under Assault: Exploitation and Abuse in a Globalizing Economy* (Armonk: M. E. Sharpe, 2001).

68. See, e.g., *Beauchamp v. Dow Chem Co.*, 398 N.W.2d 882 (Mich. 1986) (civil liability if employer knew that the injury was substantially certain to occur and intended the act which caused the injury); *Woodson v. Rowland,* 407 S.E.2d 222 (N.C. 1991) (substantial certainty test adopted); *VerBouwens v. Hamm Wood Prods.*, 334 N.W.2d 874 (S.D.1983) (same); *Suarez v. Dickmont Plastics Corp.*, 639 A.2d 507 (Conn. 1994) (same); *Bazley v. Tortorich,* 397 So.2d 475 (La.1981) (rejecting specific claim but establishing "substantial certainty" test of intention). The West Virginia court adopted a somewhat more liberal "reckless and wanton misconduct" standard. *Mandolidis v. Elkins Indus.*, 248 S.E.2d 907 (W.Va. 1978) (holding that reckless and wanton misconduct may result in civil liability). In Oregon, the court adopted the view that proof of deliberate intent to injure should focus on the question of whether the employer had an opportunity consciously to weigh the consequences of its act and knew that someone, not necessarily the plaintiff specifically, would be injured. *Lusk v. Monaco Motor Homes, Inc.*, 97 Or. App. 182, 775 P.2d 891 (1989) (despite repeated complaints from workers about exposure to toxic paints, employer refused to supply respirators); *Gulden v. Crown Zellerbach Corp.*, 890 F.2d 195 (9th Cir.1989) (workers ordered to scrub floors awash in PCBs at concentrations over 500 times the safe limit on their hands and knees over five-day period). In addition, in some states (e.g., New Jersey, California, Pennsylvania) a worker may claim that an injury was actually the result of intentional aggravation or reinjury by the employer; for example, when employers provide medical examinations (such as x-rays), conceal the discovery of injury, and the worker's health worsens as a result of continued occupational exposures, the employer may not be protected by workers' compensation immunity for this fraudulent concealment of medical information. See, e.g. *Millison v. E.I. duPont de Nemours & Co.*, 501 A.2d 505 (N.J. 1985); *Johns-Manville Produces Co. v. Contra Costa Superior Court* (Rudkin), 27 Cal. 3d 465, 165 Cal. Rptr. 858, 612 P.2d 948 (1980); *Martin v. Lancaster Battery Company, Inc.*, 606 A.2d 444 (Pa. 1992). In some states, this issue has become a battleground between the courts and the legislatures, as the legislatures responded to pressure to maintain immunity for employers and courts responded to arguments based on individualized justice. See, e.g., W.Va. Code § 23-4-2(c) and *Mayles v. Shoneys*, 405 S.E.2d 15 (W.Va. 1991).

69. News reports of this fire included the following information: the fire was the fourth to occur; the buildings were clearly substandard and lacked fire alarms or sprinklers; the company had ignored warnings to improve safety precautions. See Mary Kay Magistad, "Hundreds Die in Thai Factory Fire," *Washington Post*, May 12, 1993: A25; Michael Haddigan, "Safety Measures Haven't Kept Up with Thai Economic Growth," Associated Press, May 12, 1993, 1993 WL 4540402; Janet L. Fix, "Burned Thai Toy Factory Has Supplied U.S. firms," *U.S.A. Today*, May 13, 1993: 01A. One report included the following: "'It's not our fault,' a female guard told Reuters.' . . . The company told us to lock the doors so people would not sneak out or steal.'" Wannbovorn, "Guards: Thai Fire Victims Were Locked In," 6. According to the *Asian Wall Street Journal,* the three exits were locked to prevent pilfering. "Toy Factory Fire Shows Laxness of Safety Rules" (no byline), *Asian Wall Street Journal*, May 13, 1993: 1.

70. See Rosner, "When Does A Worker's Death Become Murder?" 537 (noting that the exit doors were locked from the outside); Berman, *Death on the Job*, 9.

71. See, e.g., *Mandolidis v. Elkins Indus.*, 248 S.E.2d 907 (W.Va. 1978) (employer deliberately removed guard that had been included by manufacturer, replaced it temporarily after an employee was injured and an OSHA inspection, and then removed it again, resulting in serious injury to worker).

72. See, e.g., *People v. O'Neil*, 194 Ill.App.3d 79, 550 N.E.2d 1090 (Ill. App. 1 Dist. 1990). The reported case involves criminal homicide charges brought against the owner of Film Recovery Systems. Film Recovery engaged in the business of extracting, for resale, silver from used x-ray and photographic film. The recovery process involved "chipping" the film product and

soaking the granulated pieces in large open bubbling vats containing a solution of water and sodium cyanide. The cyanide solution caused silver contained in the film to be released. A worker died as a result of the exposure. The indictment stated the individual defendants failed to disclose to the employee that he was working with substances containing cyanide and failed to advise him about, train him to anticipate, and provide adequate equipment to protect him. According to BNA reports, "the company's three dozen to four dozen employees, many undocumented and many Mexican workers who spoke no English, worked in unventilated conditions over the vats of cyanide solution. 'Almost daily, for at least 15 months prior to the accident, these workers complained of headaches, feeling sick, and vomiting,' Hovey said, noting that these are classic symptoms of cyanide poisoning. 'They were told to go out and get some fresh air, and if they didn't like it they could work elsewhere.' " "Guilty Pleas Entered by Former Executives in Murder Case Involving Occupational Death," (no author), *BNA Daily Labor Report*, September 16, 1993: D15.

See also *People v. Pymm*, 563 N.E.2d 1 (N.Y., 1990). According to the court's summary, mercury contamination had been an ongoing problem at Pymm Thermometer Company (PTC), posing a serious health risk to PTC's employees. Mercury vapor is highly toxic and long-term exposure to low concentrations of mercury can result in permanent neurological damage. A number of inspections dating back to the early 1970s revealed that workers at PTC's second floor manufacturing facility were not adequately protected from the dangers of mercury poisoning. OSHA conducted four inspections of the facility between 1981 and 1984. These inspections revealed hazardous working conditions in the second floor manufacturing area. Workers did not wear protective gear, such as gloves or respirators, and the workplace was dangerously contaminated with mercury. Both William and Edward Pymm, the owners, were warned of the dangers of mercury poisoning and were encouraged to adopt measures that would minimize the possibility of workers either ingesting liquid mercury or inhaling mercury vapors. PTC was twice cited by OSHA as a result of the workplace conditions observed on the second floor. In 1985, OSHA learned that PTC was operating a clandestine mercury reclamation operation in the basement of the building. The defendants had omitted the basement area from any of the earlier inspections, despite the fact that OSHA inspectors had asked to see all of the area in which mercury was being used. 563 N.E.2d at 2–3. Although seriously injured, the workers could not sue their employer in tort; New York is not one of the states with a liberalized rule regarding employer liability for intentional torts. See *Briggs v. Pymm Thermometer Corp.*, 147 A.D.2d 433, 537 N.Y.S.2d 553 (N.Y.A.D. 2 Dept., 1989) See also *People v. Chicago Magnet Wire Corp.*, 126 Ill.2d 356, 534 N.E.2d 962 (Ill., 1989 (largely Hispanic workforce was exposed to toxic chemicals without any protective gear, leading to both criminal charges and civil litigation.)

73. As occurred in the building of the Hawks Nest tunnel in West Virginia. For an account of this tragedy in which an epidemiologist estimates that about seven hundred workers (mostly itinerant and poor, many African American) died of acute silicosis in 1931, see Cherniak, *The Hawk's Nest Incident*. Again, the issue of malfeasance is key to the story: "For a long time . . . the events at Gauley Bridge were trapped locally and dissipated. Significant though racial indifference was in accounting for the press's failure to report on the plight of the tunnel workers, a story published on 20 May 1931 in the *Fayette Tribune* suggested that there were other causes: 'Rumors and reports of various conditions known to exist at the tunnel and dam project are discussed generally by residents but little first hand information is obtainable because of the 'gag rule' enforced by executives of the contracting company which employs about 1200 men. Officers of the law state that company officials refuse to converse with them and laborers do so with the fear of losing their jobs. The Tribune has been appealed to on more than one occasion to lay bare these atrocious conditions against humanity, but facts obtainable have not

been provable.'" Cherniak, *The Hawk's Nest Incident*, 51. For a fictional account of this tragedy, see Hubert Skidmore, *Hawks Nest* (New York: Doubleday Doran, 1941).

74. 29 U.S.C.A. §666.

75. Although intentional or wanton violations of OSHA do not necessarily mean that the injured employee has a tort claim against an employer, since immunity from tort is determined under state law. *Hatcher v. Bullard Co.*, 493 A.2d 908 (Conn. App. 1985).

76. See, e.g., *Danco Const. Co. v. Occupational Safety and Health Review Comm'n*, 586 F.2d 1243 (8th Cir. 1978) (employer could not avoid serious violation by hiding behind its lack of knowledge concerning dangerous working practices.)

77. Mark Rothstein, *Occupational Safety and Health Law*, 4th ed. (St. Paul, Minn.: West Group, 1998), 370, citing *Bethlehem Steel Corp. v. OSHRC*, 540 F.2d 157 (3d Cir. 1976) (state of mind required for a repeated violation is similar to that required for a willful violation).

78. See Mark Rothstein, *Occupational Safety and Health Law*, 366–71. See, also, e.g., *Potlatch Corp.*, 7 OSHC 1061 (1979); *Bunge Corp. v. Secretary of Labor*, 638 F.2d 831 (5th Cir. 1981 (agreeing with OSHRC with regard to elements of repeated violation); *Dun-Par Engineered Form Co. v. Marshall*, 676 F.2d 1333 (10th Cir. 1982) (same).

79. Rothstein, *Occupational Safety and Health Law*, 372.

80. *Frank Irey, Jr., Inc. v. OSHRC*, 519 F.2d 1200, 1207 (3d Cir. 1974), vacated by *Frank Irey, Jr., Inc. v. Occupational Safety and Health Review Com'n*, 2 O.S.H. Cas. (BNA) 1445 (3rd Cir. Dec. 20, 1974), affirmed on other grounds 430 U.S. 442 (1977).

81. See, e.g. *Intercounty Construction Co. v. OSHRC*, 522 F.2d 777 (4th Cir. 1975), cert. den. 423 U.S. 1072 (1976) (no showing of malicious intent is necessary). This decision has been followed by the federal courts of appeals in the First, Second, Fifth, Sixth, Eighth, Ninth and Tenth circuits. See Rothstein, *Occupational Safety and Health Law*, 373–74.

82. See, e.g. *People v. Pymm*, 561 N.Y.S.2d 687 (N.Y., 1990).

83. Rosner, "When Does A Worker's Death Become Murder?" 536.

84. Quoted in Wannbovorn, "Guards: Thai Fire Victims Were Locked In," 6.

85. See, for example, Article 11 of the American Declaration of the Rights and Duties of Man: "Every person has the right to the preservation of his health through sanitary and social measures relating to food, clothing, housing, and medical care, *to the extent permitted by public and community resources.*" (emphasis added) Approved by the Ninth International Conference of American States, Resolution 30, Bogota, 1948. Pan-American Union, Final Act of the Ninth Conference of American States 38–45 (Washington D.C. 1948).

86. Leary, "The Right to Health," 46 (citing the Limburg Principles).

87. Compa, "Promise and Perils," 8.

88. 29 U.S.C. §§ 651–78.

89. 30 U.S.C. §801 et seq. MSHA provides more stringent protection for miners than is provided by OSHA but is largely unaddressed in the general health and safety literature. For example, the Mine Safety and Health Administration must inspect mines at least quarterly; miners have stronger procedures to fight retaliation; and so on. There is unfortunately not space here to explore these differences or the various reasons for the differences.

90. 29 U.S.C. §651(b).

91. 29 U.S.C. §665(b)(5).

92. Health and safety standards are codified at 29 C.F.R Part 1910; 29 C.F.R. Part 1904 sets out recording and reporting requirements; 29 C.F.R. Part 1903 covers inspections, citations, and penalties. For a full description of the regulatory scheme and existing regulations, see one of the many treatises on occupational safety and health, e.g. Rothstein, *Occupational Safety and Health Law*, 4th ed. (St. Paul Minn.: West, 1998).

93. 29 U.S.C. § 652(8) and 29 U.S.C. § 654(a).

94. 29 U.S.C. §§ 657–59, 662.

95. 29 U.S.C. §666 provides for the following civil fines and criminal penalties: for willful and repeated violations not less than $5,000 and no more than $70,000; for serious violations up to $7,000; for failure to correct a hazard as required by a citation, up to $7,000 per day; for a violation causing death not more than $10,000 or imprisonment for not more than six months or both; for a second such violation: not more than $20,000 and no more than one year imprisonment; for giving advance notice of an inspection, a fine of not more than $1,000 or by imprisonment for not more than six months; for giving false statements in OSHA proceedings, not more than $10,000, or imprisonment for not more than six months, or by both; for violation of the posting requirements up, to $7,000 for each violation. The statute defines a serious violation as follows: "For purposes of this section, a serious violation shall be deemed to exist in a place of employment if there is a substantial probability that death or serious physical harm could result from a condition which exists, or from one or more practices, means, methods, operations, or processes which have been adopted or are in use, in such place of employment unless the employer did not, and could not with the exercise of reasonable diligence, know of the presence of the violation." 29 U.S.C.A. §666(k).

96. 29 U.S.C. §655(b).

97. 29 U.S.C. §669(a).

98. 29 U.S.C. §657(f)(1).

99. 29 U.S.C. §657(e).

100. 29 U.S.C. §658(b).

101. 29 U.S.C. §659(c).

102. 29 U.S.C. §657(c); 29 C.F.R. 1904.7(b)(1).

103. 29 C.F.R. §1910.1200.

104. 29 C.F.R. §1910.20.

105. 29 U.S.C. §660(c).

106. 29 C.F.R. §1977.9(c) and 29 C.F.R. §1977.12(a)(2).

107. 29 U.S.C.A. §§151 et seq.

108. 42 U.S.C.A. §§ 12101–213.

109. *Gulf Power Co. and Local Unions 1055 and 624, International Brotherhood of Electrical Workers,* 159 NLRB No. 122, 62 L.R.R.M. (BNA) 1557 (N.L.R.B., 1966) (establishing health and safety as a mandatory subject of bargaining).

110. *Plough, Inc. and International Chemical Workers Union Local No. 194,* 262 NLRB No. 141, 111 L.R.R.M. (BNA) (1982).

111. *Oil, Chemical and Atomic Workers Local Union No. 6–418 v. N.L.R.B.,* 711 F.2d 348 (D.C. Cir 1983) (union access to information regarding health and safety with exception of trade secrets and confidential medical information).

112. *Winona Industries and International Chemical Workers Union,* 257 NLRB No. 101, 107 L.R.R.M. (BNA) 1605 (1981) and *NLRB v. American National Can Co.,* 924 F.2d 518 (4th Cir. 1991) (access to firm for union's safety professionals).

113. *NLRB v. Washington Aluminum Co.* 370 U.S. 9 (1962) (concerted activity for health and safety reasons constitutes protected concerted activity for nonunionized employees).

114. *NLRB v. City Disposal Systems Inc,* 465 U.S. 888 (1984) (upholding the Interboro doctrine which established the concept of constructive concerted activity under sections 7 and 8(a)(1) of the NLRA for workers under collective bargaining agreements); *NLRB v. Washington Aluminum Co.* 370 U.S. 9 (1962) (withholding of work for health and safety reasons constitutes protected concerted activity for nonunionized employees); *Gateway Coal Co. v. U.M.W.A.,* 414 U.S. 368 (1974) (interpreting NLRA §502 during the term of a collective bargaining agreement to protect workers who confront imminently and abnormally dangerous conditions).

115. Frank Elkouri and Edna A. Elkouri, *How Arbitration Works,* 5th ed. (Washington

D.C.: Volz, Marlin M., and Goggin, 1997), 969–95 (suggesting that workers are protected from discipline in health and safety disputes); James A. Gross and Patricia A. Greenfield, "Arbitral Value Judgments in Health and Safety Disputes: Management Rights Over Workers' Rights," *Buffalo Law Review* 34 (1985): 645–91 (empirically demonstrating that this is a difficult burden for workers to meet).

116. For a review of the law in this area, see Spieler, "Perpetuating Risk?" 223–25.

117. See Burton and Chelius, "Workplace Safety and Health Regulations"; Viscusi, *Risk by Choice.* But see Spieler, "Perpetuating Risk?"; Martha T. McCluskey, "The Illusion of Efficiency in Workers' Compensation 'Reform,'" *Rutgers Law Review* 50 (1998): 657–870.

118. The specific interpretations of the ADA are too complex to summarize in this chapter. Title I of the A.D.A. governs employment, 42 U.S.C. §§ 12111–117. Regulations under Title I are at 29 C.F.R. pt. 1630 (2000). The Appendix to these regulations, 29 C.F.R. pt. 1630 app. A, provides interpretative guidance to the regulations, as does EEOC, A Technical Assistance Manual (TAM) on the Employment Provisions (Title I) of the Americans with Disabilities Act (1992), which can be found BNA *Fair Employment Practice Manual* 405:6981–7064. In addition, the EEOC has issued a number of guidances or policy statements that provide the EEOC's interpretation of specific, usually troubling, issues under ADA Title I that are relevant to workers with disability injuries: EEOC Enforcement Guidance on Disability-Related Inquiries and Medical Examinations of Employees Under the Americans with Disabilities Act (ADA) (July 26, 2000); Enforcement Guidance: Reasonable Accommodation and Undue Hardship Under the Americans with Disabilities Act (Mar. 1, 1999); EEOC Enforcement Guidance on Enforcement Guidance on Non-Waivable Employee Rights under Equal Employment Opportunity Commission (EEOC) Enforced Statutes (Apr. 11, 1997); EEOC Enforcement Guidance on the Americans with Disabilities Act and Psychiatric Disabilities (Mar. 25, 1997); EEOC Enforcement Guidance on the Effect of Representations Made in Applications for Benefits on the Determination of Whether a Person Is a "Qualified Individual with a Disability" Under the Americans with Disabilities Act of 1990 (ADA) (Feb. 12, 1997); Letter to National Labor Relations Board stating the Commission's position that, under limited specified circumstances, Title I of the ADA permits an employer to give a union medical information about an applicant or employee (Nov. 1, 1996); EEOC Enforcement Guidance: Workers' Compensation and the ADA (Sept. 3, 1996); ADA Enforcement Guidance: Preemployment Disability-Related Questions and Medical Examinations (Oct. 10, 1995); Enforcement Guidance: Questions and Answers About Disability and Service Retirement Plans Under the ADA (May 11, 1995); Interim Enforcement Guidance on the Application of the Americans with Disabilities Act of 1990 to Disability-based Distinctions in Employer Provided Health Insurance (June 8, 1993). All interpretive guidances can be found on the EEOC web site, <http://www.eeoc.gov>, as well as in the BNA Fair Employment Practices Manual.

119. Lawrence R. Mishel, Jared Bernstein, and John Schmitt, *The State of Working America, 2000/2001* (Ithaca: ILR/Cornell University Press, 2001).

120. Hugh Conway and Jens Svenson, "Occupational Injury and Illness Rates, 1992–96: Why They Fell," *Monthly Labor Review,* 121(11) (Nov. 1998): 36–58; Alan B. Kruger, "Fewer Workplace Injuries and Illnesses Adding to Economic Strength," *New York Times,* September 14, 2000: C2; Jay Causey, "Declining Workplace Injuries? Causes and Effects—A New Debate," *The National Workplace Injury Litigator,* 6 (5) (2000): 1.

121. Leslie I. Boden and John W. Ruser, "Choice of Medical Care Provider, Workers' Compensation 'Reforms,' and Workplace Injuries," unpublished paper (on file with author), showing that nonreporting under OSHA requirements increases when states tighten compensability standards for workers' compensation.

122. Kruger, "Fewer Workplace Injuries and Illnesses," C2.

123. Daniel Mont, John F. Burton Jr., Virginia Reno, and Cecili Thompson, *Workers' Compensation: Benefits, Coverage, and Costs, 1999 New Estimates, 1996–1998 Revisions* (Washington D.C.: National Academy of Social Insurance, 2001), http://www.nasi.org/publications2763/publications_show.htm?doc_id=56475&name=Workers%27%20Compensation.

124. Sidney A. Shapiro and Randy Rabinowitz, "Voluntary Regulatory Compliance in Theory and Practice: The Case of OSHA," *Administrative Law Review* 52 (2000): 97–155, 99.

125. It is difficult to document anecdotes in a manner that is an adequate counterweight to data. But the anecdotes are nevertheless troubling and persuasive. For some of the stories, see Dorothy Nelkin and Michael S. Brown, *Workers at Risk: Voices from the Workplace* (Chicago: University of Chicago Press, 1984); Joseph A. Page and Mary-Win O'Brien, *Bitter Wages* (New York: Grossman Publishers, 1973); Berman, *Death on the Job*. An empirical study of injured workers gives some of the flavor of workers' frustrations: Monica Galizzi, Leslie I. Boden, and T. Liu, *The Workers' Story: Results of a Survey of Workers Injured in Wisconsin* (Cambridge: Workers Compensation Research Institute, 1998). Muckraking stories about health and safety abuses have also appeared in the popular progressive press. See, for example Eric Schlosser, "The Chain Never Stops: Workplace Injuries in Slaughterhouses," *Mother Jones* 26 (4) (2001): 38.

126. Quoted in "Official Accuses Workers in Doomed Plant of Theft," *Orlando Sentinel Tribune*, Nov. 22, 1992, A10. For a more complete description of these events, see Spieler, "Perpetuating Risk?" 227–29 note 429. See, also Peter T. Kilborn, "In Aftermath of Deadly Fire, A Poor Town Struggles Back," *New York Times*, Nov. 25, 1991, A1; Jon Jefferson, "Dying for Work," *American Bar Association Journal* (Jan. 1993): 46. North Carolina's Retaliatory Employment Discrimination Act (REDA) N.C. Gen. Stat. § 95–240 et seq. was passed in reaction to these events. *Commissioner of Labor of North Carolina v. House of Raeford Farms, Inc.*, 477 S.E.2d 230, 234 (N.C. App., 1996).

127. See Spieler, "Perpetuating Risk?" 201–5 for a more complete description of the workings of the residual insurance market in workers' compensation.

128. U.S. General Accounting Office, *Prevalence of Sweatshops*, GAO/HEHS-95-29, November 2, 1994. See also Commission for Labor Cooperation, North American Agreement on Labor Cooperation, "*Standard" and "Advanced" Practices in the North American Garment Industry* (Secretariat of the Commission for Labor Cooperation, 2000) (noting the importance of protection for people working in the garment trades in North America).

129. Recent studies by Pauline Kim suggest that workers tend to overestimate their level of protection from discharge. Pauline T. Kim, "Bargaining with Imperfect Information: A Study of Worker Perceptions of Legal Protection in an At-Will World," *Cornell Law Review* 83 (1997): 105–60; Pauline T. Kim, "Learning and Law: Exploring the Influences on Workers' Legal Knowledge," *University of Illinois Law Review* 1999: 447–515. These findings do not really contradict the consistent anecdotes in which workers say they are unwilling to raise health and safety concerns because of concerns about possible retaliation; Kim does not ask whether the respondents would be concerned about job security, only whether they believe that retaliation would be illegal. She asks these questions of workers who are not currently employed. Further study is needed to determine the extent to which workers believe that the theoretical legal rights they identify in Kim's studies are sufficiently dependable to act upon when it comes to raising complaints, including safety complaints, at work.

130. For a recent expose on the health and safety problems in the meatpacking industry, see Schlosser, "The Chain Never Stops."

131. For a full discussion of the prevalence and cost of ergonomic injuries, see the Preamble to the Ergonomics Program Standard, 65 Federal Register 68262, Nov. 14, 2000.

132. See Congressional Review of Agency Rulemaking Act, 5 U.S.C.A. §§ 801–8. The fi-

nal ergonomics standard, published on November 14, 2000, was formally revoked by the agency on April 23, 2001, with the following notice: "Under the Congressional Review Act, Congress has passed, and the President has signed, Public Law 107–5, a resolution of disapproval of OSHA's final Ergonomics Program Standard. OSHA published the ergonomics program standard on November 14, 2000 (65 FR 68262), and the standard became effective on January 16, 2001. Because Public Law 107–5 invalidates the standard, OSHA is hereby removing it from the Code of Federal Regulations." 66 FR 20403–401, April 23, 2001.

133. *Toyota Motor Manufacturing, Kentucky, Inc., v. Williams*, 534 U.S. 184 (2002).

134. *Fingers to the Bone: United States Failure to Protect Child Farmworkers* (Washington D.C.: Human Rights Watch Report, June 2000) (the agricultural industry has 3 percent of work force, 13 percent of fatalities, 1000 deaths and 313,000 cases of occupational illnesses annually).

135. Mont, *Workers' Compensation: Benefits, Coverage, and Costs.*

136. Many of these have been described elsewhere. For discussions of the NLRA, see, e.g., Compa, *Unfair Advantage* and James A. Gross, "A Human Rights Perspective on United States Labor Relations Law: A Violation of the Right of Freedom of Association," *Employee Rights and Employment Policy Journal* 3 (1999): 65–103. For discussions of OSHA, see McGarity, *Workers at Risk*; Sidney A. Shapiro, "Occupational Safety and Health: Policy Options and Political Reality," *Houston Law Review* 31 (1994): 13–42; Clyde Summers, "Effective Remedies for Employment Rights: Preliminary Guidelines and Proposals," *University of Pennsylvania Law Review* 141 (1992): 457–546; Gross, "The Broken Promises of the National Labor Relations Act."

137. See *Schweiss v. Chrysler Motors Corp.*, 922 F.2d 473 (8th Cir. 1990) (OSHA's remedial scheme does not preempt Schweiss's state law wrongful discharge action.); *Flenker v. Willamette Industries*, Inc., 967 P.2d 295 (Kan. 1998); *Kulch v. Structural Fibers, Inc.*, 677 N.E.2d 308 (Ohio 1997) ("An at-will employee who is discharged or disciplined for filing a complaint with the Occupational Safety and Health Administration concerning matters of health and safety in the workplace is entitled to maintain a common-law tort action against the employer for wrongful discharge/discipline in violation of public policy" (syl.pt.1), recon. den. 680 N.E.2d 158, stay den. 685 N.E.2d 778, cert. den. 522 U.S. 1008 (1997); *Fragassi v. Neiburger*, 646 N.E.2d 315 (Ill. Ap. Ct. 1995). Decisions rejecting state common law discharge remedies for §11(c)-type violations include *Burnham v. Karl and Gelb, P.C.*, 745 A.2d 178 (Conn., 2000) ("the existence of this statutory remedy [for retaliatory discharge] precludes the plaintiff from bringing a common-law wrongful discharge action based on an alleged violation of [the OSHA whistle blower statute." Ibid., at 162); *McLaughlin v. Gastrointestinal Specialists, Inc.*, 750 A.2d 283 (Pa. 2000); *Grant v. Butler*, 590 So.2 254 (Ala. 1991); *Washington v. Union Carbide Corp.*, 870 F.2d 957 (4th Cir. 1989).

138. Summers, "Effective Remedies for Employment Rights," 467–68 ("because of litigation costs, all but middle and upper income employees are largely foreclosed from any access to a remedy for wrongful dismissal. This is apparent from the reported cases. Relatively few plaintiffs are hourly wage or clerical workers; the large majority are professional employees or are in middle and upper management. Middle income employees with contract claims or modest tort claims who cannot make a substantial payment in advance will be discouraged by lawyers from pursuing their claims. Lower income employees without substantial tort claims will have difficulty finding a lawyer.").

139. Notably, protections in the coal industry under the Mine Safety and Health Act and the United Mine Workers of America and Bituminous Coal Operators Agreement are better than the protections of most workers in general industry.

140. Shapiro and Rabinowitz, "Voluntary Regulatory Compliance in Theory and Practice,"

98 (citing Sidney A. Shapiro, "Substantive Reform, Judicial Review, and Agency Resources: OSHA As a Case Study," *Administrative Law Review* 49 (1997): 645).

141. Reported in "Work is Changing But Observers Wonder if OSHA is Changing With It," *Occupational Safety and Health Reporter* (BNA) (May 19, 1999): 1513, 1537.

142. Weil, "Are Mandated Health and Safety Committees Substitutes or Supplements for Labor Unions?" 4.

143. Shapiro and Rabinowitz, "Voluntary Regulatory Compliance in Theory and Practice," 98 (citing Thomas O. McGarity, "Some Thoughts on Deossifying The Rulemaking Process," *Duke Law Journal* (1992): 1385).

144. 29 U.S.C. §655(b)(5), requires that the secretary, when promulgating a standard dealing with toxic materials or harmful physical agents, "set the standard which most adequately assures, to the extent feasible, on the basis of the best available evidence, that no employee will suffer material impairment of health or functional capacity even if such employee has regular exposure to the hazard dealt with by such standard for the period of his working life." In *Industrial Union Department, AFL-CIO v. American Petroleum Institute* (The Benzene Case), 448 U.S. 607 (1980) a plurality held that in order to issue a health standard under Section 6(b)(5) the secretary must first determine that it is "reasonably necessary and appropriate to remedy a significant risk of material health impairment" 448 U.S. at 653. The secretary need not, however, conduct a cost-benefit analysis, but is instead directed to issue the standard that most adequately assures that no employee will suffer material impairment of health, limited only by the extent to which this is feasible, that is, "capable of being done." *American Textile Mfrs. Institute, Inc. v. Donovan*, 452 U.S. 490 (1980).

145. David Weil, "Enforcing OSHA: The Role of Labor Unions," *Industrial Relations* 30 (1) (1991): 20–36 (noting that unionized workplaces are more likely to receive safety and health inspections and concluding that implementation of OSHA seems highly dependent upon the presence of a union in the workplace).

146. Compa, *Unfair Advantage*.

147. See Spieler, "Perpetuating Risk," 189–201 (discussing the structure of workers' compensation insurance premium rates and issues of safety incentives).

148. As a share of wages paid to employees covered by workers' compensation, benefits declined by 38 percent between their peak in 1992 and 1999, from 1.69 to 1.05 percent of wages, while employer costs declined by 41 percent from their highest point in 1993 to 1999, or from 2.17 to 1.29 percent of wages. National Academy of Social Insurance, "Workers' Compensation Benefits Decline as a Percent of Wages for Seven Years in a Row," Press Release, May 22, 2001, http://www.nasi.org/publications2763/publications_show.htm?doc_id=57955; Mont, "Workers' Compensation: Benefits, Coverage, and Costs." As noted previously, a minority of states has expanded tort liability to second-order malfeasance. Other states have resisted.

149. See, e.g. Jeff Biddle, Karen Roberts, D. D. Rosenman, and Edward M. Welch, "What Percentage of Workers with Work-related Illnesses Receive Workers Compensation Benefits?" *Journal of Occupational and Environmental Medicine* 40 (4) (1998): 325–31; Tim Morse, Charles Dillon, and Nicolas Warren, "Reporting of Work-Related Musculoskeletal Disorder (MSD) to Workers' Compensation," 10 (3) (2000) *New Solutions*: 281–92; Tim Morse, "Economic and Social Consequences of Work-related Musculoskeletal Disorders"; Glenn Pransky, T. Snyder, Allard Dembe, and Jay Himmelstein, "Under-reporting of Work-related Disorders in the Workplace: A Case Study and Review of the Literature," *Ergonomics* 42 (1) (1999): 171–82.

150. For an analysis of this phenomenon, see Ruth Colker, "The Americans with Disabilities Act: A Windfall for Defendants," *Harvard Civil Rights-Civil Liberties Law Review* 34 (winter 1999): 99–162. See also "Symposium: Backlash Against the ADA: Interdisciplinary

Perspectives and Implications for Social Justice Strategies," *Berkeley Journal of Employment and Labor Law* 21 (2000): 1–520. For a review of the intersections between the ADA, OSHA, and workers' compensation, see Emily A. Spieler, "The Americans with Disabilities Act," in *Occupational Safety and Health Law*, ed. Randy Rabinowitz (Washington D.C.: Bureau of National Affairs, 2002).

5. A Pragmatic Assessment from the Employers' Perspective

1. See, e.g., Article 23(4) of the Declaration of Human Rights (1948) ("everyone has the right to form trade unions for the protection of his interests").

2. Even at the beginning of the last century (1900), taking conditions of employment out of competition was not a new idea. Two industrialists, Robert Owens of Wales and Daniel Legrand of France, advocated the idea in the early 1800s. Charles Hindley, a member of the British Parliament, proposed the first international treaty on labor legislation in 1833. In 1890, Otto von Bismarck convened a congress in Berlin for the purpose of establishing an international labor parliament to legislate multilateral labor conventions. The effort failed. But the concern that differing labor conditions could create a competitive advantage for one country's goods and services over those of another was one of the principal reasons leading to the formation of the International Labour Organization (ILO) in 1919 as part of the resolution of World War I in the Treaty of Versailles.

3. World Trade Organization Ministerial Conference Declaration at ¶ 4 (Dec. 1996).

4. International Labor Conference, Global Report, *Stopping Forced Labour*, Report 1 (B), 89th Sess. 13 (2001) ("The ILO Declaration is about principles and rights, not specific provisions of Conventions").

5. American Law Institute, "Restatement of the Law Third," *The Foreign Relations Law of the United States*, § 701, Comment, Vol. 2, 152 (New York: American Law Institute, 1986).

6. The American Law Institute, "Restatement of the Law," *The Foreign Relations Law of the United States*, § 701 (1986) includes the first three but not the fourth basis. This omission is undoubtedly because prior to 1986 there were no trade agreements that included or referenced workplace human rights.

7. Ibid. at § 702, note n.

8. Ibid. at §702(g).

9. Ibid. at § 702, note m.

10. Ibid. at § 701, Reporters' Note 1; §702.

11. See *Rodriguez-Fernandez v. Wilkenson*, 654F.2d 1382 (10th Cir. 1981) affirming 505 F. Supp. 787 (D. Kan. 1980).

12. See *Filartiga v. Pena-Irala*, 630 F.2d 876 (2d Cir. 1980)(involving torture in Paraguay).

13. Fisheries Jurisdiction Case (*United Kingdom v. Iceland*), I.C.J. Rep. 3, 24–26, 32 (1974).

14. *Foster & Elam v. Neilson*, 27 U.S. 253, 314 (1829).

15. *Cook v. United States*, 288 U.S. 102 (1933).

16. *Edye v. Robertson*, 112 U.S. 580, 598–99 (1884).

17. In 1988, the United States ratified the United Nations' Genocide Convention, in 1990 the Torture Convention, and in 1992 the International Covenant on Civil and Political Rights. In 1990, the United States ratified one of two ILO treaties on forced labor and in 1999, the ILO treaty on the worst forms of child labor. None of the five ratifications was unqualified, i.e., without reservations, understandings, or non-self-executing declarations as to their domestic impact.

18. Reservations are not permitted with respect to ratified ILO conventions.

19. Committee on Foreign Relations, "International Covenant on Civil and Political Rights," Exec. Rept. 102–23, 102d Cong., 2d Sess. 5 (March 24, 1992).

20. Ibid. at 5, 26–27.

21. M. Whiteman, *Digest of International Law* (Washington, D.C.: Government Printing Office, 1970), 302, 305, 309–10.

22. For example, Justice Douglas, writing for the Supreme Court in *Warren v. United States,* 340 U.S. 523, 526 (1951), disagreed with Chief Justice Stone's concurring opinion in *Aguilar v. Standard Oil Co.,* 318 U.S.724, 738 (1943), that Article 2(2) of the Shipowners' Liability Convention (ILO Convention No. 55) was not self-executing, and, instead, concluded that it was self-executing. Compare *Foster v. Neilson,* 27 U.S. 253 (1829) with *United States v. Percheman,* 32 U.S. 51 (1833) in which the court held the words "shall be ratified" to be non-self-executing in the first case but not in the second. See also Comment, "Self-Executing Treaties and the Human Rights Clauses of the United Nations Charter: A Separation of Powers Problem," *Buffalo Law Review* 25 (1976): 773, 779.

23. See, *Indemnity Ins. Co. of N.A. v. Pan American Airways, Inc.* 58 F. Supp. 338, 340 (S.D.N.Y. 1944). See also Holman, "Treaty Law-Making: A Blank Check for Writing a New Constitution," *American Bar Association Journal* 38 (1950): 707, 710. ("These clauses are included because they are appropriate and necessary to the other countries where treaties do not automatically become a part of their domestic law.")

24. See, *People of Saipan ex Rel. Guerrero v. United States Department of Interior,* 502 F.2d 90 (9th Cir. 1974), cert. denied, 420 U.S. 1003 (1974). The nature of the UN lease agreement is somewhat different, having limited precedential value in workplace human rights contexts.

25. See, for example, *Sei Fuji v. State,* 38 Cal.2d 718, 242 P.2d 617 (1952); *Camacho v. Rogers,* 199 F. Supp. 155 (S.D.N.Y. 1961); *Hitai v. Immigration and Naturalization Services,* 343 F.2d 466 (2d Cir. 1965).

26. These are the same as enumerated under the Generalized System of Preferences and other trade laws.

27. John Sweeney, president of the AFL-CIO, in a letter to Congress, dated February 8, 2001, stated that:

> While these commitments were an important breakthrough, it should be understood that they are likely to be effective only in the case of countries whose laws already conform to ILO standards, as do Jordan's. For countries whose labor laws are inadequate, much more elaborate mechanisms need to be put in place, to ensure that domestic laws are brought up to international standards on a clear timetable.
>
> Labor laws in both Singapore and Chile, two countries with which negotiations toward bilateral free trade agreements have been initiated, do not currently meet ILO standards. Therefore, it is essential that they either reform their labor laws to bring them up to international standards before a trade agreement goes into effect, or that the labor rights language included in the trade agreements contain adequate measures to ensure that such upward harmonization takes place in a timely and structured fashion.

28. Speech by Mike Moore, "The WTO: What is at Stake?" 6th John Payne Memorial Lecture, European Business School London (March 12, 2001). See http://www.wto.org/english/news_e/spmm_e/spmm54_e.htm.

29. On labor standards, the WTO contains a direct reference to prison labor and two other oblique references to worker rights in the preamble and in Article 29. Article 29 obligates contracting parties to observe principles of certain provisions of the aborted Havana Charter that was to have led to the formation of the International Trade Organization to supplant the GATT after the Bretton Woods conference in 1944. In particular, Article 7 of the Havana Charter rec-

ognized that unfair conditions, particularly in production for export, created difficulties in international trade.

30. Statement Abraham Katz, president of the U.S. Council for International Business before the Senate Finance Committee (January 28, 1999). See http://www.uscib.org/aksen128.html.

31. World Trade Organization, *Singapore Ministerial Declaration* (Doc. WT/MIN(96)/DEC, 18 Dec. 1996), para. 4.

32. Sixteen submissions were filed with the U.S. National Administrative Office, of which fourteen involved allegations against Mexico and two against Canada. Five were filed with the Mexican NAO and involved allegations against the United States. Three submissions have been filed in Canada, one raising allegations against Mexico and two raising allegations against the United States. Thirteen of the sixteen submissions filed with the U.S. NAO involved issues of freedom of association. One submission concerned the illegal use of child labor, another case raised issues of pregnancy-based gender discrimination, and the third concerned minimum employment standards. Four cases also raised issues of safety and health, while another submission raised issues of compensation in cases of occupational illnesses and injuries. Five of the U.S. submissions have gone to ministerial level consultations with Mexico on issues of freedom of association. All five Mexican NAO submissions against the United States involving plant closing, health and safety, and migrant labor resulted in ministerial consultations.

33. Edward E. Potter, *Freedom of Association, the Right to Organize and Collective Bargaining: The Impact on U.S. Law and Practice of Ratification of ILO Conventions No. 87 and No. 98* (Washington, D.C.: Labor Policy Association, 1984).

7. Voice for All

1. See, e.g., International Organization of Employers, *Policy Statement on the Social Clause* (Geneva: International Organization of Employers, 1996); Roy J. Adams and Sheldon Friedman, "Industrial Relations Implications of the New International Consensus on Human Rights in Employment," *Perspectives on Work* 2 (2) (1998): 24–27; Anne Trebilcock, "What Future for Social Clauses? Differing Institutional Approaches," paper presented at the International Industrial Relations Association's World Congress, Bologna, Italy, September 1998; ILO, "Clearing the Final Hurdle," *World of Work Magazine* 25 (1998): 13–17; UN Global Compact (http://www.unglobalcompact.org/).

2. ILO, *Your Voice at Work* (Geneva: International Labor Office, 2000).

3. In the actual document "freedom of association and the effective recognition of the right to collective bargaining" are grouped together rather than being enumerated separately. As a result commentators often refer to four core rights. Nevertheless, the specific mention of a right to collective bargaining must be considered as significant. ILO principles designate the right to bargain and the right to strike to be rights derivative from freedom of association. Thus, there was no need to explicitly make reference to a right to bargain collectively among the core rights unless the intention was to emphasize its status as a fundamental human right deserving consideration and respect on its own.

4. ILO, "Clearing the Final Hurdle."

5. Despite the notional support for the Fundamental Declaration by the U.S. Council on International Business, at the human rights conference at which this paper was first presented, Thomas Moorhead, the head of the U.S. employer delegation to the ILO conference that unanimously adopted the declaration, argued against U.S. adoption of the ILO's core human rights conventions.

6. Edward Potter, *Freedom of Association and the Right to Organize and Bargain Collectively, The Impact of U.S. Law and Practice of Ratification of ILO Conventions No. 87 and No. 98* (Washington, D.C.: Labor Policy Association, 1984).

7. Formally, the obligation to respect ILO principles with respect to freedom of association has been long standing for ILO members. The signing of the Fundamental Declaration was simply a reaffirmation of that commitment. ILO, "Clearing the Final Hurdle."

8. N. Valticos and G. von Potobsky, *International Labor Law* (Deventer, the Netherlands: Kluwer Law International, 1995).

9. B. Gernigon, A. Odero, and H. Guido, "ILO Principles Concerning Collective Bargaining," *International Labour Review* 139 (1) (2000): 33–56; John Windmuller, "Comparative Study of Methods and Practices," in *Collective Bargaining in Industrialised Market Economies: A Reappraisal,* ed. John Windmuller (Geneva: ILO, 1987), 1–149. In his widely read review of the status of collective bargaining as of the 1980s, John Windmuller, while recognizing that collective bargaining "exists in many different societies and occurs in many different forms" and that it "should be understood to refer not only to the negotiation of formal collective agreements but also to other aspects of the collective dealings between the parties" (p. 3), makes a distinction between collective bargaining and joint consultation. While both procedures bring together employer and employee representatives, the latter "differs from collective bargaining in that it is intended to be an advisory rather than a decision-making process and that it emphasises the co-operative rather than the adversary elements in labour-management relations" (p. 12). In the real world, however, it is very difficult to distinguish between one of these processes and the other in actual cases. In general, European bargaining tends to be more cooperative and less adversarial than North American bargaining. Moreover, the distinction made by Windmuller is not made in official ILO documents as the quote from Gernigon et al. indicates.

10. In various documents that inform the international human rights consensus, including, for example, the International Bill of Rights (which includes the Universal Declaration of Human Rights, and the two United Nations covenants that operationalize the UDHR—one on Civil and Political Rights and the other on Economic, Social, and Cultural Rights), these core rights have been formally considered human rights for some time. The UDHR was affirmed shortly after World War II and the covenants appeared in the 1960s. Nevertheless, until recently the international human rights movement has devoted little attention to workers' rights, leaving their defense and development to labor organizations that have not commonly drawn on the human rights consensus and the principles affirmed by that consensus. Perhaps because of this separation the ILO has only recently begun to refer to labor rights as human rights. See Virginia Leary, "The Paradox of Workers' Rights as Human Rights," in *Human Rights, Labor Rights, and International Trade,* ed. Lance A. Compa and Stephen F. Diamond (Philadelphia: University of Pennsylvania Press, 1996), 22–47.

11. Rhoda Howard and Jack Donnelly, "Introduction," in *International Handbook of Human Rights,* ed. Rhoda Howard and Jack Donnelly (Connecticut: Greenwood Press, 1987), 1–7; UN High Commission for Human Rights, *Vienna Declaration and Programme of Action* (Geneva: UNHCR, 1993) (http://www.unhchr.ch). Although arguments are from time to time put forth for the priority of some of these rights over others, as Howard and Donnelly note "virtually all states are explicitly committed to the view that all the rights recognized in the Universal Declaration are interdependent and indivisible" (p. 6). As a practical matter, however, national courts are often compelled to sort out application problems when such equal rights clash in particular instances.

12. Richard N. Block, John Beck, and Daniel H. Kruger, *Labor Law, Industrial Relations,*

and Employee Choice (Kalamazoo, Mich.: Upjohn Institute, 1996); Commission on the Future of Worker-Management Relations (Dunlop Commission), *Report and Recommendations* (Washington, D.C.: U.S. Department of Labor, 1994).

13. Sheldon Leader, *Freedom of Association: A Study in Labor Law, and Political Theory* (New Haven: Yale University Press, 1992), 28.

14. Morton G. Mitchnick, "Recent Developments in Compulsory Unionism," *International Labour Review,* 132 (4) (1993): 453–68.

15. Ibid.

16. Colin Crouch, "The Globalized Economy: An End to the Age of Industrial Citizenship?" in *Advancing Theory in Labour Law and Industrial Relations in a Global Context,* ed. Ton Wilthagen (Amsterdam: Royal Netherlands Academy of Arts and Sciences, 1998): 151–64.

17. Quoted in Herman Knudsen, *Employee Participation in Europe* (London: Sage, 1995), 115.

18. Roger Blanpain and Tadashi Hanami, eds., *European Works Councils* (Leuven, Belgium: Peeters, 1995).

19. Clyde W. Summers, "Exclusive Representation: A Comparative Inquiry into a 'Unique' American Principle," *Comparative Labour Law and Policy Journal* 20 (1) (fall 1998): 47–69.

20. James A. Gross, "A Human Rights Perspective on United States Labor Relations Law: A Violation of the Right of Freedom of Association," *Employee Rights and Employment Policy Journal* 3 (65) (1999): 351–74.

21. Block, Beck, and Kruger, *Labor Law,* 91–92.

22. Ibid., 100.

23. Richard B. Freeman and Joel Rogers, *What Workers Want* (Ithaca, N.Y.: ILR/Cornell University Press: 1999), 62.

24. Human Rights Watch, *Unfair Advantage: Workers' Freedom of Association in the United States under International Human Rights Standards* (New York: Human Rights Watch, 2000), 9.

25. Ibid., 9.

26. Freeman and Rogers, *What Workers Want,* 62.

27. Joel Rogers and Wolfgang Streeck, eds. *Works Councils, Consultation, Representation, and Cooperation in Industrial Relations* (Chicago: University of Chicago Press, 1995).

28. Paul Edwards, "Broadening the Scope of Worker Protection: The Case of Statutory Minimum Wages in the United Kingdom," Paper presented at a conference on Broadening the Bargaining Structure in the New Social Order (Toronto, Canada: York University Centre for Research on Work and Safety, May 1992).

29. Elaine Bernard, "Canada: Joint Committees on Occupational Health and Safety," in *Works Councils, Consultation, Representation, and Cooperation in Industrial Relations,* 223–30.

30. At McMaster University in Hamilton, Canada, the McMaster University Faculty Association negotiates annually with the university administration over the wages of faculty members. By mutual agreement, impasses go to final offer selection, a procedure that has been used several times. In addition to wages it is understood that the association may raise any issue of mutual concern, and subsequently, there will be joint meetings to discuss the issue and work toward a mutually acceptable resolution of it. By and large, discussions are cooperative and respectful rather than adversarial. Although from time to time the association has considered the possibility of seeking certification under the Ontario Labour Relations Act, which is modeled on the U.S. Wagner Act, it has rejected that course of action. Its reasoning has been that the current relationship is much more flexible and compatible with the nonadversarial relationship preferred by faculty than the one imposed by the Ontario legal framework. The McMaster Uni-

versity labor relationship is entirely compatible with the ILO's definition of collective bargaining, however it might be defined by those steeped in the adversarial culture of conventional North American collective bargaining.

31. Seymour Martin Lipset and Noah M. Meltz, "Estimates of Nonunion Employee Representation in the United States and Canada: How Different are the Two Countries?" in *Nonunion Employee Representation*, eds. Bruce E. Kaufman and Daphne Gottlieb Taras (Armonk, N.Y.: M. E. Sharpe, 2000): 223–30.

32. Freeman and Rogers, *What Workers Want*, 7.

33. See, e.g., Clyde W. Summers, "Employee Voice and Employer Choice: A Structured Exception to Section 8(a)(2)," *Chicago-Kent Law Review* 69 (1) (1993): 129–48.

34. Freeman and Rogers, *What Workers Want*, 7. It is ironic that in Europe where elites resisted the establishment of political democracy into the twentieth century, today both the political and economic spheres have been thoroughly democratized. Contrarily, although the United States was the pioneer of modern political democracy, "monarchically organized industry" persists into the twenty-first century. Paul Malles, *The Institutions of Industrial Relations in Continental Europe* (Ottawa: Labor Canada, 1973), 162.

35. Freeman and Rogers, *What Workers Want*.

36. A. H. Raskin, "Management Comes out Swinging," *Proceedings of the Thirty-first Annual Meeting of the Industrial Relations Research Association* (Madison, Wis.: IRRA, 1978): 223–32.

37. Richard B. Freeman and James Medoff, *What Do Unions Do?* (New York: Basic Books, 1984); Barry Hirsch, *Labor Unions and the Economic Performance of Firms* (Kalamazoo, Mich.: W. E. Upjohn Institute, 1991). The classic statement of the positive effects of unions on economic performance is Freeman and Medoff, 1984. Hirsch, 1991, makes the negative case.

38. See, e.g., Joseph Stiglitz, "Democratic Development as the Fruits of Labor," Keynote Address, Industrial Relations Research Association, Boston, January 2000 (Champaign-Urbana, IRRA, 2001) 27 pp.; Brian Langille, *Eight Ways to Think about Labour Standards and Globalization* (Geneva: Graduate Institute of International Studies, Institut universitaire de hautes études internationals, 1997).

39. The ILO has recently suspended Burma from participation in all of the organization's activities and has denied it grants and assistance because of its continued reliance on forced labor. For more information see the ILO web site at www.ilo.org.

40. ILO, *Review of Annual Reports Under the Follow-Up to the ILO Declaration on Fundamental Principles and Rights at Work* (Geneva: International Labor Office, 2000).

41. James A. Gross, "Conflicting Statutory Purposes; Another Look at Fifty Years of NLRB Law Making," *Industrial and Labor Relations Review* (October 1985): 7–18.

42. Human Rights Watch, *Unfair Advantage*.

43. Janine Goetschy and Patrick Rozenblatt, "France: The Industrial Relations System at a Turning Point?" in *Industrial Relations in the New Europe*, eds. Anthony Ferner and Richard Hyman (Oxford: Basil Blackwell, 1992): 404–44.

44. As in many countries, union membership declined in France in the 1980s despite the initiative of the government to expand collective bargaining. For a review of the reasons for this anomalous development, see Roy J. Adams, "Regulating Unions and Collective Bargaining: A Global, Historical Analysis of Determinants and Consequences,'" *Comparative Labor Law Journal* 14 (3) (spring 1993): 272–301. The 90 percent bargaining coverage rate reported in the text is based on an ILO estimate more recent than the one reported in table 7.1. International Labour Office, *Industrial Relations, Democracy, and Social Stability* (Geneva: International Labour Office, 1997).

45. See Roy J. Adams, "Realizing the Right to Bargain Collectively in Canada and the Americas," in *Globalization and the Canadian Economy: The Implications for Labor Markets, Society, and the State*, ed. Richard P. Chaykowski (Kingston, Ontario: Queen's University, 2001): 139–48.

46. Lipset and Meltz, "Estimates of Nonunion Employee Representation in the United States and Canada."

47. Freeman and Rogers, *What Workers Want.*

48. See, e.g., Hoyt N. Wheeler, "Viewpoint: Collective Bargaining Is a Fundamental Human Right," *Industrial Relations* 39 (3) (July 2000): 535–39; Labor Party of America, "Toward a New Labor Law," (Discussion paper dated July 4, 2000), available at http://www.igc.org/lpa_laborlaw.html .

49. Clyde W. Summers, "Questioning the Unquestioned in Collective Labour Law," *Catholic University Law Review* 47 (3) (fall 1998): 791–823.

50. W. Muller-Jentsch, "Germany: From Collective Voice to Co-management," in *Works Councils, Consultation, Representation, and Cooperation in Industrial Relations.*

51. Rogers and Streeck, eds., *Works Councils, Consultation, Representation and Cooperation in Industrial Relations.*

52. ILO, *Review of Annual Reports Under the Follow-up to the ILO Declaration.*

53. Dunlop Commission, *Report and Recommendations.*

54. Human Rights Watch, *Unfair Advantage.*

55. Roy J. Adams, "The North American Model of Employee Representational Participation: 'A Hollow Mockery,' " *Comparative Labor Law Journal*, 15 (1) (fall 1993): 201–11.

56. Roy J. Adams, "A Pernicious Euphoria: 50 Years of Wagnerism in Canada," *Canadian Labour and Employment Law Journal* 3 (3/4) (1995): 321–55.

8. "An Injury to One . . . "

1. International Labour Organization, *Freedom of Association and Collective Bargaining* (Geneva, Switzerland, 1994), 74.

2. National Labor Relations Act, §2(2), 61 Stat. 136, as amended, 29 U.S.C. §152 (1947).

3. Virginia Leary, "The Paradox of Workers' Rights as Human Rights" in *Human Rights, Labor Rights, and International Trade*, eds. L. Compa and S. Diamond (University of Pennsylvania, 1996), 22–47. The leading North American advocate for treating labor rights as human rights is Roy Adams. See Adams, "Labor Rights are Human Rights," *Working USA* (July/August 1999): 72–77.

4. Between 1890 and 1914, Daniel Rodgers notes, labor politics had a decidedly international tone. "From the American Knights of Labor organizers canvassing for recruits in the English midlands in the 1880s to the British and American fraternal delegates trading places at their respective annual labor union gatherings to the work of Marx's successors and the Second Socialist International, there was no missing the sharply conscious international edge to labor politics." Daniel Rodgers, *Atlantic Crossings: Social Politics in a Progressive Age* (Cambridge, Mass.: Belknap Press/Harvard University Press, 1988), 52. For the possibilities of labor internationalism in the mid-1940s, see Victor Silverman, *Imagining Internationalism in American and British Labor, 1939–1949* (Urbana: University of Illinois Press, 2000).

5. See generally, Katherine Van Wezel Stone, "To the Yukon: Local Laborers in a Global Labor Market," *Journal of Small and Emerging Business Law* 94 (93)(1999): 93–130; Adelle Blackett, "Whither Social Clause? Human Rights, Trade Theory, and Treaty Interpretation," *Columbia Human Rights Law Review* 31 (1) (1999): 31–80.

6. Harry Arthurs, "The Collective Labour Law of a Global Economy" in *Labour Law at*

the Turn of the Century, eds. R. Blanpain, Chris Engels, and Manfred Weiss (Deventer, the Netherlands: Kluwer Law International, 1998): 143–62.

7. Ibid., 145. On the other hand, the Committee on Freedom of Association accepts complaints against governments or employers or unions, although it focuses on whether a government has protected the freedom of association. Hector Bartolomei de la Cruz, Geraldo von Potobsky, and Lee Swepston, *The International Labour Organization* (Boulder: Westview Press, 1996), 101–7. For ILO actions to enforce conventions 87 and 98, see ibid., 204–10 and 224–29 respectively.

8. ILO pressure has resulted in some successes. See, e.g., Geraldo von Potobsky, "Freedom of Association: The Impact of Convention No. 87 and ILO Action," *International Labour Review* 137 (1998): 212–15.

9. Arthurs, "The Collective Labour Law," 151. See also, Harry Arthurs, "Private Ordering and Workers' Rights in the Global Economy: Corporate Codes of Conduct as a Regime of Labour Market Regulation" (forthcoming); Bob Hepple, "A Race to the Top? International Investment Guidelines and Corporate Codes of Conduct," *Comparative Labor Law and Policy Journal* (forthcoming); L. Compa and T. Darricarrere, "Private Labor Rights Enforcement Through Corporate Codes of Conduct," in *Human Rights, Labor Rights, and International Trade,* eds. L. Compa and S. Diamond (Philadelphia: University of Pennsylvania Press, 1996), 181–98.

10. Kenneth Wedderburn, *Nationalism and the Multinational Enterprise* (New York: Oceana Publications, 1973), 249.

11. Ibid., 256.

12. See, e.g., Eddy Lee, "Globalization and Labour Standards: A Review of Issues," *International Labour Review* 136 (1997): 467; Nicolas Valticos," International Labour Standards and Human Rights: Approaching the Year 2000," *International Labour Review* 137 (1998): 135; Breen Creighton, "The Internationalization of Labour Law" in *Redefining Labour Law: New Perspectives on the Future of Teaching and Research,* ed. Richard Mitchell (Melbourne: Centre for Employment and Labour Relations Law, 1995): 90–120.

13. Quoted in "Introduction: Labour Rights, Human Rights," *International Labour Review* 137 (1998): 130 (no author listed).

14. Katherine Van Wezel Stone, "Labor and the Global Economy: Four Approaches to Transnational Labor Regulation," *Michigan Journal of International Law* 16 (1995): 987.

15. Creighton, "The Internationalization of Labour Law," 92–95.

16. Christopher Arup, "Labour Market Regulation as a Focus for a Labour Law Discipline" in *Redefining Labour Law: New Perspectives on the Future of Teaching and Research,* ed. Richard Mitchell (Melbourne: Centre for Employment and Labour Relations Law, 1995): 29–61.

17. James Atleson, "Reflections on Labor, Power, and Society," *Maryland Law Review* 44 (1985): 841–42. Approximately 65 million people are employed by TNCs, 22 million of whom are in host, not home, countries. This figure represents about 3 percent of the world's total workforce. Not counted, obviously, are the large number of workers, employed by contractors, for instance, whose working conditions are in effect set by the TNCs. According to the World Bank, TNCs control 70 percent of the world's trade. In 1990, the largest 350 TNCs accounted for almost 40 percent of the world's merchandise trade; the top 500 TNCs control two-thirds of world trade. Finally, over 40 percent of international trade involves intrafirm transfers. See Tim Lang and Colin Hines, *The New Protectionism* (New York: The New Press, 1993), 34.

18. Burton Bendiner, *International Labour Affairs* (New York: Oxford, 1987), 49.

19. Jay Mazur, "Labor's New Internationalism," *Foreign Affairs* (Jan./Feb. 2000): 79.

20. Various definitions of "globalization" have been offered, often relating to the discipline of the offeror. The OECD, for instance, has provided an economic definition: an evolving pattern of cross-border activities of firms involving international investment, trade and collaboration for purposes of product development, production and sourcing, and marketing." OECD, *Globalization of Industry* (Paris: OECD), 9. Definitions favoring political and economic dimensions stress changes in the structure and operation of capitalism involving growing market integration, globalized firms, and often, the weakening or "hollowing out" of the nation state. Sociologists deemphasize a purely economic focus, stressing "the intensification of worldwide social relations which link distant localities in such a way that local happenings are shaped by events occurring many miles away and vice versa." Anthony Giddens, *The Consequences of Modernity* (Cambridge: UK Polity Press, 1990), 64. These quotations are set out in Peter Leisink, "Introduction" in *Globalization and Labour Relations*, ed. Peter Leisink (Northampton, Mass.: Edward Elgar, 1999), 4–5.

Conventional accounts have been challenged, especially on the left, without challenging the notion that capitalism has become a more universal system and that market and economic transactions are increasingly global. Some have "expressed doubts about how much production has really been internationalized, about how mobile industrial capital really is, about the very existence of 'multinational' corporations. Such critics have pointed out that the vast majority of production still goes on in nationally-based companies in single locales . . . [and] foreign direct investment has been overwhelmingly concentrated in advanced capitalist countries, with capital moving from one such country to another." Ellen Meiksins Wood, "Labor, Class, and State in Global Capitalism" in *Rising from the Ashes? Labor in the Age of 'Global' Capitalism*, eds. E. M. Wood, P. Meiksins, and M. Yates (New York: Monthly Review Press, 1998), 4.

The ILO's World Labor Report 1997–98 indicates the effect of globalization on unions in both the developed and developing world. For 65 countries between 1985 and 1995, 51 percent of the countries experienced a decline of union membership of more than 20 percent and 25 percent (16) saw a decline of between 5 and 20 percent. Only 11 percent (7) had a stable union density, 3 percent (2) had a growth of between 5 and 20 percent, and 11 percent (7) experienced a growth of more than 20 percent in union membership (Table 1.2 of the Statistical Annex).

21. Robert W. Cox, "Labor and Transnational Relations," *International Organization* 25 (1971): 555–56. See Bendiner, *International Labour Affairs*, 62–88. See also, Hans Gunter, ed., *Transnational Industrial Relations* (London: Macmillan, 1972). For a careful review of the international coordinated bargaining strategy of the International Federation of Chemical and General Workers and glass worker unions against Saint-Gobain, see Charles Levinson, *International Trade Unionism* (London: George Allen & Unwin, 1972), 8–21.

22. Cox, "Labor and Transnational Relations," 563. See also, Andreas Breitenfellner, "Global Unionism: A Potential Player," *International Labour Review* 136 (1997): 531; Harvie Ramsey, "Solidarity at Last? International Trade Unionism Approaching the Millennium," *Economics and Industrial Democracy* 18 (1997): 503; Charles Levinson, *International Trade Unionism* (London: George Allen & Unwin, 1972), 112–41.

23. Bendiner, *International Labour Affairs*, 34–72; J. P. Windmuller and S. K. Pursey, "The International Trade Union Movement" in *Comparative Labour Law and Industrial Relations in Industrialized Market Economies*, eds. R. Blanpain and C. Engels (Deventer, Netherlands: Kluwer Law International, 1993), 70–76; Andrew Herod, "The Practice of International Labor Solidarity and the Geography of the Global Economy," *Economic Geography* 71 (Oct. 1995): 341 (discussing the efforts of the United Steelworkers of America to combat the Ravenswood lockout between 1990 and 1992); Robert Taylor, "Trade Unions and Transnational Industrial Relations," Labour and Society Programme, ILO International Institute for Labour Studies, DP/99/1999.

24. Herod, "International Labor Solidarity," 357. Kim Moody, *An Injury to All: The Decline of American Unionism* (New York: Verso, 1988).

25. Kim Moody, *Workers in a Lean World* (London: Verso, 1997), 239–42.

26. ICFTU website, <www.icftu.org>, checked on February 8, 2000. See also, Bendiner, *International Labour Affairs,* 35–42. Windmuller and Pursey, "The International Trade Union Movement."

27. Philip Jennings, "Unions Respond to Changes in the Global Economy," *International Union Rights* 7 (2000): 24.

28. O. Kahn-Freund, "A Lawyer's Reflections on Multinational Corporations," *Journal of Industrial Relations* (Aug. 1972): 351, 356–57.

29. The ITF is an international trade secretariat representing 5 million members in 500 unions in 130 different countries. One of its eight major sections is road transport.

30. UPS reportedly has worldwide operations that include 340,000 employees, 500 aircraft, and 2,400 facilities in more than 200 countries.

31. This information is based on John Russo and Andy Banks, "How Teamsters took the UPS Strike Overseas," *Working USA* (Jan.-Feb. 1999): 75–87. A longer version of this article is A. Banks and J. Russo, "The Development of International Campaign-Based Network Structures: A Case Study of the IBT and ITF World Council of UPS Unions," *Comparative Labor Law and Policy Journal* 20 (1999): 543. See also, Mazur, "Labor's New Internationalism."

32. Mazur, "Labor's New Internationalism."

33. Ibid., 82.

34. For other recent examples of transnational union activities, often involving cooperative activities with nonlabor groups as well as unions, see International Labour Organization, *World Labour Report: Industrial Relations—Democracy and Social Stability, 1997–1998* (Geneva: 1997), 37–44; for the international activities of the CWA, see Larry Cohen and Steve Early, "Defending Workers' Rights in the Global Economy: The CWA Experience" in *Which Direction for Organized Labor?*, ed. Bruce Nissen (Detroit: Wayne State University, 1999), 143; Tom Juravich and Kate Bronfenbrenner, *Ravenswood: The Steelworkers' Victory and the Revival of American Labor* (Ithaca, N.Y.: Cornell University Press, 1999); David Moberg, "Striking Back: The Steelworkers Won't Let Up," *In These Times* (Oct. 3, 1999): 10.

35. Doug Imig and Sidney Tarrow, "From Strike to Eurostrike: the Europeanization of Social Movements and the Development of a Euro-Polity," Weatherhead Center for International Affairs, Harvard University, Working Paper Series, Paper No. 97–10 (1997).

36. Nevertheless, Renault may be brought before the European Court of Justice, and it was chastised by the European Parliament. A Belgium court has fined Renault 10 million Belgian francs ($264,000) for violating labor laws, which require prior notice to workers. *Wall Street Journal* (March 23, 1998): A16. *The National Law Journal* (April 6, 1998): A12. See also, "The Renault Case and the Future of Social Europe," http://ns.lex.unict/eurolabor/diritto-sociale/eiro/update2/eu_bel_2.htm.

37. *The PACE Setter,* 2 (6) (July/August 2000): 1.

38. Moody, *Workers in a Lean World,* 249–50.

39. *The Journal of Commerce,* Jan. 20, 1997.

40. Moody, *Workers in a Lean World,* 251.

41. The dispute also involved 329 Liverpool dockers who were sacked by the Mersey Dock and Harbour Company. *Lloyd's List International* (Feb., 25, 1998). Liverpool seems to be the only dock in the United Kingdom still operating under a collective bargaining agreement. See, Alexander Cockburn, "The Fate of the Neptune Jade," *The Nation* (March 23, 1998): 9.

42. *San Francisco Chronicle,* Sept. 30. 1997: C2. *Labor Party Press* 3 (3) (May 1998): 4; *Industrial Worker* (December 1997), #1607, 94 (11): 7.

43. The business press stressed that Thamesport announced that it was not a subsidiary of the Mersey Docks and Harbour Company and, thus, the "blacking" of the *Jade* was a mistake. *Lloyd's List International,* Oct. 4, 1997. See, also, "Putting the Record Straight on Picketing," *Oakland Post,* Oct. 5, 1997.

44. "British Columbia Labour Protesters Block Ship," *The Globe and Mail,* Oct. 6, 1997; Felix Chen, "NOL Ship Picketed Again in Vancouver," *Business Times* (Singapore), Oct. 7, 1997: 1.

45. Jerzy Fargnski, "Japanese Dockers Ban *Jade,*" *Australasian Business Intelligence* (Oct. 14, 1997): 2. David Hughes, "Kline, Mitsui and NYK Stand to Gain from Japanese Port Reforms," *Business Times* (Singapore), Nov. 3, 1997: 2. *Industrial Worker* (December 1997), #1607, 94 (11), 42.

46. Rick DelVecchio, "Supporters of Labor Rally Against Ship Industry Suit," *San Francisco Chronicle,* Feb. 27, 1998: A21.

47. In early 1998, the Liverpool dockers decided to end their dispute. According to Jimmy Nolan, chairman of the Shop Stewards Committee of the Merseyside Docker, the Labour government refused to intervene or use the power of the 14 percent holding it possesses in the Mersey Dock and Harbour Company. Since the dockers had been made "redundant," each docker was entitled to compensation of 28,000 pounds. Interview by Suzanne Jones at the European Workers' Conference for the Abrogation of the Maastricht Treaty, Berlin, Jan. 31–Feb. 1, 1998, e-mail from Michael Eisencher, May 8, 1998. Faced with a lack of support from those with power to assist them, the dockers took the best means available to support themselves and their families.

48. See International Labour Organization, *World Labor Report;* Deborah Greitzer, "Cross-Border Responses to Labor Repression in North America," *Michigan State University Law Review—Detroit College of Law* 3 (fall 1995): 917. Dan La Botz, "Making Links Across the Border," *Labor Notes* (August 1994): 7. See also, Lance Compa, "The International Labor Standards and Instruments of Recourse for Working Women," *Yale Journal of International Law* 17 (1992): 151, 170–71.

49. Suggested to author by Howard Kimmeldorf, professor, University of Michigan.

50. Bob Hepple, "The United Kingdom," in *Strikes and Lockouts in Industrialized Market Economies,* eds. R. Blanpain and R. Ben-Israel (Deventer, The Netherlands: Kluwer Law International, 1994), 183–85.

51. Lord Wedderburn, *Employment Rights in Britain and Europe* (London: Lawrence and Wishart, 1991), 220.

52. K. Wedderburn, *Nationalism and the Multinational Enterprise,* eds. H. R. Hahlo, J. Graham Smith, and Richard W. Wright (New York: Oceana Publications, 1973), 256. In the United States, at least, this is not surprising. United States courts and the NLRB have already made it difficult for unions to deal with multiunit and multiple-location firms and, especially, to respond to the economic power of conglomerates. Unions, like national governments and communities, tend to face the same problems of relative power and lack of information. See James Atleson, "Reflections on Labor, Power, and Society," *Maryland Law Review* 44 (1985): 841.

53. TULRA section 24(1). Primary action, on the other hand, is defined as a situation where the employer under the contract of employment in question is the employer party to the dispute. Section 224 (5). In addition, the statute reinforces the reluctance of courts to look behind the "veil" of incorporation to discover the reality of control and administration. Like the United States, the immunity for primary action is not listed simply because primary picketing has secondary effects. Section 224 (3). See Hepple, "The United Kingdom," 181–83. See also, Paul Davies and Mark Freedland, *Kahn-Freund's Labour and the Law* (London: Stevens & Sons,

1983), 321–52; K. W. Wedderburn, *Cases and Materials on Labour Law* (Cambridge, U.K.: Cambridge University Press, 1967). A classic early history of U.K. labor law is R. Y. Hedges and Allan Winterbottom, *The Legal History of Trade Unionism* (London: Longmans, Green, 1930).

54. Nicholas Blomley, *Law, Space, and the Geographies of Power* (New York and London: Guilford Press, 1994), 179–80.

55. The Employment Relations Act of 1999, enacted by the Labour party makes no change in the restrictive provisions of the prior Thatcher legislation dealing with secondary pressure. See, e.g., Lord Wedderburn, "Collective Bargaining or Legal Enactment: The 1999 Act and Union Recognition," *Industrial Law Journal* 29 (March 2000): 1.

56. Lord Wedderburn, "The New Policies in Industrial Relations Law," in *Industrial Relations and the Law in the 1980s*, eds. P. Fish and C. R. Littler (Aldershot, U.K.: Gower, 1985), 43, quoted in Blomley, *Space, and the Geographies of Power*, 180.

57. Report of the Committee of Experts on the Application of Conventions and Recommendations, International Labor Conference, 76th Sess., Rep. 111, Part 4A, 234, 238–39 (1989). See also, the ILO quotation that begins this paper. See Lee Swepston, "Human Rights Law and Freedom of Association: Development through ILO Supervision," *International Labour Review* 137 (1998): 186–90.

58. This long, complex, and vague provision bars both inducements to neutral workers as well as a strike by neutral workers on their own. Thus, the provision prohibits a strike or an inducement to engage in a strike or a "refusal in the course of his employment to use, manufacture, process, transport, or otherwise handle or work on any goods, articles, materials, or commodities or to perform any services . . . where . . . an object is forcing any person to cease using, selling, handling transporting, or otherwise dealing in the products of any other producer . . . or to cease doing business with any other person."

59. Even aside from the secondary boycott provisions, such action is traditionally treated as unprotected action, which could lead to discharge or discipline. See generally, James Atleson, *Values and Assumptions in American Labor Law*, chapter 3 (Amherst: University of Massachusetts Press, 1983).

60. *Edward J. DeBartolo v. Florida Gulf Coast Bldg & Constr. Trades Council*, 485 US 568 (1988). The court noted that it could protect handbilling because it was "much less effective than labor picketing." Ibid., 576. Whereas handbills "depend entirely on the persuasive force of the idea," picketing exerts "influences, and it produces consequences, different from other modes of communication." Ibid., 580.

61. James Pope, "The Three-Systems Ladder of First Amendment Values: Two Rungs and a Black Hole," *Hastings Law Review* 11 (1984): 192; Pope, "Labor and the Constitution: From Abolition to Deindustrialization," *Texas Law Review* 65 (1987): 1074.

62. *ILA v. Allied International, Inc.*, 456 US 212 (1982).

63. The secondary boycott prohibitions in the United States have been vigorously criticized. See, Charles Craver, *Can Unions Survive? The Rejuvenation of the American Labor Movement* (New York: New York University Press, 1993), 145–46; Paul Weiler, *Governing the Workplace: The Future of Labor and Employment Law* (Cambridge: Harvard University Press, 1990), 272–73; Dorothy Sue Cobble, "Making Post Industrial Unionism Possible," in *Restoring the Promise of American Labor Law*, eds. Sheldon Friedman et al. (Ithaca, N.Y.: ILR/Cornell University Press, 1994), 297; Marion Crain, "Between Feminism and Unionism: Working Class Women, Sex Equality, and Labor Speech," *Georgetown Law Journal* 82 (1994): 1903, 1996–99.

64. Decisions have long held that workers may not stay at work and decide which parts of their work or assigned tasks they will perform. Similarly, slowdowns are not protected. See Atleson, *Values and Assumptions*.

65. As part of an ongoing dispute between ILA-represented longshoremen and two unorganized Florida shippers, Japanese longshore unions were persuaded to aid the union by refusing to unload ships in Japan that had been loaded by nonunion workers in Florida. Prior to a ruling on the merits of the employers' unfair labor practice charge, the NLRB sought an injunction under section 10(l) of the NLRA on the grounds that the secondary boycott actually occurred in the United States as it was directed at U.S. firms and the economic pain was felt in Florida. The 11th Circuit Court of Appeals upheld the injunction on the ground that the application of the statute was not extraterritorial and, moreover, the action of the Japanese unions could be attributed to the ILA based on legal doctrines of agency, ratification, or joint venture. *Dowd v. ILA*, 975 F.2d 779 (11th Cir.1992). After the NLRB held that the ILA's actions constituted a violation of NLRA section 8(b)(4), the court of appeals for the District of Columbia held that there was no illegal secondary boycott for a variety of reasons, including the belief that the action was not taken by "employees" within the act, since the Japanese were not individuals engaged in "commerce" as defined by the NLRA. The court also denied the applicability of agency or ratification doctrines, while not clearly focusing on the interesting issue of the possible application of the NLRA beyond U.S. borders.

66. British Columbia expressly exempts from the definition of a strike a refusal to cross legal picket lines, but in other jurisdictions such refusals can be deemed a strike if some aspect of concerted activity is present. See Donald Carter, "Canada," in *Strikes and Lockouts in Industrialized Market Economies*, eds. Roger Blainpain and Ruth Ben-Israel (Deventer, The Netherlands: Kluwer Law International, 1994), 39, 43.

67. Ibid., 43.

68. In all Canadian jurisdictions, the labor injunction is the basic, usually the exclusive, civil remedy for illegal strike activity. In some jurisdictions, the agency cease and desist order has replaced the judicial injunction. Ibid., 49–50.

69. Ibid., 51. The Supreme Court of Canada has held that picketing is a form of expression protected by the charter, but it drastically limited the charter's scope to actions of the government. Significantly, a judicial injunction is not to be treated as the act of the state. See also, Bernard Adell, "Law and Industrial Relations: The State of the Art in Common Law Canada," in *The State of the Art in Industrial Relations*, eds. Hebert, Jain, and Meltz (Industrial Relations Centre, Queen's University, 1988), 128–31.

70. *Hersees of Woodstock v. Goldstein*, 2 O.R. 81 (C.A. 1963), rev'g 1 O.R. 36 (1963).

71. Kazuo Sugeno, "Japan: Legal Framework and Issues," in *Strikes and Lockouts in Industrialized Market Economies*, eds. R. Blanpain and R. Ben-Israel (Deventer, The Netherlands: Kluwer Law International, 1994), 101, 106. See generally, John Price, *Japan Works: Power and Paradox in Postwar Industrial Relations* (Ithaca, N.Y.: Cornell University Press, 1997). See Kishima Tanko Roso, Tokyo District Court, Oct. 21, 1975.

72. *Freedom of Association: Digest of Decisions and Principles of the Freedom of Association Committee of the Governing Body of the ILO*, para. 484,489, 4th rev. ed. (Geneva, 1996), quoted in B. Gernigon, A. Odero, H. Guido, "ILO Principles Concerning the Right to Strike," *International Labour Review* 137 (1998): 460; Ruth Ben-Israel, *International Labour Standards: The Case of Freedom to Strike* (Deventer, the Netherlands: Kluwer Law International, 1988), 94–96.

73. Wedderburn, *Employment Rights*, 296.

74. Felice Morgenstern, *International Conflicts of Labour Law* (Geneva: International Labour Organization, 1984), 112, 114.

75. Ibid.

76. Ibid., 115.

77. Wedderburn, *Employment Rights*, 293–96. *International Encyclopedia of Labour Law*, Part 11, Ch.5, Supp. 205 (March 1998), 609–11, Industrial Conflict, Belgium. See also, *Un-*

fair Advantage: Workers' Freedom of Association in the United States Under International Human Rights Standards (New York: Human Rights Watch, 2000).

78. Ruth Ben-Israel, "Strikes, Lockouts and Other Kinds of Hostile Actions," in *International Encyclopedia of Comparative Law, Labour Law*, ed. Bob A. Hepple (1997), 15–16.

79. Wedderburn, *Employment Rights*, 293–94.

80. Ibid. at 300.

81. Ibid. at 294.

82. Brian Etherington, "Freedom of Association and Compulsory Union Dues: Towards a Purposive Conception of a Freedom Not to Associate," *Ottawa Law Review* 19 (1) (1987): 34, cited in Adell, "Law and Industrial Relations," 114.

83. See D. Westfall and G. Thusing, "Strikes and Lockouts in Germany and Under Federal Legislation in the United States: A Comparative Analysis," *Boston College International and Comparative Law Review* 22 (1999): 29, 45–48.

84. *Freedom of Association and Collective Bargaining* (Geneva, Switzerland: ILO, 1994), 2–5. Gernigon et al., "ILO Principles," 441–45.

85. Quoted in Anthony Forsyth, *Trade Union Rights for the New Millennium* (London: International Centre for Trade Union Rights, 1988), 9. See also, Breen Creighton, "The ILO and the Internationalisation of Australian Labour Law," *International Journal of Comparative Labour Law and Industrial Law* 11 (1995): 208; Lee Swepston, "Human Rights Law and Freedom of Association: Development through ILO Supervision," *International Labour Review* 137 (1998): 186–90.

86. Ruth Ben-Israel, "Strikes, Lockouts."

87. Quoted at ibid., 15–57. See Gernigon et al., "ILO Principles," 445–47.

88. Gernigon, "ILO Principles," 446; Ben-Israel, *International Labour Standards,* 96–98.

89. A. T. J. M. Jacobs, "The Law of Strikes and Lockouts," in *Comparative Labour Law and Industrial Relations in Industrialized Market Economies*, eds. R. Blanpain and C. Engels, 6th and rev. ed. (Deventer, The Netherlands: Kluwer Law International, 1998), 471. Despite these conclusions, unions have been known to strike or threaten to strike to oppose governmental proposals or policies. See, "The Return of Trade Unions," *The Economist* (US)(Dec. 4, 1993): 53 (2).

90. A. T. J. M. Jacobs, "The Law of Strikes and Lockouts," in *Comparative Labour Law and Industrial Relations in Industrialized Market Economies*, eds. R. Blanpain and C. Engels, 6th and rev. ed. (Deventer, The Netherlands: Kluwer Law International, 1998), 472.

91. Ibid., 432.

92. Wedderburn, *Employment Rights*, 285–89.

93. Ibid., 49.

94. Ibid., 285–86.

95. S. Edlund, TCO-Tidningen (1968), quoted in K. Wedderburn, *Nationalism and the Multinational Enterprise* (New York: Oceana Publications, 1973), 253.

96. Ibid., 253–54.

97. See, for instance, Atleson, "Reflections on Labor, Power, and Society." Charles Levinson, *International Trade Unionism* (London: George Allen & Unwin, 1972), 111.

98. Levinson, *International Trade Unionism.*

99. Moody, *Workers in a Lean World,* 10.

9. "All Religions Believe in Justice"

1. Muslims understand *jihad* to be a deeply personal process of cleansing evil from their own actions as well as addressing problems in the world around them. See Toure Muhammed, "Islam and Labor," Labor in the Pulpits Insert, *Faith Works* (August, 2000), 5.

2. This historic split resurfaced in the context of the "War on Terrorism" when the AFL-CIO leadership supported the Bush administration while many Protestant and Catholic leaders with experience working in the Global South and especially the Middle East supported nonmilitary options in response to the September 11, 2001 attacks.

3. William Bloom, *Killing Hope: U.S. Military and CIA Interventions Since World War II* (Monroe, Maine: Common Courage Press, 1995).

4. Although the Catholic and mainline Protestant churches are most closely linked to the farm worker movement, it is important to remember that the first farm worker to be killed for his involvement in organizing was a Yemenite Muslim.

5. CLUE should not be confused with CLUW—the Coalition of Labor Union Women.

6. A new, and younger, leadership is now emerging in Los Angeles and around the country.

7. Two city council members who had reservations about the ordinance were absent from council chambers at the time of the vote.

8. For example, the National Council of Churches has undertaken a ten-year project to address and alleviate poverty. Reverend Bob Edgar, a former member of Congress and until the beginning of 2000, head of the Claremont School of Theology, was key to the development of this new project.

9. This figure includes some local chapters of Jobs with Justice where there is a strong involvement by members of the religious community.

10. In exchange for the increases in wages and benefits, HERE agreed to a reduction of the employers' contribution to the health fund; this concession assisted the employers without affecting the workers' overall benefit package.

11. The basket of handwritten prayers and messages draws on the practice of Jews to place the names of loved ones in the Western Wall in Jerusalem. A similar basket of names and prayers was used during interfaith services in Los Angeles sponsored by the Religious Community Against War in the Persian Gulf (1991).

12. This provision of the Worker Retention Ordinance was based on the hope that workers would prove themselves to the new employer during the three-month period and the new employer would therefore hire them on a permanent basis.

13. UNITE was formed from the International Ladies Garment Workers Union and the Amalgamated Clothing and Textile Workers.

14. The report can be found on the web at <www.sweatshop.org>.

15. For current information about faith community activities supporting worker rights, immigrant rights, and globalization, see: CLUE and the LA Living Wage Coalition: www.laane.org; National Interfaith Committee for Worker Justice: www.nicwj.org; and American Friends Service Committee: www.afsc.org.

10. Grasshopper Power

1. Wendell Berry, "Toward a Healthy Community: An Interview with Wendell Berry," *Christian Century* (October 15, 1997): 913.

2. Dan Fesperman and Kate Shatzkin, "The Plucking of the American Chicken Farmer" (two-part series), *Baltimore Sun* (February 28–March 2, 1999).

3. Cedric N. Chatterley and Alicia J. Rouverol, *I Was Content and Not Content: The Story of Linda Lord and the Closing of Penobscot Poultry* (Carbondale, Ill.: Southern Illinois University Press, 2000): 21.

Contributors

Roy J. Adams (Ph.D. University of Wisconsin) is professor of industrial relations emeritus at McMaster University in Hamilton, Canada. He has authored or coauthored more than 150 publications, including 7 books, 34 book chapters, and 49 articles in peer-reviewed journals. Internationally recognized for his work in industrial relations theory, labor policy, and international labor standards, Adams has conducted research and lectured at universities around the world. A past president of the Canadian Industrial Relations Association, Adams served as Canadian Pacific distinguished visiting professor at the University of Toronto in 1990, distinguished visiting professor at the University of Western Australia in 1996, and in 1997 received the Canadian Industrial Relations Association's Grand Dion Award for outstanding contributions to knowledge of Canadian and international industrial relations. A past director of McMaster University's innovative Theme School on International Justice and Human Rights, Adams's recent research has focused on international labor rights. In 1997 he became a founding member of the Society for the Promotion of Human Rights in Employment, whose mission is to promote awareness, understanding, and respect for core labor rights as human rights. A consultant to various international agencies such as the International Labour Organization, in 2001 he was invited to join the International Commission on Labor Rights.

James Atleson is a professor of law at the State University of New York Law School in Amherst, New York. He received his B.A. and J.D. from the Ohio State University and a LL.M. from Stanford. He has also taught at the Texas, Minnesota, Georgetown, and the University of Pennsylvania law schools.

He is the author of *Values and Assumptions in American Labor Law* (University of Massachusetts Press, 1983) and *Labor and the Wartime State* (University of Illinois Press, 1998). He has written numerous scholarly articles, published in legal journals as well as in other disciplines. Essays have been published in *Industrial Democracy in America* and *Unions and Public Policy*. Atleson has been an arbitrator since the early 1970s and a member of the National Academy of Arbitrators for many years.

LANCE COMPA is a senior lecturer at Cornell University's School of Industrial and Labor Relations in Ithaca, New York, where he teaches U.S. labor law and international labor rights. He is the author of the Human Rights Watch report *Unfair Advantage: Workers' Freedom of Association in the United States under International Human Rights Standards.*

Before joining the Cornell faculty in 1997, Compa was the first director of Labor Law and Economic Research at the North American Free Trade Agreement (NAFTA) labor commission in Dallas, Texas. At the commission, he directed labor law and labor policy studies under the North American Agreement on Labor Cooperation (NAALC), NAFTA's labor side agreement.

Prior to his 1995 appointment to the NAFTA labor commission, Compa taught labor law, employment law, and international labor rights as a visiting lecturer at Yale Law School and the Yale School of Management. He also practiced international labor law for unions and human rights organizations in Washington, D.C.

Before turning to international labor law practice and teaching, Compa worked for many years as a trade union organizer and negotiator, principally for the United Electrical Workers (UE) and the Newspaper Guild. He is a 1969 graduate of Fordham University and a 1973 graduate of Yale Law School. He also undertook studies abroad at the Institut d'Etudes Politiques in Paris, France (1967–1968), and at the Universidad de Chile in Santiago, Chile (1972–1973).

JAMES A. GROSS has published a three-volume study of the National Labor Relations Board and U.S. labor policy. The most recent volume, *Broken Promise: The Subversion of American Labor Relations Policy, 1947–1994*, was published by Temple University Press in 1995. He has also written *Teachers on Trial: Values, Standards and Equity in Judging Conduct and Competence.* His other research on various topics in labor law and labor arbitration have appeared in the *University of Buffalo Law Review, Cornell Law Review, Syracuse Law Review, Industrial and Labor Relations Review, Arbitration Journal, Labor History, Labor Law Journal, Chicago-Kent Law Review, Employee Rights and Employment Policy Journal,* and *Catholic University Law Review.*

Professor Gross teaches labor law, labor arbitration, and a course entitled values, rights and justice in economics, law, and industrial relations.

He received his B.S. from LaSalle College, M.A. from Temple University, and Ph.D. from University of Wisconsin. He is a member of National Academy of Arbitrators and on the labor arbitration panels of the American Arbitration Association, Federal Mediation and Conciliation Service, and New York State Public Employment Relations Board, as well as a panelist named in several contracts.

REVEREND JIM LEWIS is an Episcopal minister who spent seven years as missioner for the Episcopal Diocese of Delaware. He was a founder and chairperson of the Delmarva Poultry Justice Alliance.

LINDA A. LOTZ From 1996 to 1999, Linda A. Lotz was interfaith coordinator for Clergy and Laity United for Economic Justice (CLUE) in Los Angeles. She currently works in the International Program department of the American Friends Service Committee in Philadelphia. Linda is a member of the board for the National Interfaith Committee for Worker Justice and active with the Philadelphia Interfaith Committee for Worker Justice.

THOMAS B. MOORHEAD joined the United States Department of Labor as deputy under secretary for international affairs in September 2001. Prior to joining the government, Mr. Moorhead had worldwide responsibility for human resources at Carter-Wallace, Inc., where he served as vice president of human resources for more than fourteen years. Mr. Moorhead joined Carter-Wallace from Esteé Lauder, Inc., where he was senior vice president of corporate affairs. During the eleven years he was at Esteé Lauder, he was responsible for a number of administrative functions, including worldwide employee relations, internal audit, and management information services.

In 1985, 1993–96, and 2000–01, he was appointed a member of the United States delegation to the International Labour Organization (ILO) in Geneva where he served as the head of the U. S. Employer delegation for four years. In 2001 he became a member of the governing body of the ILO.

He is a member of the American Bar Association, the Association of the Bar of the City of New York, and the International Law Association. He has been admitted to practice in the states of New York and Connecticut and before the U. S. Supreme Court.

EDWARD E. POTTER is the U.S. employer delegate to the annual June ILO conference and international labor counsel to the U.S. Council for International Business. The ILO conference develops multilateral treaties that are intended to establish minimum international labor standards. In 1998, he was the employer spokesman on the conference committee that negotiated the ILO Declaration on Fundamental Principles and Rights at Work. Since June 2000, he has been the employer spokesman on the Global Report follow-up to the declaration.

Since 1981, Mr. Potter has served on a Department of Labor tripartite legal panel that examines, on behalf of the President's Committee on the ILO, the domestic law effect of ratification of ILO conventions on the United States. He has testified in both the House of Representatives and the Senate on the worker rights aspects of the North American Free Trade Agreement and ratification of United Nation's human rights and ILO conventions. In 1998, he was appointed to the National Advisory Committee of the U.S. National Administrative Office under the NAFTA labor side agreement

Since 1988, Mr. Potter has been president of the Employment Policy Foundation, a nonpartisan economic research and education foundation that focuses on workplace trends and policies. He is a senior partner in the law firm of McGuiness Norris & Williams, LLP in Washington, D.C.

His publications include *Keeping America Competitive: Employment Policy for the Twenty-First Century* (1995), *Employee Selection: Legal and Practical Alternatives to Compliance and Litigation* (2nd ed. 1986), and *Freedom of Association, the Right to Organize and Collective Bargaining: The Impact of Ratification on U.S. Law and Practice of Ratification of ILO Conventions No. 87 & No. 98* (1984), and numerous journal articles on revitalizing international labor standards.

EMILY A. SPIELER is dean and Edwin W. Hadley Professor of Law at Northeastern University School of Law. She also serves as chairperson of the Workers' Advocacy Advisory Committee, a federal advisory committee to the U.S. Department of Energy; as a member of the National Academies of Science/National Research Council Committee on the Health and Safety Needs of Older Workers; on the Workers' Compensation Steering Committee for the National Academy of Social Insurance; and as a member of the Social and Economic Consequences of Workplace Illness and Injury Implementation Team for the National Occupational Research Agenda of the National Institute for Occupational Safety and Health. In the fall of 2001 she was a Fulbright scholar on the law faculty of University College, Cork, Ireland, studying unfair dismissal and disability law in Ireland and the European Union. Before assuming her current duties, she was the Posten Professor of Law at West Virginia University College of Law where she taught courses in labor, employment law, and social policy. While in West Virginia, Professor Spieler also served as an expert for the U.S. Occupational Safety and Health Administration; as public co-chair of the Workers' Compensation Committee of the Labor and Employment Section of the American Bar Association; as commissioner of the West Virginia Workers' Compensation Fund (1989–1990); commissioner of the Human Rights Commission (1989–1998); deputy attorney general for civil rights for the State of West Virginia (1984–1987); and as a member of the governing board of the public employees health and life insurance program (1990–1998). Professor Spieler has written and spoken extensively on issues related to employment law, occupational safety and health, and workers' compensation. She is a graduate of Harvard-Radcliffe College and Yale Law School.

Lee Swepston is chief of the Equality and Employment Branch, and human rights coordinator, in the International Labor Standards Department of the International Labour Organization in Geneva.

Mr. Swepston is a U.S. citizen. He graduated from the University of North Carolina at Chapel Hill and took his legal degree at Columbia University in New York. After one year with the International Commission of Jurists, a human rights nongovernmental organization in Geneva, he joined the ILO in 1973. He has been regional adviser on International Labor Standards in English-speaking Africa and in the Caribbean, and served in other standards-related posts before taking up his present responsibilities. These include responsibility for the supervision of the ILO's standards concerning equality, indigenous and tribal peoples, and employment policy issues. His responsibilities also include coordination of the ILO's relations with other intergovernmental organizations concerning human rights questions.

Mr. Swepston is the author of a number of books and articles on international human rights, international labor standards, indigenous and tribal peoples, child labor, and related subjects.

Index